Reading God's World

Reading God's World

THE SCIENTIFIC VOCATION

EDITED BY
ANGUS J. L. MENUGE

CONCORDIA PUBLISHING HOUSE · SAINT LOUIS

Library of Congress Cataloging-in-Publication Data

Reading God's world : the scientific vocation / edited by Angus J. L. Menuge.
    p. cm.
    Includes bibliographical references.
    ISBN 0-7586-0580-3
    1. Scientists—Religious life. 2. Religion and science. 3. Vocation—Lutheran Church. 4. Science—Vocational guidance. 5. Scientists—Religious life—History. 6. Religion and science—History. I. Menuge, Angus J. L.
BV4596. S35R43 2004
261.5′5—dc22

2004018933

1 2 3 4 5 6 7 8 9 10   13 12 11 10 09 08 07 06 05 04

~

Dedicated to John Warwick Montgomery,
true Christian knight, and to his fair lady, Lanalee.

Contents

~

Acknowledgments

I would like to thank Concordia University Wisconsin, for its support of the Cranach Institute (www.cranach.org) and for granting me sabbatical leave during 2002, which enabled me to prepare the present volume. Also, I am very grateful to the Discovery Institute for providing a generous fellowship for 2002. Finally, I thank all the contributors and the editorial staff of Concordia Publishing House who worked hard and showed great patience during the preparation of the manuscript.

ANGUS J. L. MENUGE

Readers of the World

Science and Religion in Confusion

Both inside and outside the academy of science, there is a great deal of confusion about the proper roles and limits of science and religion. On the one hand, there is the idea that science has somehow abolished religion and even that science is a type of religion in its own right, promising salvation from discomfort and drudgery through air-conditioning, pharmaceuticals, and computer technology. At its most extreme, the idea of science as a type of religion gives rise to scientism, the view that science alone provides knowledge and ultimate significance for life.

On the other hand, there is a great deal of unfocused religiosity. It is widely thought that some sort of nebulous spirituality lies behind or in nature, and this provides a kind of religion shorn of tiresome moral rules and easier to reconcile with modern science. The assumption is that traditional religions, such as orthodox Christianity, are simply incompatible with science, and the conclusion is that such religions must either accommodate or die. There is thus a great deal of talk about "humility theology", combined with the background assumption that science must be allowed indefinite scope for imperialist conquest of the superstitions of the past.

Against all these notions, the contributors to this book will show that science depends on religious assumptions and will likely lose its way without them. Christianity in particular has been most successful in providing the metaphysical, epistemological, and ethical foundations for modern science. It turns out that a key to all this is the Reformation doctrine of vocation, the idea that not just clergy but all Christians are called in their stations to serve God and their neighbor. The call to be a scientist is the call to be a reader of God's world, one who interprets God's "other" book, the book of nature. The metaphysical assumption is that there is such a book inscribed with a coherent *logos*. The epistemological assumption is that human reason, because it reflects that same *logos* (albeit imperfectly), is able to read the book. Finally, the ethical assumption is that the scientist can pursue this knowledge in worship of the Creator and to serve his or her neighbor by ameliorating the consequences of the fall into sin.

Vocation and Science

At this point a natural reaction would be to claim that vocation is only a Christian idea, having relevance only to the Christian scientist. Indeed, it is true that the Christian who consciously recognizes that his or her work is a vocation will benefit immeasurably. As Nancy Pearcey argues in "How Science Became a Christian Vocation," the Christian who pursues science as a vocation will be better equipped to overcome the modern tendency to put faith and work in different compartments. For the Christian, vocation provides a bridge between faith and life that transforms the mind and directs work along God-pleasing lines. Nonetheless, the office of scientist, as any office, is ordained by God through the order of creation. This means that even the unbelieving scientist is under the dominion of the left-hand kingdom, governed by reason and natural law. In his essay, "Science and the Natural Law," William Powers shows how a natural law of reward and retribution shapes the office of even the unbelieving scientist.

Vocation also has everything to do with the origin of science. As Pearcey points out, in the Genesis account we see the "cultural mandate" in which Adam, and by extension all humans, are called to subdue creation, converting nature into culture. Science is a preeminent means of accomplishing this. But this alone does not explain why modern science is so different from its ancient and scholastic precursors. Modern science has a distinctive character, attuned to empirical discovery. This view of science was not common in ancient Greek or scholastic thought, where a belief in essences made scientists think they could intuit how nature had to be. The early modern emphasis on divine voluntarism, the idea that God was a free being who was not bound to inscribe in nature what humans anticipated, was a crucial theological change that supported the *a posteriori* turn in modern science. At the same time, the reformers, especially Martin Luther, emphasized the priesthood of all believers. As Peter Harrison shows in his essay, " 'Priests of the Most High God, with Respect to the Book of Nature': The Vocational Identity of the Early Modern Naturalist," this doctrine led to the view that a scientist was a sort of priest, worshiping in the temple of God's world. Combining the ideas of divine voluntarism and of a universal priesthood led to the understanding that the scientist was called to interpret what God had freely written. But if a priest is an interpreter, much depends on finding the best hermeneutic. In my essay, "Interpreters of the Book of Nature," it is shown how hermeneutical principles for reading nature have developed from ancient Greek science to the present, and it is suggested that intelligent design has much of value to bring to the discussion.

But again it may be objected: "So what? Even if Christianity did provide science with the boost it needed, that does not show that its contribution is essential." The objection notes that because A caused B does not imply that B requires A for its continued operation. Might not Christianity be useful scaffolding that assisted the construction of the imposing edifice we call modern science, though the building no longer has need of such support? In response, there are two main arguments to show that Christianity makes a continuing contribution to science. One argument is empirical; the other is conceptual.

The empirical argument demonstrates how a sense of vocation and the Christian assumptions it brings has led, and continues to lead, to important scientific discoveries. In his "Science and Christianity: Conflict or Coherence?" Henry Schaefer provides an impressive cast of top scientists, past and present, who not only were Christian but also approached their work in a distinctive way because of their faith. Zeroing in on the Lutheran Reformation, Peter Barker, in his "Astronomy, Providence, and the Lutheran Contribution to Science," shows how specifically Lutheran theological doctrines of providence motivated a highly successful research program in astronomy. Had a Lutheran scientist such as Johannes Kepler not viewed his work as a vocation, he would not have had the same confidence in God's providential, rational ordering of the cosmos, thus he may never have discovered his celebrated laws of planetary motion.

Focusing in even further, we consider the life of a great scientist, Robert Boyle. In "Science as Christian Vocation: The Case of Robert Boyle," Edward Davis shows how much Boyle's sense of vocation contributed to the direction of his science. It grounded his conviction that one must humbly interpret the regularities in nature freely inscribed by God, and it motivated Boyle's strong defense of the argument from design (apologetics), his exemplary piety, and his tremendous compassion for the poor, manifested both in charity and the scientific development of inexpensive chemical remedies for illness. Moving to the present day, and to the science most often considered to be in conflict with the Christian faith, Paul Boehlke's essay, "The Christian as Biologist," tells of the rewards and struggles of being both a Christian and a biologist. The Christian biologist does not always feel at home in the modern biological community. But then all Christians are citizens of two kingdoms, and none can expect to be at home in this world. In the meantime, Christians are called to witness and Boehlke clarifies what counts as success and failure when a Christian biologist tries to show his or her faith in work and conduct.

The conceptual argument shows that vocation provides the necessary philosophical basis for doing good science. In his essay, "Scientists Called to Be Like God," Nathan Jastram argues that scientists are tempted to one of two extremes. The first is that some scientists may try to rise up and claim the status of a deity. In their pride, such scientists make overblown claims that reflect their conceit of omniscience and may fall into complicity with evil, applying science to control life in ways that deny its sacred status. Like the people of Babel in Genesis 11 and like Saruman in Tolkien's *The Lord of the Rings*, these scientists build a tower that will come crashing down. In the next extreme, some scientists may be afflicted with undue modesty, afraid to carry out the mandate to understand and subdue the world in God-pleasing ways. With such a faint heart, modern science with its impressive laws and laborsaving technological innovations would never have been started. Jastram argues that applying the doctrine of the image of God to science provides what Jaki calls a "middle road" between these extremes of scientism and timidity. Kurt Marquart, in his "Science: Sacred Cow or Sacred Calling?" shows that the non-Christian Karl Popper has largely good advice for pursuing that middle road. Popper's robust realism gives confidence that there is a real world to discover, while his fallibility warns against the limitations of the human intellect. Popper remained convinced that science was rational and progress was possible, but he attacked scientism as the attempt to conflate distinct methods of understanding the world. William Powers, in his "Science and the Natural Law," shows how astute students of scientific change such as Kuhn and Laudan give reluctant witness to the constraints imposed by the scientific office but fail to provide an adequate explanation of scientific progress. By contrast, Jaki shows how science depends on metaphysical assumptions, ones ultimately grounded in Christian theology, and is thereby able to remedy the deficiencies of these secular thinkers.

The ten essays of this book are arranged into three sections. The first three essays focus on the origin of the scientific vocation and what it means to be a reader of God's world. The next four essays provide the empirical evidence that the idea of science as a vocation has had, and continues to have, an important positive influence on scientific discovery. The last three essays show how the doctrine of vocation (together with the related doctrines of the image of God and of the two kingdoms) provides the theological and philosophical resources to account for both success and failure in scientific methodology.

Origin of the Book

The idea of this book grew out of a lecture series on Science and Vocation held at Concordia University Wisconsin in the fall of 2001, sponsored by the Cranach Institute. The Cranach Institute is a think tank directed by Gene Edward Veith, whose recent book, *God at Work*,[1] is a splendid explication of the doctrine of vocation for our times. The mission of the Cranach Institute is to relate the Lutheran doctrines of vocation and the two kingdoms to every area of culture. It seemed to me, as associate director, that there had been a lack of sustained thinking about the idea that science might be pursued as a vocation, rather than merely as a prestigious and (often) lucrative profession. I had been much impressed with Nancy Pearcey's book (with Charles Thaxton), *The Soul of Science*,[2] and also with her work on rediscovering the Christian mind, so I invited her to be our keynote speaker for the series on Science and Vocation on September 11, 2001. Despite the unfolding nightmare, with great courage, clarity, and some brilliant insights that much impressed the audience, Pearcey was able to give her talk. She was then stranded in Mequon for almost a week before being able to return to her home on the East Coast. The contrast between the terrorists' gross misuse of science for evil ends and Nancy's inspiring talk, aimed at healing the fractured Christian mind and at providing meaning and a moral purpose to life, could hardly have been more stark.

A week later, on an airplane with a handful of passengers, Henry ("Fritz") Schaefer, a noted quantum chemist with almost a thousand science articles and a well-known speaker on science and Christianity, arrived in an airport where security personnel easily outnumbered civilians. Undeterred by events, Schaefer gave a super talk on the many great Christian scientists in history and the present day, and he even agreed to sit in on what was, I fear, a rather boring philosophy lecture by me! We also had the privilege of having Edward (Ted) Davis, an historian of science well-known for his work on Robert Boyle, on our campus again. He had previously appeared as a presenter for the Design and Its Critics Conference in June 2000, but because of time limits, he had not been given the chance to give his full talk. This was a chance to redress that prior curtailment, and Ted gave a beautifully illustrated presentation showing the exemplary qualities of Boyle's life as a Christian scientist.

All the way from Los Alamos, New Mexico, William Powers brought his experience as a computational physicist, philosopher, and student of theology to show how the natural law governs science. And from Concordia Theological Seminary in Fort Wayne,

Indiana, noted theologian Kurt Marquart brought out the many advantages of a Popperian perspective for a Christian understanding of science.

These five presentations became the core essays from which the collection grew. It was imperative to add some history of science focused on the Reformation. With their sterling contributions in the area, I was delighted to be able to recruit Peter Barker[3] and Peter Harrison.[4] Another deficit was the lack of an individualized reflection on what it means to be a Christian scientist in a controversial area today, and this was made good by Paul Boehlke, another former presenter at the Design and Its Critics Conference. I also knew of a scholar who had been working hard to develop the implications of the doctrine of the image of God, Nathan Jastram, chair of Concordia University's own theology division. Having seen him apply this doctrine to biomedical ethics, I asked whether he would like to consider the connection between being made in God's image and the scientific vocation in general. He was happy to oblige. My own chapter is the result of my recent work attempting to understand the idea of different hermeneutical principles for reading the book of nature. It will be obvious that I have learned much from the writings of other contributors to this volume.

Angus J. L. Menuge
Concordia University Wisconsin

Notes

1. Gene Edward Veith, *God at Work: Your Christian Vocation in All of Life* (Wheaton, Ill.: Crossway, 2002).

2. Nancy R. Pearcey and Charles B. Thaxton, *The Soul of Science: Christian Faith and Natural Philosophy* (Wheaton, Ill.: Crossway, 1994).

3. Peter Barker is author of numerous articles in the area, including "The Role of Religion in the Lutheran Response to Copernicus," in *Rethinking the Scientific Revolution,* ed. Margaret J. Osler (Cambridge: Cambridge University Press, 2000), 59–88; and with Bernard R. Goldstein, "Theological Foundations of Kepler's Astronomy," in *Science in Theistic*

Contexts: Cognitive Dimensions, Osiris, vol. 16, eds. John Hedley Brooke, Margaret J. Osler, and Jitse M. van der Meer (Chicago, University of Chicago Press, 2001), 88–113.

4. Peter Harrison, *The Bible, Protestantism, and the Rise of Natural Science* (Cambridge: Cambridge University Press, 1998).

⌣

PART I

The Origin
of the Scientific Vocation

1

How Science Became
a Christian Vocation

NANCY R. PEARCEY

Abstract

The scientific revolution was largely the product of Christian
believers, and it was fueled by a profound sense of Christian
vocation. Today, however, that sense of vocation has become rare.
In this essay, I examine the way modern thought has severed religion from the rest of knowledge in a sacred/secular dichotomy.
We will see how this split has been used to privatize and marginalize relgion, and diagnose the way the same split hamstrings
Christians in their efforts to have an impact on the public arena
and in academia. We then turn to the biblical basis for the concept of vocation and trace its historical development. Finally, we
will consider various historical figures who regarded their work
as nothing less than a calling from God. Our own heritage gives

us many inspiring and instructive models of how to recognize science as a genuinely Christian vocation.

⤳

As a young man, Johannes Kepler hoped to become a Lutheran pastor, convinced that the only way to really serve God was in the ministry. He enrolled in the university to study theology, but at the end of his studies his dreams came crashing down when university authorities suddenly transferred him to a teaching position in mathematics and astronomy. Over time, however, Kepler became captivated by these subjects and came to see that science, too, can be a calling from God—just as much as the ministry.

"I wanted to become a theologian; for a long time I was restless," Kepler wrote years later. "But now I see how God is, by my efforts, being glorified in astronomy, for 'the heavens declare the glory of God.'"[1] Kepler had discovered that science is a genuinely Christian vocation. In one of his scientific notebooks, he broke spontaneously into prayer:

> I give you thanks, Creator and God, that you have given me this joy in thy creation . . . See I have now completed the work to which I was called. In it I have used all the talents you have lent to my spirit.[2]

Notice Kepler's profound sense that he had been "called" by God to use his talents as an astronomer. He often described astronomers as "priests of God" in the book of nature.[3]

Standing at the cusp of the scientific revolution, Kepler was not alone in regarding the work of the scientist as an act of religious devotion. Throughout the sixteenth, seventeenth, and most of the eighteenth centuries, mathematical science was seen as "a religious quest," a way of honoring God by studying His creation, writes mathematician Morris Kline. "The search for the mathematical laws of nature was an act of devotion which would reveal the glory and grandeur of His handiwork."[4]

Today this concept of science as a Christian vocation has grown rare. Why is that? How have modern believers lost a robust sense of science as a calling from God? In this essay, I will examine the way modern thought has severed religion from the rest of knowledge in a sacred/secular dichotomy. We will see how this split has been used to privatize and marginalize religion and diagnose the way the same split hamstrings Christians in their efforts to have an impact on the public arena and in academia. We will then turn to the biblical basis for the concept of vocation and trace its historical development. Finally, we will consider various historical figures who regarded their work as nothing less than a calling from God. Our own heritage gives us many inspiring and instructive models of how to recognize science as a genuinely Christian vocation.

How We Lost a Sense of Christian Vocation

In saying that the concept of science as a Christian vocation has grown rare, I do not mean that believers are no longer working in the sciences. They certainly are—especially in the hard sciences. In 1969 a massive survey of American college faculty found that most scientists considered themselves deeply or moderately religious. Among mathematicians, 60 percent said they considered themselves "a religious person," and 40 percent labeled themselves "religiously conservative." In the physical sciences, the numbers were 55 and 34 percent, respectively. In the life sciences, the numbers were 55 and 36 percent. On the whole, scientists attend church in the same proportion as the general population: About 45 percent said they attend regularly.[5] Contrary to the stereotype that religion and science do not mix, the numbers make it clear that many intelligent and highly educated scientists do hold religious beliefs—which, in the United States, typically means some form of Christian belief.

In what sense, then, can we say that the idea of Christian vocation has grown rare? In the sense that these believing scientists rarely hold a Christian worldview that unifies their faith and science within a single, overarching framework. Science has become so secularized—and at the same time religion has grown so privatized—that the link between them has snapped. As a result, Christians working in the sciences often commute between two separate conceptual worlds: The sacred realm is limited to select areas of life defined as spiritual, such as worship and private morality, while the rest of life is regarded as religiously neutral or secular.

This bifurcation is what we often describe as the sacred/secular split, and one of its consequences is that Christians may be highly educated in terms of technical proficiency yet have no biblical worldview with which to interpret the subject matter of their fields.[6] As Harry Blamires lamented in his classic book *The Christian Mind*: "There *is* no longer a Christian mind,"[7]—no shared assumptions undergirding a distinctive biblically based outlook on subjects such as economics, politics, law, or science. As a result, many believers live bifurcated lives, with their faith kept separate from their professional work, running in a parallel track without ever intersecting. They may find their work engrossing and challenging, but they do not pursue it as a *Christian* vocation.

Even in Christian colleges, religion is typically a separate subject added on to the regular curriculum, rather than an integral framework shaping the interpretation of the subject matter itself. A common strategy is to inject a few narrowly defined religious elements into the classroom—such as starting the class period with prayer—then to teach the same content taught in secular colleges. "Christians in higher education are strongly, though subtly, tempted to compartmentalize our faith," says David Moberg of Marquette University. Religion is considered relevant to special areas such as church and campus religious activities. "But when we are teaching and doing our research, we usually center our attention upon the theories, concepts, and other subject matter that are conventional in our respective disciplines." Precisely. The subject matter itself is treated as if it were simply neutral knowledge, with no reference to biblical truth.

I encountered a particularly egregious example of this conceptual dichotomy several years ago while interviewing a physics professor for an article. The professor was a sponsor for a well-known campus ministry at a large secular university, someone who might be expected to have thought deeply about the relationship between his faith and his academic field of study. In the interview, I asked him to explain a Christian perspective on the "new physics" relativity theory and quantum mechanics. Claims and counterclaims have been made about the supposedly revolutionary impact of the new physics: that it demolished the Newtonian worldview that held sway for three hundred years, that it destroys determinism and makes room for free will, that it undercuts materialism, and much more. Many popular books on the subject go even further, claiming that quantum mechanics confirms Eastern metaphysics (the classic example is *The Tao of Physics*). I was eager to learn how a Christian would evaluate the unsettling and possibly overblown philosophical implications being drawn from the new physics.

To my dismay, the professor had nothing to say. He had not worked out a distinctively Christian perspective on the subject, but insisted that physics and faith were best kept in totally separate domains. His exact words were branded into my memory: "Quantum mechanics is like auto mechanics," he said. "It has nothing to do with my faith."

Now, I am sure the man was a committed believer, but obviously he kept his faith on a parallel track from his scientific work, operating completely within the limits of a sacred/secular dichotomy. He was both a Christian and a physicist—but clearly he did not have an overarching framework that brought the two together. That is, he did not regard his work in science as a *Christian* vocation.[8]

How Religion Has Been Privatized

This dichotomy between faith and vocation is not uncommon. A few years ago a massive survey of American evangelicals was conducted by Christian Smith, a sociologist at the University of North Carolina (and himself an evangelical believer), published in *American Evangelicalism: Embattled and Thriving*.[9] The survey found that most evangelicals have internalized a sacred/secular split that drastically limits the application of their faith to their professional lives and to the public arena in general.

Smith divided his subjects along a spectrum from conservative to liberal, dividing them into five categories: evangelical, fundamentalist, mainline Protestant, liberal Protestant, and Roman Catholic.[10] The good news is that on several measures of religious vitality, evangelicals came out consistently on top. For example, on their view of the Bible, 97 percent of evangelicals believe the Bible is inspired by God and without errors (compared to 92 percent of fundamentalists, 89 percent of mainline Protestants, 78 percent of liberal Protestants, and 74 percent of Catholics). Evangelicals also top the list among those who say they have committed their life to Jesus Christ as their personal Lord and Savior (97 percent), that their religious faith is very important to them (78 percent), and that absolute moral standards exist (75 percent).

Overall, the numbers are impressive. On many measures of religious vitality, it is clear that evangelicalism is doing well. Sociologists have long decreed that when a culture modernizes, religion declines—the so-called secularization thesis. But the evidence shows that evangelicalism is thriving in contemporary American culture. The secularization thesis has been disproved.

That is good news, but there is also bad news. When asked about issues in the public square—such as work, economics, politics, and public life—no one in the survey articulated an understanding of Christian vocation. Most spoke strictly in terms of individual morality and religious devotion. In other words, the only strategy offered for relating as Christians to the "secular" arena was to import "sacred" activities into it.

To draw a clearer picture, consider a sampling of the respondents' own words. Asked how to have a transforming effect on the world, one Baptist woman replied, "I just feel that if each individual lived the Christian life . . . it influences society. We just need to live the life that Christ wants us to live, the best we can, to influence society in general." A Christian charismatic told the survey takers, "For me, the solution to the world's problems is becoming a Christian, okay?" A Church of Christ man said, "Just believe in Christ and live the best you can the way He wants you to, and that would change the whole world."[11]

These answers contain a great deal of truth, of course. But notice how individualistic the categories of thought are: Most respondents appear to think only in terms of individual conversion. None spoke in terms of developing a Christian mind on these subjects or critiquing the worldviews that shape our public life.

Similar results emerged when respondents were asked how Christianity should affect the world of work and business. Most spoke only in terms of religious activities on the job. A woman from a seeker church said, "There are opportunities . . . to have Bible study on company time, a prayer breakfast, outreach of some kind." A Pentecostal man (with what sounds like a rough job) said, "I don't let them cuss excessively on my job . . . Also, we pray most of the time before we start work in the morning."[12]

Other respondents stressed their personal moral witness on the job. A Presbyterian man said Christians "should be the most honest employees they have. If you are working for someone, you shouldn't steal or take an extra ten minutes for lunch break." In fact, honesty was the single factor mentioned most often—listed by more than one out of three evangelicals. Asked if there was anything else Christians could do for the economy, a Church of Christ man said, "No, because if everybody would be honest, that's all it would take." A Baptist woman agreed, "If you [are honest], most everything will take care of itself."[13] We can only commend people who start Bible studies in the workplace or seek to exert moral influence. But something is missing when we do not hear any of the respondents expressing economic principles based on a biblical worldview or talking about having a Christian calling in their field of work.

Finally, asked about politics, a woman attending an evangelical Moravian church said, "What can a Christian accomplish in politics? Be a moral presence." A Church of Christ man said, "Why should Christians be active [in politics]? Because I think souls should be saved. . . . If I can help somebody [go to heaven] by being in the government . . . that would make me feel good."[13] Of course, Christians are called to be evangelists wherever they may be. Yet political office is not just a platform for sharing the Gospel. The respondents did not seem to have the mental categories for evaluating political systems and ideologies or for outlining a biblically based public philosophy.

The study pinpoints with deadly accuracy both the strengths and weaknesses of American evangelicals. On one hand, their hearts are in the right place: They are sincere and committed. On the other hand, their faith is completely privatized: It stays strictly in the area of personal behavior, values, and relationships. The sacred/secular split is so pervasive that even when evangelicals try to influence the secular sphere, the only strategy they come up with is ways to inject sacred activities into it, such as prayer meetings and evangelism. They do not apply a concept of Christian vocation to the work itself.

Christianity's Trade-off with Modernity

This explains why Christians have so little impact on the public square today. Polls consistently show that a large percentage of Americans claim to believe in God or to be born again, yet Christian principles have little effect on our public life. The survey shows why: Religion has been totally privatized. Most evangelicals have no understanding of how to craft Christian worldview principles to influence the public square. The Lutheran religion historian Martin Marty once wrote that a religion serves two functions—first, it is a message of personal salvation, and second, it is a lens for interpreting the world. Historically, evangelicals have been effective in the first function: preaching the Gospel and pressing for conversion. But they have not been as effective in giving people an interpretative framework for understanding the world.[15]

The upshot is that Christianity has thrived in modern culture—but at the expense of being ever more firmly relegated to the private sphere. The *private* sphere has become increasingly religious, while at the same time the *public* sphere has become increasingly secular. The result is that the divide between them has widened to a yawning chasm, and it has become harder for believers to cross that divide and to define their work in the public arena as a Christian calling.

Privatization has changed the nature of religion as well. In the private realm, religion may enjoy considerable freedom—but only because it is safely cordoned off from the "real" world of academic scholarship and public policy. Religion is no longer considered a source of serious truth claims that could conflict with public agendas. Instead, it has been reduced to what the liberal Lutheran sociologist Peter Berger calls an "innocuous 'play area,'"—

where religion is tolerated for people who need that kind of crutch, but where it will not upset any important applecarts in the larger world of politics, economics, or science.[16]

The result is that religion ends up addressing almost solely the needs expressed in the private sphere—needs for personal meaning, emotional nurturing, social bonding, family support, and so on. Almost inevitably, churches have come to appeal primarily to psychological needs, focusing on the therapeutic functions of religion. On one hand, this explains the enduring appeal of evangelicalism: People often become highly attached to a religion that addresses their emotional and practical needs. Living in an increasingly impersonal, public world, people are hungry for resources to sustain their personal and private world. Yet on the other hand, such a privatized faith represents a severely impoverished version of Christianity, a truncated view of its claims to be the truth about all reality.

As missionary Lesslie Newbigin writes, in essence, Christians have accepted a trade-off by acquiescing in the privatization process; Christianity "has secured for itself a continuing place, [but] at the cost of surrendering the crucial field."[17] That is, Christianity has survived, but it is no longer considered to be a credible claim in academia or in the public sphere. Nor is it capable of effectively challenging the dominant ideologies. As Catholic theologian Walter Kasper explains: "Secularization did not cause the death of religion" but it did cause it to become privatized as merely "one sector of modern life along with many others. Religion lost its claim to universality and its power of interpretation" of the full scope of reality.[18]

Christianity will regain its cultural power only when believers recover the conviction that it is a comprehensive worldview covering all of life—both public and private spheres. The Old Testament tells us repeatedly that "the fear of the LORD is the beginning of wisdom" (Psalm 111:10; cf. Proverbs 1:7, 9:10, and

15:33). And the New Testament teaches that in Christ "all the treasures of wisdom and knowledge" are hidden (Colossians 2:3). We tend to interpret these verses as if they referred only to spiritual wisdom, but the text places no such limitation on the term. Scripture is making the radical claim that *all* knowledge depends on religious truth—that God's revelation has provided the first principles or basic assumptions and axioms that are to guide us in every field of endeavor. God is not only the Lord of the human soul but also the Lord of nature and history. And His Word is meant to be a light to *all* our paths, illuminating the foundational truths and basic principles that apply to every vocation, including science.

The Biblical Basis for Vocation

The key scriptural source for the teaching of Christian vocation is Genesis. There we learn the purpose for which God created us—His original intention for human life. At the fall, the human race went off course, lost its way, wandered off the path. But in salvation we are brought back, returned to the way, restored to our original purpose. Redemption is not just about being saved *from* sin, it is also about being saved *to* something: to resume the task for which we were originally created.

And what was that task? In Genesis, God gives what we might call the first job description: Be fruitful and multiply and subdue the earth. The first phrase, "be fruitful," means to develop the social world and social institutions—build families, schools, cities, governments, laws. The second phrase, "subdue the earth," means to harness the natural world—plant crops, build bridges, make computers, compose songs. This passage is sometimes called the "cultural mandate" because it tells us that our original purpose was to create cultures and build civilizations. That is our original calling—nothing less.[19]

In a sense, we are called to take over God's creative work. Of course, we do not create from nothing, *ex nihilo*, as God did. Our job is to develop the powers and potentials God originally built into creation. In the first six days of the Genesis narration, God first forms, then fills, the physical universe—the sky with the sun and moon, the sea with its swimming creatures, the earth with its land animals. Then the narrative pauses, as if to emphasize that the next step is the culmination of all that has gone before. This is the only stage in the creative process when God announces His plan ahead of time, when the members of the Trinity consult with one another: Let Us make a creature in Our image, one who will represent Us and carry on Our work on earth. Then God creates the first human couple to have dominion over the earth and govern it in His name.

It is obvious from the text that the first humans are not supreme rulers, free to do whatever they wish. Instead, their dominion is a delegated authority: They are representatives of the Supreme Ruler, called to reflect His holy and loving care for creation. They are to *cultivate* the earth—a word with the same root as *culture*. The way we function as God's representatives is by building cultures and creating civilizations. That is our purpose, given in creation.

That original purpose was not abrogated by the fall. Sin corrupted every aspect of human nature, but it did not make us less than human. We were not reduced to animals or physical-chemical machines. We still reflect, through a glass darkly, our original nature as God's image-bearers. Thus even sinful people continue to "multiply and fill the earth"—they marry, raise families, start schools, organize political parties. Even sinful people continue to "cultivate the earth"—plant crops, construct buildings, make scientific findings, invent new technologies.[20] In short, after the fall, people still give evidence of having been created in the image of God. Although their efforts are distorted by sin and selfishness, they still express the human nature that God created.

Moreover, in redemption, God releases us from the guilt and power of sin to restore us to our full humanity. God does not save just our souls, while leaving our minds to function on their own. He redeems the whole person. When the Holy Spirit turns us toward God at the core of our being, everything else is meant to follow. Conversion is meant to give new direction to our thoughts, emotions, will, and habits. Our entire lives are to be offered up to God as "living sacrifices" (Romans 12:1).

The result is that we are restored to the task of working God's creation as His image-bearers. Our calling is not only to get to heaven but also to cultivate the earth. The ideal human existence is not eternal leisure, an endless vacation—or even a monastic retreat into prayer and meditation—but creative effort expended for the glory of God and the benefit of other people. Any honest labor can be dedicated to God and endowed with dignity as service done in obedience to the cultural mandate.

Yet our vocation is not something *we* do for God, a notion that puts the burden on us to perform and achieve. Instead, our vocation is a way we participate in *God's* work. We are given the privilege of carrying out His purposes on earth. In "tilling the ground," we participate in the work of God Himself. For God is engaged not only in the work of salvation but also in the work of preserving and maintaining His creation.

Martin Luther liked to say that our occupations are God's "masks"—His way of working in a hidden manner through human means. In the church, God works though Word and Sacrament. In the world, He works through human vocations. In our work, we are God's hands, God's eyes, and God's feet as we care for His creation.

There are times, says the Lutheran writer Gene Edward Veith, when God works directly and miraculously, as when He fed the Israelites manna from heaven. But ordinarily He feeds people through the work of the myriads of workers in agriculture, transportation, food processing, and retailing. God may heal the sick miraculously, as Jesus did in the New Testament. But God works just as surely through the work of doctors, nurses, and health care specialists. God may rout an enemy army miraculously, as He did in the Book of Judges. But in everyday life, He protects us from evil through police officers, attorneys, judges, and from outside enemies through the military. He raises children through parents, teachers, pastors, and soccer coaches.[21] Even nonbelievers can be "masks" of God, avenues of His providential love and care.

The theological term that covers vocation is *sanctification*. After justification, we are called to a gradual and continuous growth in grace and virtue—and one avenue of that growth is in the vocations in which we serve God by serving one another. The message of the church must include both justification and sanctification, equipping the saints to carry out God's work in the world and to fulfill the cultural mandate.

History of the Concept of Vocation

The concept of Christian vocation is the product of a long historical development. The early church faced a Greek culture that denigrated the material world as the place of chaos and corruption. The Greek philosophers (especially Plato) drew a stark distinction between matter and spirit, teaching that the material world was not as good or as valuable as the spiritual world. Sometimes matter was even regarded as outright evil. Not surprisingly, the Greeks taught that salvation could be attained only through ascetic exercises aimed at liberating the spirit from the "prison house" of the body so it could ascend to God.

Work, especially manual labor, was relegated to slaves, while philosophers enjoyed leisure to pursue the higher things of the intellect. Many historians believe this is one reason the ancient world did not develop experimental science. The intellectual elites had no interest in dirtying their hands with actual experiments, and they had disdain for the ordinary farmers and craftsmen who might have acquainted them with a hands-on knowledge of nature.

Against Greek culture, the church fathers stood firmly opposed to the denigration of God's creation. Matter is not evil, they insisted; it is the creation of a good God and bears the stamp of His handiwork.[22] The church fathers wrote extensively on the beauties of nature and on the moral lessons it teaches.[23] Yet perhaps unavoidably, they still absorbed some of the attitudes of the surrounding Greek culture (after all, it was the dominant conceptual worldview at the time). Many began to reflect a Platonic asceticism: Throughout the Middle Ages, those considered *really* committed to their faith were those who withdrew from ordinary work and social life to live celibate lives devoted to prayer and meditation. The word *vocation* was used strictly of religious callings (priest, monk, or nun), which were conceived as separate from ordinary human communities and endeavors.

For the medieval mind, then, there were essentially two classes of Christians and two levels of salvation. Believers were presented with a choice: Either they could separate themselves from ordinary life and devote themselves full-time to specialized spiritual disciplines or they could accept a second-order piety, sojourning in the old world and trying to find time to add spiritual exercises on top of their earthly duties.

The tide began to turn in the late Middle Ages, with the rediscovery of the works of Aristotle, who taught that nature itself is good. The Dominicans began to use Aristotle's categories to defend the biblical teaching of the goodness of creation. As one historical account explains, Albert Magnus, the teacher of Thomas Aquinas, argued that "the natural world was good and was evidence of the work of a single good Creator, and should therefore be studied."[24]

This new attitude swept in like a flood with the Reformation. The reformers soundly rejected the spiritual elitism of the Middle Ages—the two-tiered system that ranked religious professionals above lay Christians—in favor of the priesthood of all believers. Luther was the first to use the word *vocation* to talk about the calling of a merchant, farmer, weaver, or homemaker. Running a business or a household is not the least bit inferior to being a priest or a nun, Luther argued, because these endeavors are ways of obeying the cultural mandate. These activities are God's "masks," ways of participating in His work of maintaining and caring for His creation.

Luther maintained that Christian vocation is not a separate state that exists parallel to the creation order of family and work but is embedded within it. That is why Paul instructs believers to retain the places in life to which God has "called" each of us (1 Corinthians 7:17, 20)—a word with the same root as *vocation*. Elaborating on this theme, Luther wrote: "It is pure invention that pope, bishop, priests, and monks are called the spiritual state while princes, lords, artisans, and farmers are called the temporal estate. This is indeed a piece of deceit and hypocrisy." By this, Luther did not mean to eliminate the priesthood; rather, he wanted *all* Christians to be priests and to recognize that whatever office they held respresented a call from God. "All Christians are truly of the spiritual estate, and there is no difference among them except that of office." Luther appealed to 1 Corinthians 12, where Paul says that Christians form one body yet every part has its own work, its own office, its own trade by which it serves the rest of the body. No calling is inferior to any other—all are necessary for the proper functioning of the body.[25]

Moreover, the good works required of Christians are not extraordinary deeds that we must take time out from ordinary life in order to perform. Consider the Ten Commandments, Luther said: After the first table, which commands us to direct our entire lives to God alone, the second table relates to the outworking of that faith in everyday life. The Fourth Commandment (honor your mother and father) takes for granted that we live in the context of family and, by extension, the larger kinship group and society, with its authority structures. The Fifth Commandment (do not murder) talks about our responsibility for one another's bodily welfare and, by implication, emotional and psychological welfare. The Sixth Commandment (do not commit adultery) takes for granted the sexual relationship of marriage as the basis for the family. The Eighth Commandment (do not bear false witness) assumes the existence of a juridical system and, more broadly, the social world created by words and communication. The Seventh, Ninth, and Tenth Commandments (do not steal, do not covet) all presume the existence of private property, which assumes that we have engaged in fruitful work to produce that property within the context of some appropriate exchange of goods and services. In short, the commandments address ordinary people, living and working in ordinary human communities. We do not have to escape into secluded cloisters to live out God's call.[26]

Luther contrasted the monastic call *from* the world with the biblical call *into* the world. He once illustrated the point colorfully in a Christmas sermon, reflecting on the shepherds. After meeting the Savior, "These shepherds do not run away into the desert, they do not don monk's garb, they do not shave their heads, neither do they change their clothing, schedule, food, drink nor any external work. They return to their place in the fields to serve God there."[27]

The other major reformer, John Calvin, joined Luther in promoting a high view of human labor. Indeed, he articulated a view of work so distinctive that it later came to be called the

Protestant work ethic. "He taught that the individual believer has a vocation to serve God in the world—in *every* sphere of human existence—lending a new dignity and meaning to ordinary work," explains Alister McGrath.[28] Calvin taught that Christ is the Redeemer of every part of creation, including culture, and that we serve Him in our everyday work of building a culture. This general enhancement of the dignity of work served to endorse scientific work as well.[29]

So did Calvin's view of knowledge, which stressed that no part of creation can be rightly understood apart from its relation to God. Whereas Plato had explained the order of the universe in terms of abstract ideals (matter is ordered by rational form), Calvin explained its order by God's Word or Law. God's creative decree gives things their "nature" or identity and makes them what they are. It governs both human life (moral law) and the rest of the universe (natural law). We moderns tend to place morality in a completely different category from science, but for Calvin both were examples of God's Law. The only difference is that humans must choose to obey the moral law, whereas natural objects have no choice but to obey the laws of physics or electromagnetism. If we look at the world through Calvinist glasses, we see God's Law permeating every corner of the universe, God's Word constituting its orderly structure, and God's goodness in every fiber of its being.

And if God is the source of all created reality, then nothing can be rightly interpreted apart from Him. God's laws for nature are the source of the order and patterns that scientists investigate (science). His laws for human life form the principles of justice (politics), creative enterprise (economics), aesthetics (the arts), and even clear thinking (logic). Psalm 119:89–91 (ESV) says God's laws structure all of reality: "Your word is firmly fixed in the heavens" and "all things are Your servants." Thus all areas of knowledge, not just theology and ethics, are related to Him.

The implication is that there is no "neutral" subject matter that can be understood rightly apart from divine revelation. God's word is a light to *all* our paths. Christians cannot complacently abandon "secular" areas of knowledge to nonbelievers, just so long as they allow us some restricted "sacred" area where we are free to sing hymns and read Bible verses. Our calling is to "take *every* thought captive to obey Christ" (2 Corinthians 10:5 ESV, *emphasis added*), constructing a biblically based framework on every subject.

A Christian Vocation in Science

Having opened with a quotation from Kepler, let's return now to him and to the other early modern scientists to learn how they treated science as a Christian vocation. Our own history provides several effective models for taking Christianity as a framework for doing science. John Hedley Brooke proposes a helpful taxonomy of five functions that Christian beliefs played in the early days of the scientific revolution. We often forget that this was a time when science was the new kid on the block, so to speak, and it had to contend for acceptance as a valid calling against an often hostile academic culture.[30]

Presuppositions for Science

To begin with, Christian teachings provided crucial presuppositions for the scientific enterprise. For example, the very possibility of doing science depends on the existence of regular, predictable patterns in nature—what we refer to as "laws of nature." As historian A. R. Hall has pointed out, the concept of natural laws appeared in medieval Europe alone and nowhere else. The use of the word *law* in the context of natural events "would have been unintelligible in antiquity," Hall explains. Only "the Hebraic and Christian belief in a deity who was at once Creator and Lawgiver rendered it valid."[31]

To moderns, the idea of lawful patterns in nature has become so commonplace that we think of it as common sense. Not so, says Kline. The idea of laws in nature was not a product of observation but a deduction from biblical faith. The early modern scientists "were sure of the existence of mathematical laws underlying natural phenomena and persisted in the search for them because they were convinced *a priori* that God had incorporated them in the construction of the universe."[32] In short, the concept of natural law was an assumption that preceded any actual scientific observation.

The *ontological* presupposition of laws built into the structure of the universe was linked to the *epistemological* presupposition that the human mind is capable of detecting those laws. As Brooke writes, the early scientists assumed that "the human mind had been created in such a way that it was matched to the intelligibility of nature."[33] For example, Kepler once wrote: "God, who founded everything in the world according to the norm of quantity [mathematics], also has endowed man with a mind which can comprehend these norms."[34]

Or, as we might say theologically, humans are created in the image of God. Our confidence that scientific knowledge is reliable has its basis in the biblical doctrine that human reason reflects, in some measure, the divine reason. Thus the doctrine of creation (of the world and the human mind) provided the basic ontological and epistemological presuppositions for the scientific enterprise.

Sanctions for Science

Second, Christian teachings have functioned to sanction or justify the pursuit of science. Proponents of the new science "would often argue that God had revealed himself in two books—the book of His words (the Bible) and the book of His works (nature)," explains Brooke. "As one was under obligation to study the former, so too there was an obligation to study the latter."[35] Such an argument was persuasive because the imagery of two books was a longstanding tradition reaching back to the church fathers. St. Augustine wrote: "Some people, in order to discover God, read books. But there is a great book: the very appearance of created things . . . Why, heaven and earth shout to you: 'God made me!' "[36]

If the imagery of two books was so inspiring, why did it take centuries for modern science to arise? The answer, as Peter Harrison[37] has pointed out, is that science had to wait until a new method was developed for *interpreting* the book of nature. And that depended, in turn, on a new method for interpreting the Bible.

The church fathers focused their attention on the four "spiritual" meanings of Scripture—what they termed the typological, moral, allegorical, and analogical. They did not actually deny the literal, historical meaning of the text, but it held far less interest for them. Indeed, in the medieval period, the common mentality virtually lost all sense of the historicity of biblical events. As Berndt Moeller[38] explains, the reason the "spiritual" senses of Scripture seemed far more important was that they made the text relevant by showing how God continues to work in the lives of believers in an on-going manner. Scriptural events happened long ago, but spiritual analogies and typologies of those ancient events could take place in the believer's spirit today.

For the medieval believer, where God was most tangibly and directly at work was in the Sacraments. "What the Bible only reported, happened daily in the Mass," Moeller writes. The reconciliation of God and humans took place again as the past event (Christ's death and resurrection) was actualized in the present on the altar. In fact, for medieval believers, this present actualization became the main focus, so "the living contemplation of the Church and her possession of divine things . . . took the place of retrospective consideration of the past saving act." The result was a loss of historical consciousness: "Medieval contemplation of a present God brought about a cyclical understanding of history, for which time lost its linear character, and was not movement but only repetition and continuation."[39]

The same mentality that was applied to the book of God's Word was also applied to the study of God's world. When St. Augustine talked about the book of God's world, he meant that the physical world was overlaid with multiple layers of moral, spiritual, and allegorical meanings. For example, as late as 1512, when Albrecht Dürer designed a large triumphal arch for emperor Maximilian I, he placed at the top several symbolic animals, among them a lion (representing fear), a dog wearing a stole (representing the judgment of kings), a crane on a raised foot (a guard against enemies), and a bull (courage with temperance). "In other words, animals were part of a visual language; they were symbols. . . . Animals were living characters in the language of the Creator."[40] Reading the book of nature meant deciphering these spiritual and allegorical meanings. Think of this as the Proverbs 6:6 approach to nature: "Go to the ant, you sluggard!" Nature taught spiritual and moral lessons.

How was the allegorical reading of nature replaced by a modern, scientific reading? The answer, says Harrison, lies in the Protestant Reformation. By rejecting the allegorical method of interpreting Scripture (God's Word), the reformers made it possible to reject the allegorical method of reading nature (God's world). By championing a literal, historical method of biblical interpretation, the reformers likewise began to think of nature in a more literal way. For Luther, the historical events *were* spiritual: The events themselves were laden with spiritual meaning and import, and there was no need for any additional layers of "spiritual" interpretation superimposed upon them.

As a result, theologians began to look at the early chapters of Genesis with a new interest in what really happened. The church fathers had interpreted Adam's dominion over the animals as a metaphor for the dominion of reason over the passions. They had interpreted the command to "be fruitful and multiply" to mean the cultivation of the virtues, the "fruits" of the spirit. Thus redemption was strictly personal and internal—it was defined as regaining mastery over the passions and developing the virtues. St. Augustine interpreted the paradise to be restored strictly as a paradise within.[41]

After the Reformation, however, theologians began to pay greater attention to the historical aspect of Genesis. They began to insist that the command to have dominion meant the mastery of *nature*, not of the passions. The fall was emphasized as an event within history—and by the same token, redemption began to be understood as a process of reversing the fall within history (at least in part), not merely a transcendent event at the end of time. Scholars began to speak of recovering dominion over nature through scientific knowledge—using science to reverse the process of deterioration set in motion by the fall and thereby to improve the human condition.[42]

One of the most important shifts was a new understanding of the story of Adam naming the animals. To name something was to express its essence or nature, its properties and relations to one another—which in turn implied a process of analyzing, categorizing, and classifying. Thus Luther wrote of Adam: "Because of the excellence of his nature, he views all the animals and thus arrives at such a knowledge of their nature that he can give each one a suitable name that harmonizes with its nature."[43] Adam's perfect knowledge of the natural world was lost at the fall, of course, but there was hope that it could be recovered once more in redemption. Luther exulted that "we are now again beginning to have the knowledge of the creatures which we lost in Adam's fall."[44]

The recovery of Adam's knowledge was also regarded as the means for recovering his original position as God's ruler and representative on earth. "By controlling and subduing the world, human beings would be restored to their original position as God's viceroy on earth," Harrison explains. "Redemption, in short, did not entail as it did for Augustine, flight from the material world . . . but rather an ordered knowledge of the natural world."[45]

For example, in the seventeenth century, Thomas Sprat wrote: "This was the first service, that *Adam* perform'd to his *Creator*, when he obey'd him in mustring, and naming, and looking into the *Nature* of all the *Creatures*." Indeed, Sprat asserts that if there had been no fall, then Adam's investigation of nature would have been "the only *religion*."[46] In short, Sprat regarded science, the study of nature, as nothing less than the original worship of God. Thus scientific knowledge was justified by construing it as an attempt to recover or reconstruct Adam's original knowledge of creation, which would also be the means of restoring human dominion over nature.

Motives for Science

Third, Christian faith supplied motives for studying nature, the first being to praise God for His wonderful works. The early modern scientists were convinced that the study of God's creation was a means of bringing glory to God by revealing His wisdom and ingenuity. As Kline writes: "Each discovery of a law of nature was hailed as evidence of God's brilliance rather than the investigator's."[47] To use Sprat as an example once more, he wrote that one benefit of scientific study is that the scientist "will be led to admire the wonderful contrivance of the *Creation*; and so to apply, and direct his praises aright."[48]

A second motivation for studying nature was for the purpose of apologetics. One effect of the scientific revolution was to give natural theology a huge boost because the new scientific knowledge filled out in much greater detail the amazing order and complexity of the world. This was not a matter of using mystery and ignorance to dazzle the ignorant; it was rather that the positive findings of the astonishing complexity and elegant harmonies in nature seemed to provide ever-mounting evidence for a supreme Intelligence as its source. For example, both Newton and many of his followers regarded his stunning findings as evidence for a Creator. Roger Cotes, in his preface to the second edition of Newton's *Principia*, wrote that the book "will be the safest protection against the attack of atheists, and nowhere more surely than from this quiver can one draw forth missiles against the band of godless men."[49] Robert Hooke, a polymath of the scientific revolution, argued that nature works by such "stupendous contrivances" that it is foolish "to think all these things the production of chance"; clearly, they are "the works of the Almighty."[50]

A third motivation for studying nature was Christian humanitarianism, searching for means to alleviate suffering and tedium. Indeed, the very concept of social improvement or amelioration grew from the biblical teaching on creation because it implied that the world is contingent, not necessary (in contrast to most Greek thought). As Christopher Kaiser writes: "The Greek philosophers, almost without exception, viewed matter as eternal and uncreated. If there was a God, he had to do the best he could with the prescribed properties of matter."[51] By contrast, the biblical doctrine of creation stated that God had freely created the world *ex nihilo*, without any external constraint or limitation— and therefore, He could also change and restore it. The brokenness of creation was not intrinsic and inherent. It was a temporary state that God had already begun to heal.

Moreover, God had assigned to His redeemed people the obligation of participating in His work of healing and restoration—using the tools of knowledge and creativity. As P. M. Rattansi writes, Christian principles "imposed a religious obligation to make such [scientific] study serve the twin ends of glorifying God and benefiting fellow-men."[52]

Thus the writings of many of the early scientists are suffused with moral concern to help the poor and the sick. For example, Paracelsus grounded his calling as a physician in the commandment of Jesus that we love our neighbor as ourselves. As Kaiser explains: "The work of the physician was, therefore, a ministry of God's grace as much as the preaching of the gospel was. . . . The doctor acted not for himself but for God."[53]

The application of science to technology was justified in the same terms—as a means of serving God by ameliorating suffering. As Lynn White puts it, biblical faith engendered "a religious urge to substitute a power machine for a man where the required motion is so severe and monotonous that it seems unworthy of a child of God."[54] The early development of modern science is impossible to explain apart from the Christian moral vision.

Scientific Methodology

Fourth, Christianity played a role in regulating scientific methodology. The debate over whether the order in the world is contingent (a product of God's will) or rationally necessary (a product of God's intellect) played an enormous role in the history of scientific methodology. Many historians have pointed out that the rise of voluntarist theology (emphasizing God's will) supported the idea of a contingent creation, which in turn helped to inspire an empirical methodology within science. For if creation could have been different from what it is, then all *a priori* methods for deducing what *must* be the case are inadequate.

Instead, we must observe and experiment in order to discover what is in fact the case.[55]

The concept of a contingent creation was developed especially by the nominalist philosophers, such as William of Ockham, who greatly influenced the reformers. It is significant that the concept of contingent order was often spoken of using a legal metaphor: God is a king who lays down laws for His kingdom. In fact, the most common word was *covenant*. The order in nature was covenantal, contingent on God's will and promise. (The idea of covenant was, of course, to become a staple in Reformed theology.)

In *Omnipotence, Covenant, and Order,* Francis Oakley explains the concept of contingent order in this way: Although God cannot be bound by any of His creations, He can freely choose to bind Himself "to follow a stable pattern in dealing with his creation. . . . If God has freely chosen the established order, he *has* so chosen, and while he can dispense with or act apart from the laws he has decreed, he has nonetheless bound himself by his promise and will remain faithful to the covenant that, of his kindness and mercy, he has instituted with man."[56]

Debates over necessity and contingency took place first in theology and were later translated into the language of philosophy of science. How the translation process took place is the theme of Margaret Osler's *Divine Will and the Mechanical Philosophy: Gassendi and Descartes on Contingency and Necessity in the Created World*.[57] The concept of necessity found expression in the view that the laws of nature describe the essences of things. Epistemologically, this meant that at least some things could be known *a priori* and that this knowledge would be certain or demonstrative—which led to various forms of determinism. As an example, Osler discusses the thought of Rene Descartes. By contrast, the concept of contingency found expression in the view that the laws of nature are merely observed regularities. Epistemologically, this meant they could be known only empirically and that knowledge is merely probabilistic. Osler's example here is Pierre Gassendi.

To elucidate the concept of contingency, consider the seventeenth-century philosopher and mathematician Marin Mersenne. In rejecting Kepler's notion that the planetary orbits could be inscribed within the five regular Greek solids, Mersenne argued that the structure of the solar system was only one of an infinite number of possibilities—and *therefore* it depended on the free and unconstrained will of God, not on any preconceived rational pattern.[58] Similarly, Mersenne objected to Aristotle's claim that the earth must be at the center of the cosmos. "For Mersenne there was no 'must' about it," writes Brooke. "It was wrong to say that the centre was the earth's *natural* place. God had been free to put it where He liked. It was incumbent on us to find where this was."[59] As these examples show, theological debates over divine voluntarism became the basis for an empirical methodology within science.

The Content of Scientific Theories

Fifth, religion has at times provided substantive content for scientific theories—what Brooke calls the *constitutive* role of religious beliefs. The idea that Scripture gave information that could direct actual scientific theorizing became possible only after the reformers had developed the historical hermeneutic described earlier, with its new interest in the historical events of Scripture. Almost immediately, scholars began trying to identify physical mechanisms for events described in Scripture.

There was intense speculation on the geographic location of the Garden of Eden, heaven, purgatory, and hell. (Harrison cites extensively from original source materials on each of these points, demonstrating how widespread this new interest was.) Many early scientists (e.g., Thomas Burnet, William Whiston, John Woodward, Nicholas Steno) began to suggest physical mechanisms for the flood (here we see the beginnings of modern flood geology). Others proposed natural forces to explain the end of the earth and its destruction by fire. For if creation was an historical reality, then so was the end time (here we see the beginnings of millennialism). Still others proposed various biological mechanisms to account for the resurrection of the body at the end of history.

Clearly, many of these speculations were overenthusiastic in their attempts to locate physical mechanisms for events that the Bible portrays as miraculous. The theologically orthodox, such as Robert Boyle, insisted that even if physical mechanisms were found, these events were nonetheless effected "not by or according to the ordinary course of nature, but by his [God's] own power."[60] Others, such as Leibniz, went further down the road to naturalism, regarding the resurrection of the body as merely another kind of natural process. The main point, however, is that there was a dramatic shift in mentality toward the conviction that Scripture gives genuine information for the realm of science and history—a conviction that functioned as a powerful stimulant to scientific inquiry.

One example is the seventeenth-century botanist John Ray, who is credited with offering the first biological (as opposed to logical) definition of species. The great challenge for natural history at the time was how to find a guiding principle for delimiting species. Botanists were asking: Should plants be classified according to their root system, leaf shape, blossom, fruit, or habitat? Based on his understanding of Genesis 1, Ray proposed that a species consists of all the descendants of a male-female pair created by God—just as the human race consists of all the descendants of the original human pair, Adam and Eve. Hence Ray's definition of species centered on reproduction. No matter how widely they may appear to differ, individuals belonged to the same species if they were descended from the same parents.[61]

With the rise of population genetics, the most commonly accepted modern definition of species likewise centers on reproduction: A species is defined as a group that is capable of interbreeding because it shares a common gene pool and is reproductively isolated from other groups.[62]

Another example, cited often by modern creationists, is the story of Matthew Maury, the founder of modern oceanography. Upon reading Psalm 8, which talks about the creatures that "pass through the paths of the seas," Maury decided he would find the "paths" spoken about in the passage. In other words, he set out to find regular currents in the oceans. Although mocked by some of his colleagues, he studied old ships' logs and performed experiments with bottles weighted to float at different depths, becoming the first to develop charts of the ocean currents.

Maury then proceeded to Ecclesiastes 1:6: "The wind blows to the south and turns to the north; round and round it goes, ever returning on its course." The text inspired him to theorize that there might be established wind currents as well—which indeed there are. A memorial of Maury in Richmond, Virginia, calls him the "Pathfinder of the Seas, the Genius Who First Snatched from the Ocean and Atmosphere the Secret of Their Laws. His Inspiration, Holy Writ, Psalm 8:8, Psalm 107:23, 24, and Ecclesiastes 1:6."

Conclusion

The biblical doctrine of vocation can have a transforming effect on anyone who takes it seriously. When we regard our scientific work as a "mask" of God, our day-to-day lives are lifted up to an astonishing level of dignity and significance. As Veith writes, a sense of vocation is nothing less than "the spirituality of ordinary life."[63]

One of Klaus Bockmuehl's books is divided into two sections, which are subtitled *gifts* from the Gospel and *tasks* arising from the Gospel.[64] Interestingly, his chapter on Christian vocation is placed in the first section, as one of the gifts we receive through Christ. Bockmuehl's point was that our work is not meant to be a matter of merely expending our own energy to earn a living and make a reputation, to feed our own ego or to pursue our own passions. These aims are too small for a human being made in the image of God. We have been created to serve a larger purpose than our own interests and success. Instead, our work is a gift from God, an invitation to participate in His own work of reversing the harmful effects of the fall, healing what is broken, and creatively making new things out of the original materials of His creation. As Bockmuehl puts it, God's call on our lives, His invitation to play a part in His own unfolding plans and purposes for history, liberates us from our natural egocentricity or from mindless drifting, boosting us to a new level of purpose and meaning.

The doctrine of vocation heals the split between sacred and secular so we no longer live divided, fragmented lives. Instead, we are empowered to offer up everything we do in love and service to God. As St. Paul said, "Whatever you do, do all to the glory of God" (1 Corinthians 10:31 ESV). The promise of vocation is the joy and power of an integrated life, transformed on every level by the Holy Spirit, so our whole being participates in the great drama of God's plan of redemption.

Notes

1. Gerald Holton, *Thematic Origins of Scientific Thought: Kepler to Einstein* (Cambridge, Mass.: Harvard University Press, 1988), 70. I have adapted the translation slightly.
2. Cited in Christopher Kaiser, *Creation and the History of Science* (Grand Rapids: Eerdmans, 1991), 127.
3. Holton, *Thematic Origins of Scientific Thought,* 70. See also Margaret Wertheim, *Pythagoras' Trousers: God, Physics, and the Gender Wars* (New York: Random House, Times Books, 1995), 71.
4. Morris Kline, *Mathematics: The Loss of Certainty* (New York: Oxford University Press, 1980), 34–35.

5. Rodney Stark and Roger Finke, *Acts of Faith: Explaining the Human Side of Religion* (Berkeley: University of California Press, 2000), 53–54.

6. For an extended treament of the sacred/secular split and its history, and the need to craft a comprehensive Christian worldview, see my *Total Truth: Liberating Christianity from Its Cultural Captivity* (Wheaton, Ill.: Crossway, 2004).

7. Harry Blamires, *The Christian Mind: However Should a Christian Think?* (Ann Arbor: Vine Books, 1997), 3 (*emphasis added*).

8. I did end up writing that article on the new physics, which I later exapanded to form two chapters in *The Soul of Science: The Christian Faith and Natural Philosophy* (Wheaton, Ill.: Crossway, 1994). There I make it clear that physics has always been a place where profound philosophical questions have been hammered out, such as determinism versus freedom, the relationship between miracles and natural law, whether life is reducible to physics and chemistry, and how divine providence operates in a physcial world. In our own day, some overweening physicists even claim that mantle of cultural priests, giving their books titles like *The Mind of God, The God Particle,* and *The Theory of Everything.* It is astonishing that a Christian professor could treat physics as though it were a neutral, technical topic with no relationship to Christian truth.

9. Christian Smith, *American Evangelicalism: Embattled and Thriving* (Chicago: University of Chicago Press, 1998).

10. The labels were based on self-definition: If a respondent identified himself as an evangelical (whether Presbyterian or Lutheran or whatever), he was placed in the evangelical category, while if he identified himself as a liberal (whether Presbyterian or Lutheran or whatever), he was slotted into the liberal category. The resulting number of evangelicals is smaller (7 percent of the population) than in most other surveys, where respondents are identified according to standards imposed by the survey-taker, such as the type of church attended or specific doctrinal beliefs held.

11. Smith, *American Evangelicalism*, 188, 190.

12. Smith, *American Evangelicalism*, 203.

13. Smith, *American Evangelicalism*, 204, 206.

14. Smith, *American Evangelicalism*, 194.

15. Martin Marty, *The Modern Schism: Three Paths to the Secular* (New York: Harper & Row, 1969), 40, 57, 92, 96.

16. Peter Berger, *Facing Up to Modernity: Excursions in Society, Politics, and Religion* (New York: Basic Books, 1977), 18. Berger uses the phrase to refer specifically to the private sphere of the family, but it is an apt description of the private sphere more generally.

17. Lesslie Newbigin, *Foolishness to the Greeks: The Gospel and Western Culture* (Grand Rapids: Eerdmans, 1986), 19.

18. Walter Kasper, "Nature, Grace and Culture: On the Meaning of Secularization," in *Catholicism and Secularization in America: Essays on Nature, Grace, and Culture,* ed. David L. Schindler (Huntington, Ind.: Our Sunday Visitor, Communio Books, 1990), 38.

19. See my chapter "Saved to What?" in Charles Colson and Nancy Pearcey, *How Now Shall We Live?* (Wheaton, Ill.: Tyndale, 1999).

20. See Al Wolters, *Creation Regained: Biblical Basis for a Reformational Worldview* (Grand Rapids: Eerdmans, 1985).

21. Gene Edward Veith, *The Spirituality of the Cross* (St. Louis: Concordia, 1999), 74. See also Veith, *God at Work: Your Christian Vocation in All of Life* (Wheaton, Ill.: Crossway, 2002).

22. Charles Norris Cochrane, *Christianity and Classical Culture* (New York: Oxford University Press, 1957), 239, 342, 390, 417.

23. See Clarence J. Glacken, *Traces on the Rhodian Shore: Nature and Culture in Western Thought from Ancient Times to the End of the Eighteenth Century* (Berkeley: University of California Press, 1967), chapter 5, "Earth as a Planned Abode for Man."

24. Roger French and Andrew Cunningham, *Before Science: The Invention of the Friars' Natural Philosophy* (Aldershot, England: Scolar Press, 1996), 183.

25. LW 44:127, 130. Cited in Karl Froehlich, "Luther on Vocation," *Lutheran Quarterly,* XIII (1999): 195–207, at http://www.elca.org/jle/articles/vocation/article.froehlich_karlfried.html.

26. Steven A. Hein, "Luther on Vocation: Ordinary Life for Ordinary Saints," at http://www.issuesctc.com/resource/archives/hein.htm. Originally published in the *Reformation & Revival Journal,* 8:1 (Winter 1999): 121–42.

27. LW 52:37, cited in Froehlich, "Luther on Vocation."

28. Alister McGrath, "Calvin and the Christian Calling," *First Things* 94 (June/July 1999): 31–35.

29. Ian Barbour, *Issues in Science and Religion* (New York: Harper & Row, Harper Torchbooks, 1966), 48–49.

30. John Hedley Brooke, *Science and Religion: Some Historical Perspectives* (New York: Cambridge University Press, 1991), 19–33.

31. A. R. Hall, *The Scientific Revolution, 1500–1800: The Formation of the Modern Scientific Attitude* (Boston: Beacon Press, 1954), 171–72.

32. Kline, *Mathematics,* 35.

33. Brooke, *Science and Religion,* 19.

34. Cited in Holton, *Thematic Origins of Scientific Thought*, 68.

35. Brooke, *Science and Religion*, 22.

36. Cited in Glacken, *Traces on the Rhodian Shore*, 204.

37. Peter Harrison, *The Bible, Protestantism, and the Rise of Natural Science* (Cambridge: Cambridge University Press, 1998). The themes of this section are treated in greater detail in Nancy Pearcey, "Recent Developments in the History of Science and Christianity," and "Reply," *Pro Rege* 30, no. 4 (June 2002): 1–11 and 20–22.

38. Berndt Moeller, "Scripture, Tradition, and Sacrament in the Middle Ages and in Luther," in *Holy Book and Holy Tradition*, ed. F. F. Bruce and E. G. Rupp (Manchester: Manchester University Press, 1968), 113–35.

39. Moeller, "Scripture, Tradition, and Sacrament," 123–24, 126.

40. William B. Ashworth Jr., "Natural History and the Emblematic Worldview," in *Reappraisals of the Scientific Revolution* (Cambridge: Cambridge University Press, 2000), 306–7.

41. Harrison, *Bible, Protestantism, and the Rise of Natural Science*, 209.

42. Harrison, *Bible, Protestantism, and the Rise of Natural Science*, 59, 230.

43. Harrison, *Bible, Protestantism, and the Rise of Natural Science*, 249. See also James L. Bono, *The Word of God and the Languages of Man: Interpreting Nature in Early Modern Science and Medicine, Vol. 1: Ficino to Descartes* (Madison: University of Wisconsin Press, 1995), 55ff.

44. Cited in Bono, *Word of God and Languages of Man*, 71. Bono deals extensively with the theme of Adam's naming the animals and with attempts after the Reformation to recover Adam's original language.

45. Harrison, *Bible, Protestantism, and the Rise of Natural Science*, 60–61; see also 250–51.

46. Cited in Harrison, *Bible, Protestantism, and the Rise of Natural Science*, 231.

47. Kline, *Mathematics*, 35.

48. Cited in Harrison, *Bible, Protestantism, and the Rise of Natural Science*, 231.

49. Roger Cotes, preface to the second edition of Newton's *Principia*, in *Newton's Philosophy of Nature: Selections from His Writings*, ed. H. S. Thayer (New York: Hafner, 1953), 134.

50. Cited in Nancy R. Pearcey and Charles B. Thaxton, *The Soul of Science: Christian Faith and Natural Philosophy* (Wheaton, Ill.: Crossway, 1994), 71.

51. Kaiser, *Creation and the History of Science*, 36. On the Neoplatonist concept of creation as a necessary "emanation" of God's being, and how this

idea filtered into medieval thought, see Arthur O. Lovejoy, *The Great Chain of Being* (Cambridge: Harvard University Press, 1990, first published in 1936), esp. 67ff. See also Jaroslav Pelikan, *Christianity and Classical Culture: The Metamorphosis of Natural Theology in the Christian Encounter with Hellenism* (New Haven: Yale University Press, 1993), chapter 16, "Cosmos as Contingent Creation."

52. P. M. Rattansi, "The Social Interpretation of Science in the Seventeenth Century," in *Science and Society*, ed. Peter Mathia (Cambridge: Cambridge University Press, 1972), 2 3.

53. Kaiser, *Creation and the History of Science*, 119.

54. Lynn White, "What Accelerated Technological Progress in the Western Middle Ages?" in *Scientific Change*, ed. A. C. Crombie (New York: Basic Books, 1963), 290–91.

55. The case for the importance of voluntarist theology was made most notably by Cambridge philosopher Michael Foster, writing in the 1930s. See M. B. Foster, "The Christian Doctrine of Creation and the Rise of Modern Natural Science," in *Mind* 43 (1934), reprinted in *Science and Religious Belief: A Selection of Recent Historical Studies*, ed. C. A. Russell (London: University of London Press, 1973).

56. Francis Oakley, *Omnipotence, Covenant, and Order* (Ithaca: Cornell University Press, 1984), 62.

57. Margaret Osler, *Divine Will and the Mechanical Philosophy: Gassendi and Descartes on Contingency and Necessity in the Created World* (Cambridge: Cambridge University Press, 1994).

58. Brooke, *Science and Religion*, 26.

59. John Brooke and Geoffrey Cantor, *Reconstructing Nature: The Engagement of Science and Religion* (New York: Oxford University Press, 2000), 20.

60. Cited in Harrison, *Bible, Protestantism, and the Rise of Natural Science*, 154.

61. See Pearcey and Thaxton, *Soul of Science*, 101–2.

62. This definition has to be qualified in cases of nonsexual reproduction.

63. Veith, *Spirituality of the Cross*, 71.

64. Klaus Bockmuehl, *Living by the Gospel: Christian Roots of Confidence and Purpose* (Colorado Springs: Helmers & Howard, 1986).

2

"Priests of the Most High God, with Respect to the Book of Nature"

The Vocational Identity of the Early Modern Naturalist

PETER HARRISON

Abstract

Most historians agree that the vocation of "scientist" came into being only in the nineteenth century. However, it does not follow that those involved in the study of nature in preceding eras had no sense that they were involved in a distinct calling. Johannes Kepler once remarked that astronomers were "priests of the most high God, with respect to the book of nature." Taking Kepler's observation as a point of departure, this chapter shows how a number of early modern naturalists came to regard the study of nature as an essentially religious vocation, comparable in certain respects to the priesthood. The trope "the book of nature" played an important role in this development. By the same token, priest-scientists also were able to point to the religious significance of the formal study of nature, and thus justify their pursuit of scientific interests that had traditionally been regarded as beyond the scope of the clerical profession. These developments serve to show the importance of religious motivations in early modern science and demonstrate the role played by theological considerations in the social legitimation of scientific activities.

Introduction

Strictly speaking, during the era of the scientific revolution there were no scientists. In the early modern period, "science" was not, indeed could not have been, a specific profession. At this time there were three official vocations—medicine, law, and theology. These were understood in their original sense as specific callings to service both of God and of commonwealth. As a consequence, those individuals engaged in the study of nature often found themselves attempting to show how what we call "science" could be a legitimate pursuit for someone engaged in one of the three official professions.[1] Only in this way could the formal study of nature be regarded as useful to society on the one hand and divinely sanctioned on the other. While medicine, perhaps, seems closest to "science" as we currently understand it, many who devoted themselves to the study of nature sought to reconcile their scientific proclivities not with the practice of medicine but with the priestly vocation. In this chapter I shall explore early modern notions of vocation with a view to showing how the priestly calling was of central importance for the self-understanding of a number of those who played vital roles in the emergence of modern science.

"Science" and the Vocational Dilemma in the Early Modern Period

In the seventeenth century neither science nor scientists existed as we understand them today. According to historian Nicholas Jardine: "No Renaissance category even remotely corresponds to 'the sciences' or 'the natural sciences' in our senses of the terms."[2] The same was true for much of the eighteenth century. The closest equivalents during this period were "natural philosophy," which sought causal explanations for natural phenomena, and "natural history," which provided descriptions of natural objects.[3] Also, no European language had the word *scientist*—a word that first entered the English lexicon in 1834.[4] Those whom we typically regard as early modern "scientists" were thus variously categorized by their contemporaries as mathematicians, philosophers, savants, virtuosi, or naturalists.[5]

Strictly, these various categorizations were not professions in the modern sense because the modern professions, like the designation "scientist," came into being only in the nineteenth century.[6] The three recognized vocations—those of the ministry, law, and medicine—paralleled the structure of the university education because undergraduates typically would study arts before proceeding to the "higher faculties" of theology, law, or medicine. Moreover, these vocations were then understood in their etymological sense as a divine call to serve both God and humanity and were distinguished from other callings inasmuch as they required literacy, education, and training. The clergy served to teach and prepare the laity for salvation—a considerably narrower role than that of their medieval counterparts—while lawyers saw to matters of civil rights and property, and physicians concerned themselves with physical health. Of these, the clerical office retained something of the special status it had inherited from the Middle Ages. Protestant Reformer John Calvin

(1509–1564) had thus observed that while "God inspires special activities, in accordance with each man's calling," yet it remained the case that "the dignity of the ministry [is to] be held among us in highest honor and esteem, even as the most excellent of all things."[7]

The absence of a specific linguistic category of "scientist" was also reflected in the structures of social institutions. The one place that we might expect to have catered for the professional ambitions of would-be scientific investigators—the university—made little provision for research into the natural world. Few university chairs were devoted to natural philosophy and fewer still to natural history. Between 1660 and 1750, only 4 percent of university chairs were set aside for those professing the natural sciences, and of this 4 percent most were devoted to mathematics, medicine, and natural philosophy.[8] In England, at the turn of the eighteenth century, Oxford, Cambridge, and Gresham College combined had only ten such professorships divided among medicine, mathematics, and natural philosophy.[9] In the last decade of the seventeenth century, clergyman and naturalist John Ray (1627–1705) could thus complain: "I am sorry to see so little Account made of real *Experimental Philosophy* in this University [i.e., Cambridge], and that those ingenious Sciences of the *Mathematicks* are so much neglected by us." Instead, Ray observed: "We content ourselves with the knowledge of Tongues, and a little skill in Philosophy, or History perhaps and Antiquity, and neglect that which to me seems more material, I mean Natural History and the Works of the Creation."[10] The dominance of the university curriculum by the humanities persisted until the end of the nineteenth century.

Compounding this difficulty was the fact that the normal path taken by arts graduates would see them progress at graduation to professional studies. At England's ancient universities, for example, the statutes of the colleges typically enshrined the principle that upon graduating with an arts degree, students would take up theology. Indeed, to be elected fellow of a college—the mechanism for becoming a member of the university—one was expected to take holy orders. This generated considerable difficulties for those whose first choice of study was natural history or natural philosophy. Certainly fellowships were available in the other two professions—medicine and law—yet it was by no means clear that these were any more compatible with investigations into nature than was the clerical office. In any case, these fellowships were quite scarce and competition for them was fierce.

All of this meant that there were limited institutional opportunities for those who wished to devote themselves solely to the pursuit of the natural sciences. Aspiring natural philosophers might seek patronage from royalty or the aristocracy. For example, Galileo (1564–1642) resigned from the Chair of Mathematics at Padua to take up a position in the Tuscan court of the Medici. Such posts, while generally more lucrative than university appointments, often involved the distraction of teaching duties and the intrigues of palace politics. Moreover, patrons could be fickle and their whims could prove fatal, as René Descartes (1596–1650) was to discover. His premature death was precipitated by a chill contracted while teaching mathematics to the demanding Swedish monarch Queen Christina, whose preference was for lessons at 5 A.M.—even on the coldest of Swedish winter mornings. In England, where there were fewer opportunities for royal patronage, employment might be found with well-off families seeking tuition for their offspring. In some cases these convenient arrangements provided time for private study. Thomas Hobbes (1588–1679) was fortunate enough to find himself in such a situation. There were, of course, the first amateur societies—the Royal Society of London, the Parisian Académie des Sciences, and the Roman Academia dei Lincei. But while these provided venues for the exchange of ideas, they offered little by way of continuing financial support for those wishing to devote themselves solely to the study of the natural world.

Gentlemen of wealth and leisure, of course, could fund their own scientific pursuits, if they had the talent and inclination. The most famous of such gentlemen was Robert Boyle, Earl of Cork (1627–1691), whose independent means enabled him to equip himself with laboratory facilities and devote his life to the pursuit of experimental philosophy. The Royal Society of London, according to its first historian, was made up chiefly of such men of independent wealth. Bishop Thomas Sprat informed readers of *History of the Royal Society* (1667) that the society "entertains many men of *particular Professions*, yet the farr greater Number are *Gentlemen*, free, and unconfin'd."[11] Some historians have even argued that the gentlemanly status of these early "scientists" was a crucial factor in establishing the trustworthiness of scientific observations and reports of experiments, and thus played a key role in the establishment of notions of scientific truth.[12] The standing of these gentlemen not only established their general trustworthiness but also provided some guarantee of independence from financial and political interest, and from the tendency to exploit science for the purposes of social advancement.

Finally, those within the recognized professions—theology, law, or medicine—might devote all or part of their time to scientific pursuits though, as we shall see, a clerical career was often argued to be incompatible with extracurricular activities.

The absence of any socially sanctioned scientific professions brought with it a considerable degree of personal uncertainty about the legitimacy of a divine call to the pursuit of science. The personal conviction of such an "inner" divine calling was widely regarded as a vital component of any vocational commitment, yet in the absence of a socially appropriate station that might validate that inner call, the personal conviction itself became questionable. In short, the lack of a formal category of "scientist" was sufficient for many to call into question the validity of any conviction concerning a particular calling to devote one's life exclusively to the study of the natural world. In the case of the ministry, for example, whatever the sincere belief of the individual, an inner call was to be independently validated by an appropriate social authority. Calvin had thus distinguished between "the outward and solemn call which has to do with the public order of the church" and "that secret call of which each minister is conscious before God."[13] The mark of legitimacy of the inner call to the ministry was always the external confirmation of that call by the church. Without this, there was always the danger that the seeking of an office, particularly one that required the highest intellectual gifts, was prompted by "ambition," "avarice," or "selfish desire."[14]

Furthermore, discernment of one's calling was a matter of considerable import. Devout Protestants, in particular, held that God had a single vocation in mind for each individual. "The Lord's calling" observed Calvin, is "the basis of our way of life." God, he insisted, "has appointed duties for every man in his particular way of life. And that no one may thoughtlessly transgress his limits, he has named these various kinds of living 'callings.'"[15] Calvin's view of the matter subsequently was to become commonplace in Reformed theology. Preaching in 1621 on the text of 1 Corinthians 7:24 ("Brethren, let every man wherein he is called, therein abide with God." KJV), Robert Sanderson (1587–1663) admonished the congregation at St. Paul's Cathedral to observe the rule "that every man (notwithstanding his calling unto liberty in Christ) abideth in *that station* wherein God hath placed him." There were, he went on to point out, general and particular callings. The general calling was "to the faith and obedience of the *Gospel* and to the embracing of *the Covenant* of grace and of mercy and salvation by Jesus Christ." Our particular calling, however, "is that wherewith GOD enableth us, and directeth us, and putteth us on some *special* course and *condition of life* wherein to employ our selves, and others." Sanderson insisted that every person "should have an *inward Calling* from God, for his particular course of life." This inward call was to be confirmed by an "outward calling," which came from the church or Commonwealth.[16]

These considerations represented not merely some official theological position but had an impact on the way all educated individuals conceptualized their life's work. For example, John Locke (1632–1704) subscribed to the notion of a general and particular calling and also to the exclusive nature of the professions: "For a man to understand fully the business of his particular calling in the commonwealth, and of religion, which is his [general] calling as he is a man in the world, is usually enough to take up his whole time; and there are few that inform themselves in these, which is every man's proper and peculiar business, so to the bottom as they should do."[17] Of the clerical calling in particular, Locke held that it must exclude all extraneous considerations: "The office of a minister of the Gospel requires so the whole man, that the very looking after their poor was, by the joint voice of the twelve apostles, called 'leaving the word of God, and serving of tables.' Acts iv. 2." Locke went on to defer to the opinion of "a learned prelate," according to whom "the pastoral care is to be a man's entire business, and to possess both his thoughts and his time."[18] It was considerations such as these that led to Locke, during his own vocational crisis, to avoid the singular set of commitments that he believed accompanied the clerical life and that would have curtailed his broader philosophical activities.

To see the impact of these general considerations on specific individuals, we need look no further than the careers of Kepler, Newton, Locke, and Ray.[19] In a letter to his old teacher Michael Maestlin, Johannes Kepler (1571–1630) conveyed his personal sense of conflicting vocational aspirations: "I wished to be a theologian; for a long time I was troubled, but now see how God is also praised through my work in astronomy."[20] Kepler had initially studied theology at Tübingen, intending to become a Lutheran minister. But here he encountered Maestlin, who first encouraged his interest in astronomy. Obviously, at some point Kepler managed to reconcile these apparently conflicting commitments. Certainly, his fortunes in his chosen occupation bear testimony to the vocational uncertainties faced by those who chose to pursue astronomy. Upon graduating, Kepler first taught mathematics at the Protestant faculty in Linz, but was forced to leave and take up private teaching because he did not subscribe to the Formula of Concord. He subsequently went to Prague as Tycho Brahe's assistant and succeeded him in 1601 as Imperial Mathematician—the highest post to which a European mathematician could aspire. However, the machinations of the counter-reformation led to his removal from that post and his life ended in extreme poverty.

In England Isaac Newton's early career was also somewhat precarious. His position at Trinity College during the 1670s was beset with considerable uncertainties because, though it was his desire to pursue natural philosophy, the prescribed career path demanded that he proceed to one of the three professions. Newton knew full well that though he could continue to hold the Lucasian Chair of Mathematics, he could not remain a Fellow of Trinity without seeking ordination. With Newton's Arian sympathies, he felt that he could not, in all good conscience, subscribe to the Trinitarian formula of the Thirty-nine Articles. Thus, as in the case of Kepler, the official religious "tests" were to imperil his scientific career. In 1673 Newton had sought a fellowship in law that would have relieved him of the responsibility of ordination, but he was unsuccessful. Fortunately, two years later Isaac Barrow, his predecessor in that now distinguished chair, sought and obtained dispensation for Newton, and indeed for all subsequent incumbents.[21]

Others who were to play a significant role in the foundation of the modern sciences were similarly fortunate. John Locke, whose opinion on the exclusive nature of the clerical office we have already discussed, was able to remain a student at Christ Church, Oxford, only because a royal dispensation relieved him of the obligation of ordination.[22] For a time it had seemed that Locke would have to abandon his philosophical and scientific interests and devote himself fully to a clerical career. At Cambridge, the naturalist John Ray found himself in the same predicament—"I must of necessity enter orders" he wrote, "or else live at great uncertainties, and expose myself to the mercy of men for my livelyhood." At this time Ray thus resolved to "bid farewell to my beloved and pleasant studies and employments, and give myself up to the priesthood, and take to the study of that which they call divinity."[23] He was ordained in 1660, yet as we shall see, managed to successfully combine a clerical and scientific career.

In sum, then, during the sixteenth and seventeenth centuries there was limited social space for the professional practice of what we call "science." Those engaged in one of the three sanctioned callings, on the strictest interpretation of their professional responsibilities, should have found little time to accommodate scientific interests. How did such laymen as Kepler and Boyle come to understand their vocations? Moreover, how was it that clerics such as John Ray could come to regard the study of nature as a legitimate component of the theological vocation, and thus consistent with clerical calling?

Priests of Nature and the Priesthood of All Believers

The early modern period witnessed two developments that made social space available for the dedicated pursuit of the sciences. First was the view, prosecuted by the Protestant reformers, that the clerical vocation was not different in kind from other vocations. This enabled non-clergymen who were involved in the pursuit of the "sciences" to make a plausible claim to be engaged in a sanctified or priestly activity. Second, and equally important, was the development of the discipline of physico-theology—a mixed science that combined natural philosophy (or "physics") with theology. The emergence of this field of enquiry legitimated the study of nature for those engaged in clerical professions because to study nature now meant to be engaged in an appropriately theological activity.

To obtain a sense of the significance of the first development it is necessary to understand how the early modern conception of distinct vocations differed from the earlier medieval notion of distinct estates. During the Middle Ages the occupational status of individuals was determined by their "estate." The clergy formed one of three vertical estates of Christendom, the other two being the aristocracy and the laity.[24] The spiritual estate of the clergy was superior to the temporal estates. The elevated status of the clerical estate was mirrored in the university curriculum because just as the clergy were acknowledged to be superior to the laity, so theology was superior to the other sciences. Furthermore, it was assumed that the most academically gifted students would proceed to the study of theology then to a clerical career.

This hierarchical division of estates was subjected to acute criticism during the Reformation when Luther, and to a lesser extent Calvin, rejected the notion of a religious class different in kind to the other estates. "It is pure invention," railed Luther, "that pope, bishops, priests and monks are called the spiritual estate while princes, lords, artisans, and farmers are called the temporal estate." "All Christians," he insisted, "are of the spiritual estate, and there is no difference among them except that of office."[25] This doctrine, which subsequently became known as "the priesthood of all believers," also received support from Calvin.[26] In Protestant lands, these theological contentions led to structural reform of the clerical office. The clergy were no longer distinguished by their estate but came to be regarded as one "calling" among others. This meant that in principle, if not always in practice, anyone could fulfill a priestly office.

It is in this context that we are to understand Johannes Kepler's conviction that the study of astronomy could count as a priestly activity. Having been torn between a socially sanctioned career in theology and the pursuit of "science," he eventually came to the view that astronomy was no less a religious vocation than theology. The whole world, Kepler was to write, was "the temple of God" and "the book of Nature." To contemplate nature was thus to engage in "true worship to honor God, to venerate him, to wonder at him."[27] That an astronomer might be able to discharge a sacerdotal function would have been inconceivable in the older understanding of "estates." The Protestant notion that all believers, in principle, could be "priests" thus made possible Kepler's contention that the astronomical calling was, in effect, a priestly one.

Kepler was not the only lay scientist to claim a priestly status. Robert Boyle also argued that the world was the "temple" of God and that this gave warrant to the priestly vocation of investigators of the natural world. Boyle observed: "Philosophers of almost all religions have been, by the contemplation of the world, moved to consider it under the notion of a temple."[28] A number of Boyle's contemporaries also subscribed to the notion of the world as God's temple. Cambridge Platonist Henry More (1614–1687) described the universe as "the temple of God," claiming that its human inhabitants were priests who should be "invested as it were and adorned with the Knowledge of the Laws and Measures of the Creation." More himself, while in holy orders, argued that the true priest must be armed with a knowledge of philosophy (science): "I make account I began to *adorn my Function*, and amongst other Priestly Habiliments, in particular to put on the Λόγον or *Rationale*. . . . every *Priest* should endeavour, according to his opportunity and capacity, to be also as much as he can, a *Rational* man or *Philosopher*."[29]

If More had thought that a formal knowledge of nature was appropriate knowledge for a priest, Boyle conversely had held that acquisition of such knowledge could confer a priestly status on a layman. "If the world be a temple," he wrote, "man sure must be the priest, ordained (by being qualified) to celebrate divine service not only in it, but for it." Like Kepler, Boyle concluded that the investigation of nature was an act of worship. The rational contemplation of nature was "the first act of religion, and equally obliging in all religions." Natural philosophy was nothing less than the "philosophical worship of God." He went on to suggest that "discovering to others the perfections of God displayed in the creatures is a more acceptable act of religion, than the burning of sacrifices or perfumes upon his altars."[30] For Boyle, ordination in this "priesthood" called for a knowledge of the operations of the natural world. In short, the true priestly vocation could be followed only by those familiar with the workings of nature.[31] Other naturalists followed Boyle's lead on this issue. The physico-theological writer Noël Antoine Pluche wrote in his best-selling *Spectacle of Nature* that man is the priest of all the creatures because by discovering their perfections, he articulates their "Tribute of Praise to him who has formed them for his glory."[32] The notion of the "priest of nature" was thus one way to argue for the religious status of the naturalist.

Interpreters of the Book of Nature

Another image of the natural world, exploited by both Kepler and Boyle to vindicate their vision of the priestly role of natural philosophers, was that of the "book of nature." According to the standard early modern use of the metaphor, God has provided us with two books, the natural world and the book of Scripture. Both communicate something of the divine nature. As English physician Thomas Browne (1605–1682) expressed it: "Thus there are two books from whence I collect my divinity: besides that written one of God, another of his servant Nature—that universal and public manuscript that lies expansed into the eyes of all."[33] Of course, the metaphor of the book of nature was not new. But Kepler and the other early modern figures who would follow him in exploiting this metaphor used it in quite a new sense.

During the Middle Ages, the notion of "the book of nature" was intimately related to the allegorical interpretation of Scripture. From the time of the church fathers, allegorical interpretation had involved determining the transcendental meanings of natural objects. Aquinas and Augustine had both taught that to know the literal meaning of the words of Scripture, one must ascertain the objects to which the words referred. To determine the allegorical sense, however, one needed to elucidate the meaning of those objects.[34] Thus at the literal level, the word *lion* referred to the object "lion." However, at the allegorical level, the natural object "lion" could refer to Christ or Satan or even the head of the household. Reading the book of nature in the Middle Ages had thus called for the elucidation of the mystical religious meanings of objects the key to which was provided by the book of Scripture.

The Renaissance and Protestant Reformation brought a renewed emphasis on the literal sense of Scripture, and the long-standing system of allegorical meanings collapsed. As a consequence, the world of natural objects was liberated from the business of biblical exegesis. The natural world now lay open to new ordering principles, and the nascent natural sciences were to provide these.[35] Henceforth, nature was understood mathematically and taxonomically, rather than in terms of its transcendental meanings.[36] The book of nature, in short, now offered itself up to alternative hermeneutical practices. Mathematics provided one such hermeneutical key. The language of this book of nature, Kepler wrote in the preface to his *Mysterium Cosmographicum* (1596), was the language of geometry. Mathematics, then, was like a holy language, and the discovery of the mathematical nature of the universe was akin to the exposition of God's other book—the Bible.

Other astronomers would also exploit the "book of nature" metaphor to give religious legitimacy to their scientific pursuits. Galileo, as is well known, insisted that the book of nature was written in the language of mathematics:

> Philosophy is written in this grand book, the universe, which stands continually open to our gaze. But the book cannot be understood unless one first learns to comprehend the language and read the letters in which it is composed. It is written in the language of mathematics, and its characters are triangles, circles, and other geometrical figures without which it is humanly impossible to understand a single word of it.[37]

Exegesis of the book of nature was for Galileo, as for Kepler, a religious act. In the opening pages of the work that would ultimately lead to his condemnation by the Inquisition, Galileo explained why the vocation of natural philosopher is to be most highly regarded:

> He who looks the higher is the more highly distinguished, and turning over the great book of nature (which is the proper object of philosophy) is the way to elevate one's gaze. And though whatever we read in that book is the creation of the omnipotent Craftsman, and is accordingly excellently proportioned, nevertheless that part is most suitable and most worthy which make

His work and His craftsmanship most evident to our view.[38]

Insistence on the mathematical coding of the natural world brought with it the implication that only those with the requisite mathematical skills were capable of expounding this book. Thus skill in mathematics conferred a special status in the interpretation of nature comparable to that traditionally exercised by a priesthood that had been possessed of both the requisite skills in Latin and knowledge of the authoritative and delimiting interpretations of Scripture sanctioned by the church.

Robert Boyle was another who regarded the study of nature to be not only a religious act but also one that was closely akin to the exegetical task of reading Scripture. Just as rare historical works require an expert interpreter, so, too, with the book of nature:

> For the book of nature is to an ordinary gazer, and a naturalist, like a rare book of hieroglyphicks to a child, and a philosopher: the one is sufficiently pleased with the oddness and variety of the curious pictures that adorn it; whereas the other, is not only delighted with those outward objects, that gratify his sense, but receives a much higher satisfaction, in admiring the knowledge of the author, and in finding out and inriching himself with those abstruse and veiled truths dexterously hinted in them.[39]

If Kepler and Galileo had found in mathematics the interpretative key of the book of nature, for Boyle it lay in experimentation and dissection. These were the means by which the deceptive appearances of things could be penetrated, enabling the exploration of deeper meanings. Of the unsavory practice of dissection, a messy and manual business, Boyle was to admit: "I confess its instructivenesse hath not only so reconciled me to it, but so enamoured me of it, that I have often spent hours much less delightfully, not only in courts, but even in libraries, than in tracing those forsaken mansions, the inimitable workmanship of the omniscient Architect."[40]

The two related metaphors—"priests of nature" and "book of nature"—played a vital rhetorical role in establishing the vocational respectability of the study of nature by providing it with a theological sanction. The deployment of these expressions paved the way for the eventual emergence of a hybrid discipline— physico-theology—that would represent an important synthesis of "science" and "religion" that persisted virtually until the end of the nineteenth century. Physico-theology was the hyphenated discipline that brought with it respectability for the hyphenated vocation of the clergyman-naturalist.

Physico-theology and the Clergyman-Naturalist

While the doctrine of the priesthood of all believers was to confer on the formal study of nature the sanctity of a priestly vocation, the emergence in the late seventeenth century of the discipline of physico-theology was to provide professional clergymen with a justification for studying nature as an integral part of their vocation. If, as John Locke had held, the office of a minister of the Gospel was so all-consuming as to exclude all secular pursuits, the vocational designation "clergyman-naturalist" would be oxymoronic. This was clearly not the case for the eighteenth century and for much of the nineteenth, owing in large measure to the birth of this new, mixed discipline. Whereas the metaphors "temple of nature" and "book of nature" provide an informal indication of how the study of nature might be regarded as a sanctified activity, with the emergence of a new disciplinary category— "physico-theology"—came the formal recognition that the study of nature was no less a theological activity than the preaching of sermons or the exposition of Scripture.

The seventeenth century had witnessed the rise of a number of "mixed" disciplines. The traditional Aristotelian division of the sciences that had held sway throughout the late Middle Ages and into the Renaissance had distinguished three speculative sciences—metaphysics (also known as "sacred science" or "theology"), mathematics, and natural philosophy (or "physics").[41] Aristotle had sounded cautions against the transgression of these disciplinary boundaries, though some admixture of mathematics and natural philosophy was admitted in the so-called "subordinate" sciences.[42] In a sense, many of the achievements of the seventeenth century came as a consequence of ignoring Aristotle's injunctions against mixing the disciplines, in particular by using mathematics in the sphere of natural philosophy. The growth of the discipline of "physico-mathematics" was a consequence of this development, and the title of Newton's magnum opus—*The Mathematical Principles of Natural Philosophy* (1687)—provides an important clue to Newton's view of the role of mathematics in natural philosophy.[43]

The term "physico-theology" represents another novel combination of two of the three speculative sciences. The term "physico-theological" first appeared in English in 1652, but it was Boyle who provided the first formal account of this approach in 1688.[44] For Boyle, the Christian philosopher must resort to theological explanations to provide a complete account of the natural world. This, for Boyle, was an account that would be consistent with both nature itself and scripture.[45] In addition, this new discipline could be exploited against unbelievers to demonstrate the rationality of theistic belief. In short, physico-theology would demonstrate how the book of nature and Scriptures were in complete harmony and link natural theology with the new approaches to the study of nature. The physico-theological approach advocated by Boyle eventually gave rise to the eighteenth-century discipline "physico-theology." The title of the mixed discipline first appears, appropriately enough, in the title of the Boyle Lectures given by William Derham in 1711/1712: *Physico-Theology: Or a Demonstration of the Being and Attributes of God from the Works of His Creation* (1713). This work was followed by similar titles and others that represented increasingly specialized fields of interest—Friedrich Lesser's *Insecto-Theologia* (1738), Peter Ahlwart's *Bronto-Theologie* (1745), and John Balfour's *Phyto-Theology* (1851).[46] In each of these instances it was the task of the physico-theologian to show how nature provided evidence of the wisdom and goodness of the Deity. This was principally achieved by highlighting the myriad instances of design or "contrivance" in nature and by pointing out how living things had been purposefully created to serve human or divine ends.

In sum, the discipline of physico-theology provided the motivation for individuals to study nature and, equally important, gave natural history a coherent theoretical structure. The emergence of physico-theology as a discipline also invested the study of nature with a new and more dignified status. The remarkable popularity of physico-theology as a genre provided additional social sanction for this activity. Crucially, moreover, it made it possible for naturalists to argue that they were pursuing a kind of theological vocation and for clergymen to claim that the study of nature was not merely a diverting sideline but an integral element of their priestly duties. John Ray's classic work of physico-theology—*The Wisdom of God Manifested in the Works of His Creation* (1691)—was thus a compilation of sermons delivered in the Chapel of Trinity College, Cambridge. Indeed, in this work, Ray argued that part of the prescribed duties of the Sabbath should be contemplation of the works of nature:

> It may be (for ought I know, and as some Divines have thought) part of our business and employment in Eternity to contemplate the works of God. . . . I am sure it is part of the business of a Sabbath-day, and the Sabbath is a Type of that eternal Rest; for the Sabbath seems to have been instituted for a commemoration of the Works of the Creation.[47]

Natural history, thus conceived, was an activity of divine worship to be directed by one with the requisite knowledge of nature.

Secularization and a New Priesthood

The word *scientist*, as mentioned at the outset, first entered the English lexicon in the nineteenth century.[48] Its introduction met with considerable resistance, no doubt partly because of the common, though erroneous, view that it was an American barbarism. However, by the end of the nineteenth century the term had achieved wide acceptance. The success of this new designation is not merely a semantic curiosity because it was largely a reflection of the general growth of distinct professions during this period. More importantly, the appearance of the term *scientist* signaled the end of that typically eighteenth- and nineteenth-century phenomenon of the priest-naturalist. Over the course of the nineteenth century deliberate moves were afoot to elevate the status of the natural sciences and of those who were its practitioners. This could only take place, many believed, if the social powers of the priesthood were challenged and the domination of the university curriculum by theology and the humanities brought to an end. In this zero-sum game there had to be losers, and the diminution in the social status and authority of the clergy was a direct consequence of the elevation of "the scientist." Henceforth, it is the scientist who is the authoritative purveyor of true and useful knowledge.[49]

It is significant that the nineteenth century also witnessed the establishment of the first professional bodies for scientific practitioners. The British Association for the Advancement of Science, to take the most obvious example, was established during the 1830s. The founding of such societies brought a new status for those engaged in the pursuit of science and a distinct and exclusive set of professional commitments.[50] As we have seen, whereas previously in many of the scientific disciplines—and in natural history in particular—clergymen had played a predominant role, this was to change dramatically over the course of the century.[51] In addition, in the memberships of the various scientific associations there was a significant shift in professional commitment. Whereas in the early and middle decades of the nineteenth century Anglican clergymen had typically dominated both the membership and the offices of these societies, by the end of the century they were in a minority. The deliberate attempt on the part of some of the newly designated "scientists" to replace the clergy at the pinnacle of the professions was accompanied by a rhetoric that suggested the sciences were a kind of surrogate religion. "Darwin's bulldog," Thomas Huxley (1825–1895), thus wrote that he and his scientific brethren were members of a "church scientific."[52] The appearance of the word *scientist* is thus symptomatic of a new phase in the understanding of the study of the natural world and its relation to theological interests.

Conclusion

In the twenty-first century, when scientists make public profession of a religious commitment, such convictions are usually deemed irrelevant to scientific practice. Theological considerations themselves are not thought to play any substantial role in the sciences, and even their motivational role is generally disregarded. However true this may be of our own era, the history of the scientific vocation demonstrates that this was not always so.

This history also has important lessons for the more general question of the relationship between science and religion. After all, science and religion are not disembodied practices but represent activities carried out by individuals. In an important sense, then, there is no relationship between science and theology as such because sets of convictions, whether theological or scientific, exist only in the minds of persons. It is for this reason that scientific and religious biographies should have a central place in any historical account of the relationship between "science" and "religion." To the case in point, consideration of the vocational dilemmas faced by early modern figures makes it clear that religious convictions played a vital role in the creation of a vocational space for the study of nature and in the sanctioning of scientific activity. The anachronistic image of the "secular scientist," projected backward onto this period, can at times blind modern investigators to this situation, leading them to overlook the centrality of theological convictions in the motivations of early modern investigators of nature. At that time, the practice of the "new science" called for equally new notions of vocation. The office of "priest of nature" was the result of a rethinking of traditional notions of the priestly calling and played an important role in the development of natural philosophy and natural history, and thus of modern science itself.

Notes

1. On this general issue see Mordechai Feingold's excellent essay, "Science as a Calling: The Early Modern Dilemma," *Science in Context* 15 (2002): 79–119.
2. Nicholas Jardine, "Epistemology of the Sciences," in *The Cambridge History of Renaissance Philosophy*, eds. Charles Schmitt and Quentin Skinner (Cambridge, 1988), 685. See also Jardine, "Demonstration, Dialectic, and Rhetoric in Galileo's Dialogue," in *The Shapes of Knowledge from the Renaissance to the Enlightenment*, eds. Donald R. Kelley and Richard H. Popkin (Dordrecht; Boston: Kluwer Academic Press, 1991), 101–21.
3. Andrew Cunningham, "Getting the Game Right: Some Plain Words on

the Identity and Invention of Science," *Studies in History and Philosophy of Science* 19:3 (1988): 365–89; Cunningham, "How the Principia Got Its Name: Or, Taking Natural Philosophy Seriously," *History of Science* 28 (1991): 377–92; Peter Harrison, "Natural History," in *Wrestling with Nature: From Omens to Science*, eds. Ronald Numbers and Michael Shank (Chicago, forthcoming). For the medieval and Renaissance understanding of "natural philosophy," see William Wallace, "Traditional Natural Philosophy," in *The Cambridge History of Renaissance Philosophy*, 201–35.

4. Sydney Ross, " 'Scientist': the Story of a Word," *Annals of Science* 18 (1962): 65–86.

5. For some of these labels, see Christoph Lüthy, "What to Do with Seventeenth-Century Natural Philosophy? A Taxonomic Problem," *Perspectives on Science* 8 (2000): 164–95 (esp. 176f.); Helmut Holzhey, "Der Philosoph im 17. Jahrhundert," in *Grundriss der Geschichte der Philosophie. Reihe 17. Jahrhundert*, ed. Jean-Pierre Schobinger (Basel, 1993), 1:3–30 (13f.); Peter Burke, *A Social History of Knowledge: From Gutenberg to Diderot* (Cambridge, 2000), chapter 2; Joseph Freedman, " 'Professionalization' and 'Confessionalization': The Place of Physics, Philosophy, and Arts Instruction at Central European Academic Institutions during the Reformation Era," *Early Science and Medicine* 6 (2001): 334–52.

6. W. J. Reader, *Professional Men: The Rise of the Professional Classes in Victorian England* (London: Weidenfeld & Nicholson, 1966); M. S. Larson, *The Rise of Professionalism: A Sociological Analysis* (Berkeley: University of California Press, 1977), chapter 1.

7. John Calvin, *Institutes of the Christian Religion*, 2 vols., ed. J. McNeill, trans. F. Battles (Philadelphia: Westminster Press, 1960), 1:276; 2:1,055. Cf. Philip Melanchthon, *Orations on Philosophy and Education*, ed. Sachiko Kusakawa (New York: Cambridge University Press, 1999), 184.

8. John Gascoigne, "The Eighteenth-Century Scientific Community: A Prospographical Study," *Social Studies of Science* 25 (1995): 575–81 (577f.).

9. Feingold, "Science as a Calling," 95.

10. John Ray, *The Wisdom of God Manifested in the Works of Creation* (London, 1691), 125, 123f.

11. Thomas Sprat, *The History of the Royal Society* (London, 1667), 57.

12. See especially Steven Shapin, *A Social History of Truth: Civility and Science in Seventeenth-Century England* (Chicago: University of Chicago Press, 1994).

13. Calvin, *Institutes*, 2:1,062. Cf. Calvin, *Tracts and Treatises on the Refor-*

mation of the Church, 3 vols., trans. H. Beveridge (Grand Rapids: Eerdmans, 1958), 3:281ff.

14. Calvin, *Institutes*, 2:1,062.

15. Calvin, *Institutes*, 1:724.

16. Robert Sanderson, *XXXVI Sermons* (London, 1689), 204, 205, 220, 226.

17. John Locke, *Of the Conduct of the Understanding*, 5th ed., ed. Thomas Fowler (Oxford: Clarendon Press, 1901), 42. Locke nonetheless argued in this context that the exclusive nature of the professions militated against the attainment of universal knowledge.

18. John Locke, *Third Letter concerning Toleration, Works*, 12th ed. (London, 1823), 6:171.

19. For the examples of Newton, Locke, and Ray, I am indebted to Feingold, "Science as a Calling."

20. Johannes Kepler, *Gesammelte Werke* (Munich, 1937–1945), 8:40. For Kepler's own account, Johannes Kepler, *Selbstzeugnisse*, ed. Franz Hammer, trans. Esther Hammer (Stuttgart-Bad Constatt, 1971), 61–65.

21. Richard Westfall, *Never at Rest: A Biography of Isaac Newton* (New York: Cambridge University Press, 1980), 330–33. But cf. Feingold, "Science as a Calling," 96f.

22. Locke, *Essays on the Law of Nature* (Oxford: Clarendon Press, 1954), 19.

23. John Ray, quoted in Feingold, "Science as a Calling," 95.

24. Rosemary O'Day, "The Clergy of the Church of England," in *The Professions in Early Modern England*, ed. Wilfred Prest (London; New York: Croom Helm, 1987), 25–63.

25. Martin Luther, "To the Christian Nobility of the German Nation (1520)," in *Three Treatises* (Philadelphia: Fortress, 1970), 12.

26. Calvin, *Institutes*, 1:502; 2:1,473.

27. Johannes Kepler, *Mysterium Cosmographicum*, trans. A. M. Duncan (Norwalk, Conn.: Abarus, 1999), 53.

28. Robert Boyle, *Some Considerations Touching the Usefulness of Experimental Natural Philosophy*, in *The Works of the Honourable Robert Boyle*, 6 vols., ed. Thomas Birch (Hildesheim: Georg Olms 1966), 2:31. For an early account of Boyle's notion of the priest-scientist, see H. Fisch, "The Scientist as Priest: A Note on Robert Boyle's Natural Theology," *Isis* 44 (1953): 252–65.

29. Henry More, *A Collection of Several Philosophical Writings*, 2nd ed. (London, 1662), v; More, *An Antidote against Atheisme* (London, 1653), 103. Cf. George Herbert, "Providence," line 13; Henry Vaughan, "Christ's Nativity," lines 11f.; John Smith, *Select Discourses* (London, 1660), 433f.; Francis Bacon, *A New Organon*, I.cxx, in *The Works of*

Francis Bacon, 14 vols., eds. James Spedding and Robert Ellis, (London, 1860), 4:106; Thomas Traherne, "Centuries," 1.31; Joseph Addison, *The Spectator* 564 (9 July 1714): 805.

30. Boyle, *Usefulness of Natural Philosophy*, in *Works*, 2:62f.

31. Boyle, *Usefulness of Natural Philosophy*, in *Works*, 2:32.

32. Noël Antoine Pluche, *Spectacle de la Nature*, 5th ed., 7 vols. (London, 1770), 1:390.

33. Thomas Browne, *Religio Medici, Hydriotaphia, and The Garden of Cyrus*, ed. Robin Robbins (Oxford: Clarendon Press, 1972), 1.16 (16f.).

34. See, e.g., Augustine, *On Christian Doctrine*, 1.ii.2; Aquinas, *Summa theologiae* 1a. 1, 10; Hugh of St. Victor, *Didascalicon* V.2–3.

35. For this transition, see Peter Harrison, *The Bible, Protestantism, and the Rise of Natural Science* (Cambridge: Cambridge University Press, 1998), and Harrison, "Fixing the Meaning of Scripture: The Renaissance Bible and the Origins of Modernity," *Concilium* 294 (2002): 102–10.

36. On mathesis and taxonomy as new ordering principles, see Michel Foucault, *The Order of Things* (London: Tavistock, 1987).

37. Galileo Galilei, *The Assayer*, in *Discoveries and Opinions of Galileo*, trans. Stillman Drake (New York: Doubleday, 1957), 237f.

38. Galileo Galilei, *Dialogue Concerning the Two Chief World Systems— Ptolemaic & Copernican*, trans. Stillman Drake (Berkeley: University of California Press, 1962), 3.

39. Boyle, *Usefulness of Natural Philosophy*, in *Works*, 2:6. Cf. the previously unpublished manuscript "Of the Study of the Book of Nature" in the new edition of Boyle's works: *The Works of Robert Boyle*, eds. Michael Hunter and Edward B. Davis (London: Pickering and Chatto, 2000), 8:145–72.

40. Boyle, *Usefulness of Natural Philosophy*, in *Works*, 2:7.

41. Aristotle, *Metaphysics*, 1,025b–1,026a.

42. Aristotle, *Posterior Analytics*, 75a–b; *Metaphysics*, 989b–990a; *On the Heavens*, 299a–299b. See also Amos Funkenstein, *Theology and the Scientific Imagination* (Princeton: Princeton University Press, 1986), 35–37; 303–7.

43. Cunningham, "How the Principia Got Its Name."

44. The first appearance of the term "physico-theological" (with due respect to the *Oxford English Dictionary*) is in Walter Charleton, *The Darknes of Atheism Dispelled by the Light of Nature: A Physico-Theological Treatise* (London, 1652). Boyle used the term in the title of his *Physico-Theological Considerations about the Possibility of the Resurrection* (London, 1675). For Boyle's explanation of the term, see *A Disquisition about the*

Final Causes of Natural Things (London, 1688), 104f. John Ray subsequently used the expression in the title of his *Three Physico-Theological Discourses* (London, 1693).

45. Boyle, preface to *A Disquisition*, 29, 80.

46. F. C. Lesser, Insecto-Theologia (Frankfurt und Leipzig, 1738); Peter Ahlwardt, *Bronto-Theologie, oder Vernünftige und theologische Betrachtungen über den Blitz und Donner* (Greifswalde & Leipzig, 1745); John Balfour, *Phyto-Theology; or, Botanical Sketches intended to illustrate the works of God in the structure, functions, and general distribution of plants* (London & Edinburgh: Johnstone and Hunter, 1851).

47. Ray, *Wisdom of God*, 124.

48. Ross, " 'Scientist': The Story of a Word."

49. Frank Turner, "The Victorian Conflict between Science and Religion: A Professional Dimension," *Isis* 49 (1978): 356–76; Richard Yeo, "Science and Intellectual Authority in Mid-Nineteenth-Century Britain," in *Science in the Public Sphere* (Aldershot: Ashgate, 2001), 5–31.

50. John Hedley Brooke, *Science and Religion: Some Historical Perspectives* (New York: Cambridge University Press, 1991), 5, 50; David Livingstone, "Science and Religion: Toward a New Cartography," *Christian Scholar's Review* 26 (1997): 270–92. Adrian Desmond, *Archetypes and Ancestors: Palaeontology in Victorian London: 1850–1875* (Chicago: University of Chicago Press, 1984).

51. On the role of the clergy in natural history, see Patrick Armstrong, *The English Parson-Naturalist: A Companionship between Science and Religion* (Leominster, Herefordshire, 2000).

52. See George Levine, "Scientific Discourse as an Alternative to Faith," in *Victorian Faith in Crisis*, eds. Richard J. Helmstadter and Bernard Lightman (Stanford: Stanford University Press, 1990), 225–61; Livingstone, "Science and Religion," 273; Colin R. Russell, "The Conflict Metaphor and Its Social Origins," *Science and Christian Belief* 1 (1989): 3–26; Adrian Desmond, *Huxley*, 2 vols. (London: Michael Joseph, 1997), 2:244–48; Adrian Desmond and James R. Moore, *Darwin* (London: Michael Joseph, 1991), 560–61; Bernard Lightman, *The Origins of Agnosticism: Victorian Unbelief and the Limits of Knowledge* (Baltimore: Johns Hopkins University Press, 1987), chapter 5.

3

Interpreters of the Book of Nature[1]

ANGUS J. L. MENUGE

Abstract

It is commonplace to speak of nature as a book. But we often do not reflect on the importance of a sound hermeneutic and of what difference this makes to the scientific vocation. The scientist is called to interpret nature, so we should ask which hermeneutical principles will best aid that calling. This essay attempts to show how transformations in the nature as text metaphor were pivotal for both success and failure in the scientific vocation. Why did anyone ever open the book in the first place? What was it about the medieval reading of nature that held back empirical science? What role did the Reformation revolution in hermeneutics, emphasized by Peter Harrison (1998), play in the emergence of the modern vocation of scientist? How can both the rise of natural theology and its critique be understood in terms of rival interpretations of the natural text? These and other questions will be addressed by way of showing that hermeneutics is critical in evaluating competing perspectives on the interplay between science and religion. It is argued that intelligent design has much to contribute to discussions about the vocation of nature's interpreter.

Introduction

The idea of nature as a book provides one of the richest and most often appropriated metaphors for the natural world. Plato, Aristotle, the Stoics, and Christians have all seen the work of the scientist as tracing out the *telos* or *logos* inscribed in nature by some demiurge or god. Critics of design, from Francis Bacon[2] to Daniel Dennett, also see science as a kind of reading. Bacon urged that nature was a text that, to be rightly understood, must not be anticipated but humbly interpreted.[3] Dennett concludes evolutionary biology must employ "artifact hermeneutics"[4] to discern what biological structures are adaptations for. Nonetheless, for Dennett, the text is written by the blind process of natural selection, not via the agency of an author. The metaphor of nature as text is congenial to both proponents and critics of intelligent design. The vocation of natural interpreter calls to both believers and unbelievers in the Author of the text.

In this essay, I will trace the history of the idea that nature is a book from early Greek science through the Middle Ages and Reformation, culminating in the rise and critique of natural theology. First (section 2), we will try to understand how science got started: What prompted some people to stand back from their busy lives to open the book of nature in the first place? Next (section 3), we will draw on the recent work of Peter Harrison, who argues persuasively that the Reformation provided the crucial hermeneutical change that overcame scholasticism and made modern science possible. Then (section 4), we will move to the great controversy between natural theology and its critics. This we will consider as fundamentally a drama about rival hermeneutics and the proper limits of theological and scientific interpretation. Finally (section 5), we will consider what intelligent design has to contribute to this discussion.

Opening the Book

Before science can start, humans must understand that nature is congenial to systematic study. They must believe that the vocation of science is possible. Not all ways of understanding nature support this assumption.[5] Animism and polytheism suggest that nature itself is sacred, so it would be sacrilege to dissect it, and also that nature is governed by a multiplicity of local deities and is thus too heterogeneous and capricious to support universal laws. Excessive spiritualism or exclusive concern for eternal truth may disparage nature as the realm of transience, *maya* (illusion), or corruption, making science's systematic study a pointless or even sinful diversion.[6]

Even Plato had tendencies in the latter direction but overcame them by proposing a more fruitful connection between the eternal and the temporal. If the eternal realm is fundamentally orderly and rational, and the temporal universe is a copy, then if the copy preserves enough of the original qualities, it should be intelligible to human reason. Speaking for Plato, Timaeus says that "the world has been framed in the likeness of that which is apprehended by reason and mind,"[7] that is, in the (imperfect) likeness of the Forms. The cosmos was understood as an organism, "a living creature truly endowed with soul and intelligence by the providence of God."[8] While moderns will find this picture anthropomorphic, the assumption that the cosmos is an intelligent organism like us at least guarantees that nature's order is intelligible to humans, making the vocation of science possible.

Despite this nudge forward for science, Plato's philosophy inhibited its full potential. For one thing, he distinguished a corrupt sublunary realm from the superlunary region, where alone entities truly fulfilled their *telos*: "The sublunary part was . . . a partial failure." Because of this distinction in Plato's vitalistic universe, he "deprived it of a thorough, universally valid orderliness."[9] Although Plato had the genius to suggest that much of physics could be reduced to geometry, thereby anticipating Descartes, Kepler, and other giants of the scientific revolution,[10] he did not think that geometry was valid for the corruptible Earth, a view hardly congenial to terrestrial physics. The major problem was that Plato divorced essences or forms from *concreta* so the only universal truths were found in the eternal realm. Thus science was viewed as speculating about the eternal mind on the basis of its temporal image, an activity that could at best yield approximations.

A decisive move away from this picture was made by Plato's great student Aristotle, who suggested that essences were actually contained in substances. If this is true, then scientific analysis of substance can hope to rival mathematics in its ability to discern forms. Aristotelian metaphysics made it possible to think that science could discover necessary connections (laws) by examining the essences of particulars. Because the Platonic realm was rational, when Aristotle imported it into particulars, these were predicted to conform to rational principles. Science became the project of discerning what a substance's nature was, which would tell us what it was inclined to do, and thus predict its characteristic behavior. The mentalism of Plato's approach to the universe was thus displaced but not eliminated.[11]

In addition to the material and efficient causes still recognized throughout contemporary science, Aristotle also emphasized the formal and final causes. Looking at the development of embryos into chickens, Aristotle observed a programmed series of changes, which he supposed derived from the characteristic form of chickens contained in the embryo. Although contemporary science has challenged the claim that DNA is the exclusive determinant of development, it is not absurd to suggest that the discovery of DNA partially confirmed Aristotle's insight about embryogenesis. Outside of biology, however, modern science sees much less use for formal causes because typical physical objects are taken to be passively obedient to external laws rather than enacting active principles within themselves. Even less popular is Aristotle's idea that each substance has some final end that provides a teleological explanation of its current behavior. Teleology of this kind is rejected by most contemporary scientists, except in the case of a human or other observable intelligent agents. Yet both the laws of thermodynamics and various anthropic principles are suggestive of a universe that has a certain in-built direction. Darwinists such as Gould have claimed that were the evolutionary tape rewound and played again, it is most unlikely that life as we know it would re-evolve. However, theistic evolutionists, self-organizers, and proponents of intelligent design would expect similar patterns to emerge, pointing to the fine-tuning of physical constants and the stability of species as evidence. Some Darwinists also concede that what Dennett calls "forced moves in the game of design"[12] would channel natural selection along somewhat predictable paths.

Aristotle sets out an early form of the design inference, arguing that if we find a natural entity whose development corresponds to an artifact that we know is designed, we can conclude that the natural entity is designed as well. Swallows make nests and spiders make webs and Aristotle concluded that these products are artifacts produced for a purpose.[13] When Aquinas taught Aristotle to speak like a Christian, he extended this argument by pointing out that if the swallow and spider lack the intelligence to direct their craft, it must instead be located in their creator and director (Aquinas's Fifth Way). Before Humean skepticism about the discernibility of God's purposes and the various recent attempts to reduce intelligence to unintelligent causes, this seemed a persuasive argument to most people. Thomist hermeneutics take us from the text all the way to its author, in cheerful disregard of postmodern claims that the author is "dead" or unrecoverable.

Christianity also provided some additional presuppositions that helped science along its way. That this is so seems to many a matter of historical record, though it does not follow that these presuppositions cannot be detached from Christianity and supported on independent grounds.[14] Christians contributed the idea that the entire universe was created *ex nihilo* by a single, rational being. As we saw, Greek science had supposed that the universe was bifurcated into the perfect heavens governed by celestial physics and the corruptible sublunar realm subject to terrestrial physics. A rational God who is sovereign of all can be expected to make no such distinction. As Jaki argues, even Buridan in the Middle Ages seems to have grasped this point, which is implied by his willingness to understand celestial motion by comparison to such mundane terrestrial examples as moving a smith's wheel and the long-jump.[15] It was not until Newton that a comprehensive set of universal laws was developed and the distinction between celestial and terrestrial physics finally abolished. Despite his unorthodox Arianism, Newton shared with Buridan a strong belief in a single, rational creator of the universe, and this certainly founded his faith that universal laws were available for discovery. The theological hermeneutic that insists the book of nature is the work of a single, coherent author has been fruitful for science.

By distinguishing the Creator from the creation while retaining the idea that the creation was good, Christianity removed the universe's sacred status, making its study and dissection morally permissible, while upholding the value of matter against the Gnostic disdain for it.[16] And if God is identified with the Logos, a principle of rational order, and one in whose image we are made, there is a foundation for Plato's expectation of an intelligible, orderly universe.[17] It seems undeniable that this assumption is one that can never be justified from the bottom-up (that is, from human perceptions of phenomena) because it is essentially equivalent to solving the insoluble problem of induction. The pragmatic need for a faith in natural order seems to be a prerequisite for doing science, and it is a major challenge for naturalism to justify this faith.[18] In all of these ways, the idea of divine design has helped science, not so much by providing specific theories but by legitimating general research programs directed toward the discovery of universal laws. The secularist may grant the historical value of this theological scaffolding but claim it has been used to build a materialist edifice that no longer has need of it. Conversely, quite a few philosophers, myself included, are coming to the conclusion that scientific materialism cannot justify its foundational assumptions independently of theism.[19]

Still, it must be admitted that Christianity has not always been a friend to science. To be sure, most contemporary scholars agree that the Enlightenment picture of the Dark Ages as an authoritarian stifling of science is an overdrawn caricature that ignores important scientific advances in both mathematics and theoretical physics.[20] But it is undeniable that scholasticism impeded the development of modern empirical science and that some Christian assumptions were partly to blame for this.[21]

From Scholasticism to Modern Science

There is little doubt that the scholastic scientists of the medieval period related textual interpretation to nature in unhelpful ways. Not only Scripture but also all classical works were taken as authoritative. It was supposed that Adam's knowledge before the fall was much more complete than our own, and that even after the fall, early texts retained many great insights now in danger of being lost through the progressive corruption of the human mind. Thus Peter Harrison argues that "the mastery of nature at which thirteenth and fourteenth century minds aimed, amounted to a reconstruction of a past body of knowledge, the ruins of which could be discovered in those texts of the ancients."[22] Not only that, scholasticism followed the obsession of the early church fathers with allegorical interpretations of the text. This was extended from Scripture to the study of nature, so a hermeneutics of nature aimed not at accurate description of the facts about an entity but discernment of its symbolic meaning. These meanings were thought to reside in authoritative texts, making empirical investigation of the world unnecessary.

> The turn to nature as an entity in its own right was a turn to texts about nature . . . Such was the nature of the scholastic method that discovery took place through exegesis and argument rather than by observation and experiment.[23]

As a result, medieval bestiaries evince quite credulous acceptance of a variety of nonexistent creatures (harpies, unicorns, centaurs, satyrs, and more). These books also include unsubstantiated fables about real creatures, going back at least as early as St. Ambrose, such as the claim that the pelican's mother wounds itself in Christlike manner to revive its young.[24]

Behind this approach to the study of nature lies the assumption that natural objects, especially animals and plants, are designed by the creator to educate humans, in particular, to teach moral lessons. This assumption is one that encourages the human mind to intuit and anticipate essential meanings in an armchair fashion, rather than carefully investigate the natural facts. The idea that nature *must* be a certain way effectively precludes our checking out whether this is the case. In that sense, Bacon was surely right to complain that an *a priori* notion of design is an idol of the mind, deadly to scientific progress. It also warrants an important distinction between the hermeneutics of theology and science. *Theologically*, we can assert that God works providentially. In this sense, granted God's revelation, we do have *a priori* knowledge of design. However, this does not imply that *science* can anticipate the means God will use or His final purpose. If design has a scientific role, it must be the more modest one of an *a posteriori* conclusion. As a result, science needs a different, more modest, hermeneutic from theology.

Oddly enough, it was improvements in textual analysis that partly explain the fall of scholasticism.[25] The emerging science of textual criticism revealed that current copies were frequently corrupt, motivating a search for the original text. In the process of sorting out variant meanings to make sense of the original, it became necessary to actually investigate the natural world directly, to see which interpretation made most sense. At this point, a crucial move was made from following the claims of the ancients to following the scientific method that the ancients had used to substantiate those claims. We might think of this in terms of a distinction Susan Blackmore makes between two ways of copying memes (that is, discrete memorable units, such as advertising jingles or the aphorisms of an ancient writer).[26] The medieval scientists moved from copying the product (the writings) to copying the instructions (the procedures the ancient scientists used to discover which statements were true). The exegesis of ancient texts could no longer progress without some exegesis of nature itself. However, as soon as scientists followed this path, they discovered all sorts of embarrassing errors and omissions, even in the original texts. By the time North America was discovered, it became obvious that there were many flora and fauna of which Aristotle was completely ignorant.[27]

But there was something else that had to happen before modern science could appear. Medieval thought was still mired in the idea that not only words but also things are invested with a variety of symbolic meanings. The Bible and nature alike were viewed as a storehouse of allegory. As Harrison argues, the Reformation was decisive in its rejection of this view, proposing a new hermeneutic for both Scripture and the book of nature. Martin Luther, John Calvin, and others believed that allegorical interpretations allowed all sorts of false or unnecessary doctrines to occlude the simple Gospel message of the Bible. While not denying the possibility of secondary, metaphorical interpretations, they insisted on the primacy of the literal meaning of the text. When the same approach was carried over to the natural world, symbolic meanings were rejected in favor of accurate, factual description. In the case of both revelation and the book of nature, the reformers insisted that we should humbly confine ourselves to discovering what the text actually and clearly says, avoiding anticipatory flights of fancy. This outburst of intellectual humility was essential to science's decisive turn toward the *a posteriori*.[28]

When demonstrable fact, not traditional commentary, is paramount, it becomes possible for theologians to uphold God's Word and for scientists to uphold nature as their final epistemic authorities. This hermeneutical change was decisive in shaping the modern vocation of natural interpreter.

> In freeing persons to make determinations about the meaning of the book of scripture without deferring to authorities, the reformers had at the same time made room for individuals to make determinations about the book of nature, unfettered by the opinions of approved authors.[29]

The Reformation emphasis on total depravity and the sovereignty of God made it inappropriate for a mere human to claim to discern through unaided reason the symbolic meanings and ultimate purposes of God. Some of these purposes are revealed by Scripture and can be read via the theological hermeneutic. But at best, the scientist could hope, like Lutheran astronomer Johannes Kepler, to discern the patterns God had left behind in nature and, in this limited way, to think God's thoughts after Him.

Nonetheless, the idea of design was still important in shaping scientific work. As Peter Barker argues, Lutheran theology provided grounds for expecting nature to obey a discernible *logos*.

> The specifically Lutheran doctrines of the ubiquity and the Real Presence of Christ in the host are the basis for the Lutheran belief in the universal presence of a providential deity, whose design or plan may be known through the study of nature.[30]

Contrary to the assumption that Luther was anti-science, his emphasis on real presence and providence predisposed him in favor of modern science. This explains the fact that Luther gave free rein to Erasmus Reinhold, Georg Rheticus, Caspar Peucer, and other Lutheran astronomers at the University of Wittenberg, allowing them to pursue the revolutionary Copernican heliocentric model, though it seemed to many to conflict with both Scripture and common sense.[31] The greatest of the Lutheran scientists was Johannes Kepler, who saw God as the geometer of the universe and who maintained that fallen humans retain a "natural light" of rational intuition so "the geometrical part of God's providential plan for the world would be accessible to human beings through the natural light."[32]

> More generally, the rise of modern science depended on a fundamental change from a world which is ordered symbolically by resemblances to one which is ordered according to structural similarities, or abstract mathe-

matical relations, and always, at a higher level, divine purposes.[33]

In this perspective the distinct hermeneutics of science and theology are part of an integrated whole, so, for example, the problem of natural evil disclosed by empirical science is addressed by applying the theological doctrine of providence. The theological ideas that harmful or noxious creatures exist as agents of divine justice or as fillings for otherwise unoccupied levels of the "Great Chain of Being" or as foils to show off the finer creatures more clearly or as spurs to human soul-building or simply as instruments of some divine purpose unknown to us were all developed at length, with the understanding that they were complementary, rather than irrelevant, to science. Likewise, Robert Boyle, a paragon of Christian science, saw scientific work as fulfilling God's purposes by producing medicines and technologies to aid our neighbor and partially restore the effects of the fall.

Although Christianity—in the form of allegorical scholasticism—was certainly to blame for medieval stagnation in science, it is also true that it was the reinvigorated Christianity of the Reformation that came to the rescue. By limiting the scientist's vocation to the task of reading God's book of nature without an anticipatory gloss, the reformers encouraged an explosion of scientific discovery.

Natural Theology and Its Critics

The powerful integration of science and religion that began on the continent later flourished in the predominantly British school of natural theology. What remained of Aristotle after the birth of modern science was widespread, though not universal, commitment to final causes. However, no longer were these causes viewed as occult essences within substances, as Aristotle had supposed. Rather, final causes could be discerned by straightforward investigation of the benefits of a phenomenon to humanity. Work along these lines varied from the sensible (Walter Charleston's study of the uses of blood, respiration, and muscles[34]) to the suspect (Henry More's claim that rivers are designed as natural quarries of stone[35]) to the outrageously Panglossian. Perhaps Noël Pluche gets the prize for the latter category, with the suggestion:

> The woodworm, which eats the hull of ships, actually contributes to harmonious international relations, for it provides opportunities for some countries to sell to others pitch with which to protect ships' hulls: "Thus does this little Animal, which we so much complain of as being troublesome and injurious to us, become the very Cement which unites these distant nations in one common Interest."[36]

At this extreme, science became an exercise in post hoc rationalization with the doubtful aim of defending God's wisdom. At the same time, wiser heads such as those of Robert Boyle, William Harvey, Robert Hooke, and John Ray argued that the microscope reveals an organic world brimming with evidence of design, regardless of whether we can discern its ultimate purpose.[37] Boyle was more careful to distinguish the theological from the scientific hermeneutic, confining his scientific investigation to the material mechanisms. Convinced that matter was completely passive and unable to give an ultimate explanation of its own order, Boyle was free to draw the theological conclusion that this order evinced divine design.[38] Indeed, Boyle was concerned that science should not try to mingle the divine and the natural, as occurred in the immanent spiritism of van Helmont's active principles, because this mingling tended to pantheism and denied God's free and sovereign will over His creation.[39]

Although distinct from science, natural theology has undoubtedly contributed to science by motivating careful examination of the functioning of physical and biological systems. For example, medicine began to flourish when scientists asked questions such as what the heart, lungs, and other parts of the circulatory system are for. Indeed, the identification of these physical structures *as* a circulatory system presupposes a functional stance of analysis, and this was contextually motivated by a belief in divine providence. But natural theology also came under increasing criticism, some friendly and some not so friendly.

As superior telescopes revealed the vastness of space, the possibility of extraterrestrial life was first discussed. To many people it no longer seemed credible that humanity, residing in a tiny part of a huge universe, was the sole beneficiary of nature. This led to a decisive move away from anthropocentric to a more broadly cosmological design.[40] The universe may be designed by God to serve the purpose not only of human beings but also of other intelligent life.

At a more conceptual level, some philosophers, including Bacon, Descartes, and Hobbes, objected in various ways to the reliance of natural theologians on final causes. Bacon argued that the natural theologians were unwilling to accept the limits of human understanding and the inevitability of "brute facts" that admit no further explanation. Instead, Bacon charges, humans project their own agency onto the world, supposing that a being like themselves is the ultimate explanation of mystery: "As it strives to go further, [the human mind] falls back on things that are more familiar, namely final causes, which are plainly derived from the nature of man rather than of the universe."[41] Bacon here warns against the human tendency to read human psychological categories into the universe beyond the warrant of the evidence. Hobbes made much the same point in critiquing the use of final causes in dynamics:

> [M]en measure, not only other men, but all other
> things, by themselves; and because they find themselves
> subject after motion to pain, and lassitude, think every-
> thing else grows weary of motion and seeks repose of its
> own accord.[42]

Descartes also thought science should focus on the mathematical properties of matter in motion and that the idea of final
causes was "premised on a false analogy from human actions and
motivations"[43] to the divine. On the other hand, Harrison argues
that the critics of final causes overplay their hand.

> The search for divine purposes in the natural order pro-
> vided a clear religious warrant for a pursuit which might
> otherwise have been regarded as the accumulation of
> vain and futile knowledge, little different from the book-
> ish and unprofitable endeavors of the encyclopaedists.
> The scientific achievements of men such as Robert Boyle
> and John Ray give the lie to Bacon's assertion of the
> baleful influence of final causes.[44]

It is true that Boyle did not regard final causes as part of
physical science,[45] which he believed was concerned only with the
secondary causes operative in material mechanisms.[46] Nonetheless, final causes were a crucial theological motivation for asking
scientifically fruitful questions.[47]

Against the idea of integrating the scientific and theological
hermeneutics, Bacon argued that the words of Scripture and of the
book of nature are of different kinds: "Heretical religion as well as
fanciful philosophy derives from the unhealthy mingling of divine
and human."[48] Moreover, some argued that the more nature is
viewed providentially, the more acute is the problem of evil.
Although some of the theodicies for natural evil were ingenious,
many were rather strained. Also, there were many different ways of
accounting for the same evil, and no clear way to adjudicate which
of these was correct. From these considerations, many concluded

that natural theologies were engaging in fanciful speculation with no relevance to the empirical demonstrations of science.

Despite his rejection of final causes in physics, Descartes grounded science in the confidence that, if we restrain our errant will, we are capable of understanding the rational, and especially geometric, order of the universe. But both Christian theology and agnostic skepticism gave grounds for doubting this optimistic view of human cognitive powers. The reformers took total depravity to mean that human will and reason is unable to know God personally without regeneration. But does this depravity also darken the human understanding of the book of nature? A radical form of theological skepticism would argue that human reason is no longer analogous to the divine, so scientific realism is doomed to failure. Perhaps scientific theories do not justify ontological commitments but merely provide useful calculation devices that capture the right predictions. The agnostic Hume also tends in this direction, arguing powerfully that there is no way to justify the scientific practice of induction, thus there is no basis for the assumption that science can discover the true categories and regularities of nature.

The obvious way out of this skeptical miasma is to appeal to some transcendent and authoritative word. But as the Enlightenment progressed, modernist philosophers concluded that such a word was both epistemically inaccessible and practically dispensable. In his *Dialogues Concerning Natural Religion*, Hume saw a Divine Designer as only one of many hypotheses that save the phenomena, discerning that metaphysics is radically underdetermined by the totality of natural facts. However, Kant strove to restore the confidence in human reason that Hume had lost. Impressed with the triumph of Newton, himself a firm believer in providence and final causes, Kant attempted to understand Newton's laws of motion as synthetic *a priori* statements, that is, necessary truths of our experience, as geometry appeared to him to be. In this way Kant hoped to escape Humean skepticism about induction and to provide a foundation of rational certainty for science that did not depend on some inaccessible or nondemonstrable revelation. While Newton himself appealed to the divine to explain the formation and stability of planetary orbits, Laplace followed the Kantian line and argued that he no longer had need of such a hypothesis.

Skepticism was replaced by a confidence in human reason that made appeals to religious foundations seem redundant. Although Kant himself was Christian, there is no doubt that his thinking encouraged the move from an interventionist natural theology to Deism. If Kant and Laplace were right about the inherent rational order of the cosmos, surely the universe is more like a carefully crafted machine than a living organism. While organisms need constant support and attention, an automaton devised by a perfect engineer might easily be supposed to require no further intervention, making of God a sort of cosmic Maytag repair man, with nothing left to do except read the papers. Aesthetically, some preferred the idea of a God who got it right the first time and had no need to tinker with His handiwork.[49] Pushed too far, of course, this made the incarnation itself a source of embarrassment. But it was just at this time that naturalistic criticism of the Bible began to suggest that the Bible was full of legendary material and that the miracles did not really happen. For those who could not bear such a distant, uncaring God, pantheism and varieties of nature worship got God back into nature, sacrificing His transcendence to maintain His immanence. Such a God could easily be identified with the life force or spirit of progress that came to dominate in the eighteenth and nineteenth centuries. He was, of course, British.

But even by the nineteenth century, the criticisms of Bacon, Descartes, Hobbes, Hume, and Kant had not unseated the argument for design. Although many had unorthodox ideas about the

101

nature of God, these ideas were not incompatible with His being a designer, and *The Bridgewater Treatises* were influential because, despite the skeptical worries about final causes, no one had a serious rival theory. To say that the divine might not be analogous to the human or that our faculties might not be able to discern divine purposes falls short of a demonstration that this is the case. Only a plausible reading of the natural text that makes appeal to a designer superfluous could justify outright rejection of the design hypothesis.[50]

Such a reading was provided by Charles Darwin's *The Origin of Species* (1859). Darwin's most important philosophical insight involved a careful distinction between the appearance and reality of design. Neither Darwin nor his most vigorous contemporary spokesman, Richard Dawkins, had any doubt that biological systems appear to be designed. This is why it is so worthwhile to treat creatures, organs, and biochemical structures as artifacts or machines. Nonetheless, just because something appears to be designed does not mean that it actually is. Darwin's contribution was to supplement this philosophical distinction with a hypothesis that would account for the appearance of design in nature without invoking a designer. Darwin argued that living creatures diversify through a process of descent with modification, where some source of variation (unknown to Darwin) led to both advantageous and disadvantageous traits among a species' progeny. The structure of the environment and competition for the crucial resources of food and mates jointly act as a sieve, tending to the extermination of the maladapted and the increase of the well-adapted. Because well-adapted creatures are those with traits that happen to suit their environment, this process of entirely natural selection fosters the illusion that the traits were explicitly designed for this purpose.

The process is thoroughly mechanistic and, some felt, quite ruthless and wasteful, making it hard to see how a loving God could carry out His providential plans through such means. Deism, which was already on the theological scene, was co-opted as a means of keeping God's hands clean of the blood that ran from tooth and claw. It might be possible to explain why God would allow such goings on, but His active involvement in them seemed unjustifiable to many. Still, if evolution meant progress (a doubtful inference from Darwin's theory),[51] perhaps one could think of a World Soul or Life Force propelling us ever closer to enlightenment. The carnage of the primitive past was regrettable, but possibly justified if it eventually produced people as civilized as Victorians. However, some felt there was simply no way to get God off the hook. If Darwin was right about how life develops, then natural evil seemed to be an essential part of the process and the conclusion must be that either God lacks one of the traditional attributes (omniscience, omnipotence, or holiness)[52] or He does not exist at all. Others were more determined to retain an orthodox Christian faith. Following Karl Barth, the Neo-Orthodox placed the salvific Gospel events (*Geschichte*) in a separate self-validating realm of suprahistory where they could not be falsified by the facts of history, no matter how recalcitrant. The Gospel events then show that the Lord is a loving God, regardless of what natural science turns up. However, it was pointed out by many that this falsifies the true "scandal" of the incarnation— that God became man in the same grimy history that the rest of us inhabit—and that it also removes the distinctive advantage of historicity that Christianity holds over the plethora of other religions and cults.[53] Those who (rightly, in my view) insisted that God really acted in the same history about which science speaks and who were troubled by the Darwinian process concluded that there was no option but to reject much of Darwin's theory. To this group, as to many Christians today, Darwin's account is incompatible with the idea that God creates things good and continues to sustain and care for His creation.

Other approaches attempt to defang Darwin by showing that one can have one's cake and eat it too. Some claim that the hermeneutic of science cannot uncover spiritual truths, so the medieval and Reformation hope for an integrated interpretive strategy for both Scripture and nature must be abandoned. The problem of evil in nature only occurs if we read the scientific facts spiritually, but this, it is claimed, is to confuse science and theology. Perhaps Bacon was right that "heretical religion as well as fanciful philosophy derives from the unhealthy mingling of divine and human." One natural outcome of this line of thinking is Gould's model of theology and science as Non-Overlapping Magisteria (NOMA), with science the authority on natural fact and theology the arbiter of morality and ultimate meaning. This, however, is a "two spheres" approach, not unlike Barthianism, in which the Gospel and Christian moral teachings are not upheld as objective truth. By divorcing theology from the realm of objective fact, it appears to make religious statements purely subjective, denying the full reality of God's action in the world. Most recently, proponents of intelligent design argue that the natural text is not being given a fair reading because of the background assumption of methodological naturalism. Should nature have anything to say of the supernatural, this assumption serves as a gag order, producing a censored and mutilated text akin to Thomas Jefferson's Bible.

Intelligent Design

Intelligent design raises red flags for some who see it as returning to the confusion of science and theology, of which some of the natural theologians were certainly guilty. Walter Thorson has developed this criticism with impressive sophistication, arguing on theological and methodological grounds that science proper is not in the business of detecting divine design.[54] Thorson agrees with intelligent design that the mechanistic, reductionist paradigm of physics is unable to account for the "functional logic" of biochemical structures, and he agrees that it is natural and warranted by the objective facts for Christians who are scientists to infer a designing intelligence. However, Thorson argues that this inference is not a scientific but a theological one. First, Thorson rightly notes that a foundational requirement of science is that its findings be accessible to all competent investigators, regardless of their spiritual condition. Second, Thorson claims on scriptural grounds that "transcendence means that God and God's agency in creation cannot be subjected to scrutiny by the *unrepentant and autonomous* rational powers of humans."[55] Unregenerate humanity cannot "name" God in the sense of identifying who He is or what He is doing in creation.

In my view, Thorson's second claim is largely, but not entirely, correct. Thorson is absolutely right that unregenerate humans cannot gain a *personal* knowledge of God by their own reason; this is clearly incompatible with salvation by grace alone. But at least the more careful proponents of intelligent design would point out that one can detect the marks of an *unknown* agency, just as the pagans of Acts 17 had an altar to an unknown God. What is more, this agency might not even be personal: It might be the impersonal *logos* of the stoics. That we can detect design without knowing the agent or its motives is clear from human cases. Ancient archaeological finds include artifacts whose maker and purpose no one can identify.

Second, I think Thorson goes too far in limiting natural knowledge of God. Paul's Epistle to the Romans implies that the reason the unbeliever is "without excuse" is because he or she has *impersonal* knowledge of God.

> The wrath of God is being revealed from heaven against all the godlessness and wickedness of men who suppress the truth by their wickedness, since what may be known about God is plain to them, because God has made it

plain to them. For since the creation of the world God's invisible qualities—His eternal power and divine nature—have been clearly seen, being understood from what has been made, so that men are without excuse. (Romans 1:18–20)

It is clear from these verses that the unbeliever does detect the *anonymous* agency of God; in other words, the unbeliever can see the marks of God's agency and even the qualities of the agent *without attributing either of them to God.* It is not, as Thorson seems to claim, that these marks or qualities are inaccessible to the unbeliever and violate the requirement that scientific evidence must be accessible to all competent investigators. The reason the unbeliever continues to reject this knowledge is not cognitive but volitional impairment. Unbelieving scientists can access the marks of design, but their wills are opposed to interpreting it as evidence of a designer. If science is the search for objective knowledge, it should not be constrained by the fact that some wish to suppress that knowledge when it clearly, though anonymously, implicates the divine. Intelligent design may or may not turn out to be fruitful for science. But so long as it only claims to detect anonymous design, I do not think it muddles the distinction between scientific and theological hermeneutics, which Thorson so rightly insists on. Science may detect altars to an unknown God. Theology will proclaim who that God is.

Thorson, however, wishes to restrict the notion of "design" to the functional logic of living things, so we may speak of a creaturely but not a divine *telos.* Consequently, Thorson maintains that, insofar as it points to a divine designer, intelligent design remains part of natural theology—not natural science.

In defense of this conclusion, Thorson gives two main arguments. First (T1), Thorson argues that intelligent design perpetuates "Aristotle's baneful influence"[56] because it makes a premature

appeal to a final divine cause, discouraging scientists from looking for "possible *further meanings*" in living things. Second (T2),
Thorson argues that because we can understand the creaturely
telos "on its own terms,"[57] appeal to divine design is redundant in
natural science.

I will try to show that a careful proponent of intelligent
design can handle both objections.[58] In response to T1, I argue
that one can defend divine design without incautious appeal to
direct intervention. In response to T2, I argue that legitimate scientific inferences are not closed under naturalistic consequences,
even with the enriched notion of nature proposed by Thorson.

Indirect Divine Agency: Response to T1

The worry that premature appeal to divine design will
inhibit scientific discovery is legitimate. However, a proponent of
intelligent design can eschew the naïve view of divine agency that
creates this problem. Consider an analogy from Reformation theology. According to Luther, God continues His creative work
through the vocations of human beings. While God could provide our daily bread *ex nihilo*, He typically works through the
means of bakers, truck drivers, and store clerks.[59] Although God
can create directly, He often chooses to use means. We should
expect the same pattern when we investigate the world scientifically. God certainly can produce events directly (miracles), but
He can also work through the laws of nature or by other means. It
seems to me, however, that intelligent design can grant all this
and that this has an important consequence: Inferring that an
effect is designed is not the same as inferring that the proximal
cause of that effect is the designer and in no way discourages further examination of the cause.

This point is clear even with human design. Suppose that
you are handed a piece of paper with a beautiful fractal pattern.
Initially, you are tempted to suppose it sprang directly from the

mind of an artist. Then you discern the telltale dots that evidence digital production, and you infer that it is computer output. The computer is not an intelligent designer, but the output still points to intelligent design. There is no known, unaided natural process that transfers fractal patterns onto paper in just this way. Because the proximal cause is a mindless computer, you realize that the intelligence lays further back, in the minds of computer programmers and users. But you are not discouraged from investigating how the computer generated the output.

Likewise, we should not simply cry "Divine Intervention!" upon discovery of biological systems that exhibit "complex specified information." We need not assume that the systems were created directly by God, and we should be interested both in their "functional logic" and their proximal causes. However, this does not show that the design inference is unscientific. If a forensics expert infers that a bullet found in Madagascar was fired by a gun in Brooklyn, the inference is not undermined by the discovery that the bullet was mailed all over the world before arriving in Madagascar. Proponents of design can agree on the importance of investigating the naturalistic chain of causes that resulted in a designed event. However, these causes are at best conduits of design, the means of transmitting complex specified information. These conduits help to explain why such information is present at a particular time and place, but they no more explain the origin of that information than water pipes explain the origin of water.

The Design Inference and the Displacement Problem: Response to T2

Thus, in the human case, the fact that designers work through means neither undermines the design inference nor discourages the examination of those means. The claim of intelligent design is that the same point holds in cases of supernatural design. As Del Ratzsch has argued, the logic is surprisingly straightforward.[60] There are certain things of which unaided nature is incapable, but which humans can do. When we discover such things, we infer that they are human artifacts, even if we do not know how or why they were manufactured. Suppose that we discover marks of design that no human (or other natural being) could produce, such as ancient biological information or the fine structure constants of cosmology. It seems that we are using the same kind of inference in both cases, so if the former inference is scientific, the latter is also scientific.

The point is strong when the characteristic necessarily has no naturalistic explanation. For example, Robert Koons argues as follows: "By definition, the laws and fundamental structure of nature pervade nature. Anything that causes these laws to be simple, anything that imposes a consistent aesthetic upon them, must be supernatural."[61] Why deny that inferences of this sort are scientific just because they do not happen to be closed under *naturalistic consequences*?

The point is strengthened by attending to Dembski's "Displacement Problem."[62] Dembski argues that naturalistic processes can shuffle Complex Specified Information around but cannot create it *de novo*. Consequently, following the information trail through various conduits only displaces the problem of the information's origin. Suppose now we consider the functional logic of a living structure. Thorson may be right that we can understand how the creature works synchronically "on its own terms," without considering its possible origin. However, there is also the diachronic question of the means by which such a structure was produced. This, too, is a legitimate scientific question. As we examine the chain of natural causes that terminate in the structure, suppose we discover that complex specified information is never generated but only rearranged in various ways. Suppose further that we can show that no known naturalistic process can generate such information, while we do know that intelligent agents can produce it.[63] If there is no plausible natural candidate, why is it unscientific to *suggest* that the origin of this information is a supernatural being? Of course, the claim may be false, and it may be refuted by the discovery of some new natural process that does not merely displace the problem. Yet design inferences do not need to be saddled with theological finality. As putative scientific claims, they lay themselves open to empirical refutation in just the same way as the claims of the naturalist. But if there is no naturalistic solution to the displacement problem, limiting ourselves to the creaturely would deprive science of discovering an important truth.

Conclusion

Science began when nature appeared to be intelligible—something one might read like a book. Tracking the transformation and diversification of the nature as text metaphor provides a useful means of understanding the successes and failures of science. Science stagnates when a hermeneutic for the natural text encourages a dogmatic presumption (or anticipation) of nature's proper course, as occurred in the Middle Ages. It is essential, therefore, to distinguish an *a priori* theological hermeneutic from the *a posteriori* hermeneutic appropriate for science. Nonetheless, the scientific and theological hermeneutics are not unrelated. A good scientific interpretation is one that allows nature to speak for itself, yet is motivated by and connected to an overarching frame of meaning provided by revealed theology. Such a method of reading nature was essential to the birth of modern science, but there is no guarantee it will continue to prevail. There are now many rival hermeneutics, and some of these, by detaching natural processes from their divine direction, provide fragmentary or incoherent readings.[64] A good way to assess the overall worth of a *perspective* (that is, a family of hermeneutics) on the relation between science and religion is to examine its overall success in providing a full and integrated reading of the texts, which means both Scripture and the book of nature. Intelligent design holds the promise of providing a coherent and unified perspective, thereby supporting the faithful Christian who is called to interpret the book of nature.

Notes

1. This chapter is adapted from two of my recent articles, "Interpreting the Book of Nature" and "Indirectness and the Displacement Problem: A Reply to Walter Thorson," both in the journal of the American Scientific Affiliation (ASA), *Perspectives on Science and the Christian Faith* 55:2 (June 2003): 88–98 and 102–103 respectively. I am indebted to Walter Thorson for his acute and insightful comments, to an anonymous referee of *PSCF* for many helpful suggestions, and to Ted Davis for advice about Robert Boyle. The mistakes that remain are all mine.

2. Francis Bacon rejected the idea of final causes in science, seeing them as camouflaging our ignorance of the real causal explanation of the phenomena. See Lisa Jardine and Michael Silverthorne, eds., *The New Organon* (Cambridge: Cambridge University Press, 2000), Bk. 1, LXV and Bk. 2, 11.

3. Bacon's *The New Organon* contrasts the "true" method of science, which proceeds via *a posteriori* induction from particulars (the "Interpretation of Nature"), with the *a prioristic* analysis of nature according to preconceived intuitions of essences (the "Anticipation of Nature"), which was employed by Aristotelian scholasticism. See Bk. 1, XXVI–XXXIII, and Bk. 2 as an outline of the method of interpretation.

4. See Daniel C. Dennett's *Darwin's Dangerous Idea* (New York: Simon & Schuster, 1995), 212–20.

5. No one has made this point more vigorously than the historian and philosopher of science, Stanley Jaki. He has further pointed out that impoverished conceptions of nature tend toward stagnation and "still-births" in science. For a recent statement, see Jaki's *The Savior of Science* (Grand Rapids: Eerdmans, 2000).

6. Because our ancestors were almost universally religious, a fruitful theology of nature was practically, if not logically, essential to the birth of science. While this view was typically rejected by Enlightenment thinkers, it is uncontroversial among contemporary historians of science. See, for example, Margaret Osler's recent collection, *Rethinking the Scientific*

Revolution (Cambridge: Cambridge University Press, 2000), in which important essays show the connections between theological ideas and the development of modern science. The general point is also well made in the first chapter of Nancy R. Pearcey and Charles B. Thaxton, *The Soul of Science* (Wheaton, Ill.: Crossway, 1994).

7. Timaeus 29a. See Edith Hamilton and Huntington Cairnes, eds., *The Collected Dialogues of Plato: Including the Letters* (Princeton: Princeton University Press, 1963), 1162.

8. Timaeus, 30b, *Collected Dialogues*, 1163.

9. Stanley Jaki, *Bible and Science* (Front Royal, Va.: Christendom Press, 1996), 77.

10. If, indeed, there was a scientific revolution, a matter of much recent dispute. See, for example, the exchange between the late Betty Jo Dobbs, who questions the aptness of the revolution metaphor in her essay "Newton as Final Cause and First Mover," and Richard S. Westfall, who defends it in his "The Scientific Revolution Reasserted," both in *Rethinking the Scientific Revolution*, ed. Margaret Osler (Cambridge: Cambridge University Press, 2000).

11. *Physics*, 194a, 28–30, in *The Basic Works of Aristotle*, ed. Richard McKeon (New York: Random House, 1941), 239.

12. Dennett, *Darwin's Dangerous Idea*, 128–135.

13. *Physics*, 199a, 20–33, in *The Basic Works of Aristotle*, 250.

14. Although Jaki is vigorous in his argument that alternatives to Christianity, both religious and secular, do not in fact provide as fertile a soil for science. That is his main thesis in *The Savior of Science*.

15. Jaki, *Savior of Science*, 54–58.

16. Jaki, *Savior of Science*, 79–81.

17. Jaki, *Savior of Science*, 83.

18. For example, Robert Koons argues that naturalism is inconsistent with the view that science is a reliable guide to ontology. See Koons, "The Incompatibility of Naturalism and Scientific Realism," in *Naturalism: A Critical Analysis*, eds. William Lane Craig and J. P. Moreland (London: Routledge, 2000), 49–63. In the same volume, Michael Rea argues that naturalism cannot even justify its commitment to physical objects because they have modal characteristics whose spatio-temporal instantiation naturalism cannot account for. See Rea, "Naturalism and Material Objects," in *Naturalism: A Critical Analysis*, 110–32.

19. I develop this case at length in my book, *Agents Under Fire: Materialism and the Rationality of Science* (Lanham, Md.: Rowman & Littlefield, 2004).

20. For example, the foundational work of the Mertonian mathematicians on the kinematics of average velocity and Buridan's own impetus theory.

21. Although it can and should be disputed whether these assumptions were doctrinally sound.

22. Peter Harrison, *The Bible, Protestantism, and the Rise of Natural Science* (Cambridge: Cambridge University Press, 1998), 67.

23. Harrison, *Bible, Protestantism, and the Rise of Natural Science*, 67–68.

24. Harrison, *Bible, Protestantism, and the Rise of Natural Science*, 24–25.

25. Harrison, *Bible, Protestantism, and the Rise of Natural Science*, 70.

26. Susan Blackmore, *The Meme Machine* (New York: Oxford University Press, 1999), 61–62.

27. Harrison, *Bible, Protestantism, and the Rise of Natural Science*, 82–92.

28. Jaki, a devout Roman Catholic, has a more negative view of the Reformation, arguing that the literalism of Luther and Calvin is responsible for bibliolatry and the excesses of creationism. See *Bible and Science*, 109–11.

29. Harrison, *Bible, Protestantism, and the Rise of Natural Science*, 101.

30. Peter Barker, "The Role of Religion in the Lutheran Response to Copernicus," in *Rethinking the Scientific Revolution*, 62. Applied to the Lord's Supper, the Lutheran terms for the presence of Christ's body are sacramental union and multi–voli–presence. They do not derive from ubiquity but from the Scripture principle that God's Word is the final authority, that He cannot be hemmed in by the human use of reason, and that the plain mandate of Christ—"This is My body"—can only be interpreted faithfully as it is, not as "signifies" or some other sinful human invention. The classical Reformed position follows the Heidelberg Catechism and associated theologians by calling the Lutheran position a kind of ubiquity.

31. Barker, "Role of Religion," 62–72.

32. Barker, "Role of Religion," 84.

33. Harrison, *Bible, Protestantism, and the Rise of Natural Science*, 162.

34. Harrison, *Bible, Protestantism, and the Rise of Natural Science*, 170.

35. Harrison, *Bible, Protestantism, and the Rise of Natural Science*, 171.

36. Harrison, *Bible, Protestantism, and the Rise of Natural Science*, 175. The embedded quote is from Noël Pluche, *Spectacle de la Nature: or Nature Display'd*, 5th rev. and corrected ed. (London: 1770), 3:318.

37. Harrison, *Bible, Protestantism, and the Rise of Natural Science*, 172–76.

38. See Pearcey and Thaxton, *Soul of Science*, 88.

39. See Pearcey and Thaxton, *Soul of Science*, 87.

40. Harrison, *Bible, Protestantism, and the Rise of Natural Science*, 177–82.

41. Bacon, *New Organon*, Bk. I, XLVIII.

42. Hobbes, *Leviathan*, I.2, in *The English Works of Thomas Hobbes of Malmesbury*, ed. William Molesworth (Aalen: Scientia, 1962), 3:3f.

43. Harrison, *Bible, Protestantism, and the Rise of Natural Science*, 183.

44. Harrison, *The Bible, Protestantism, and the Rise of Natural Science*, 184.

45. Here I am reading "physical science" as equivalent to what Boyle called "natural philosophy."

46. However, Boyle did not think that life had a mechanistic explanation. He does seem to have allowed final causes in biological science, as Ted Davis confirmed in private communication. See also Pearcey and Thaxton, *Soul of Science*, 88.

47. In particular, it was divine final causes that led Boyle to expect material mechanisms to obey laws. Boyle did not think that matter would obey such laws if simply left to its own devices, unlike the deistic mechanists. Rather, the orderly behavior of matter depended on God's "general concourse" with the world. See Pearcey and Thaxton, *The Soul of Science*, 88.

48. Bacon, *The New Organon*, Bk. I, LXV.

49. Kenneth Miller argues that the dichotomy between a nature in which God can intervene and a Deistic nature is a false one because he thinks there is a third alternative: "an active and present God . . . can work His will . . . in ways consistent with scientific materialism" (Miller, *Finding Darwin's God: A Scientist's Search for Common Ground between God and Evolution* [New York: Cliff Street Books, 1999], 217.) In this view God does not need to intervene in a special way (except for miracles) because He is always involved in shaping creation through the ordinary means of His laws.

50. The hypothesis seemed to have the *a posteriori* support of the scientific hermeneutic, as well as the *a priori* support of the theological hermeneutic.

51. Undirected evolution has no fixed and final goal. Consequently, there is no way to define an absolute metric for progress. The best one can do is talk of relative progress, progress in adapting to the currently operative fitness landscape, which may change tomorrow.

52. If God is not omniscient, perhaps He does not know about some of the evil; if He is not omnipotent, perhaps He cannot prevent it; and if He is not holy, perhaps He does not want to do so. Such a being might be a god, but not the God of Abraham, Isaac, and Jacob, and perhaps not one particularly worthy of worship.

53. One of the staunchest opponents of Barthian theology is John Warwick Montgomery. See, for example, his devastating critique, "Karl Barth and Contemporary Theology of History," chapter 5 in *Where Is History Going? A Christian Response to Secular Philosophies of History* by J. W. Montgomery (Minneapolis: Bethany, 1969), reissued by the Canadian Institute for Law, Theology, and Public Policy, Inc.

54. Walter R. Thorson, "Legitimacy and Scope of 'Naturalism' in Science," *Perspectives on Science and the Christian Faith*, 54:1 (March 2002): 2–21.

55. Walter R. Thorson, "Thorson Replies . . .," *Perspectives on Science and the Christian Faith* 54:1 (March 2002): 42–46, 43.

56. See "Aristotle's Baneful Influence" in Thorson's response to my essay, *Perspectives on Science and the Christian Faith* 55:2 (June 2003).

57. See "A Creaturely Telos" in Thorson's response to my essay, *Perspectives on Science and the Christian Faith* 55:2 (June 2003).

58. I do not dispute that some proponents of design may be vulnerable to the objections Thorson makes. If so, however, this arises from their operating with an inadequate conception of divine agency and is not essential to the intelligent design program.

59. See Gene Edward Veith, *God at Work: Your Christian Vocation in All of Life* (Wheaton, Ill.: Crossway, 2002), especially chapters 1–2.

60. Del Ratzsch, *Nature, Design and Science: The Status of Design in Natural Science* (Albany: State University of New York Press, 2001). Ratzsch defends the legitimacy of inferring supernatural design; see especially chapters 9–10.

61. Robert Koons, "The Incompatibility of Naturalism and Scientific Naturalism," in *Naturalism: A Critical Analysis*, eds. William Lane Craig and J. P. Moreland (London: Routledge & Kegan Paul, 2000), 49–63, (55).

62. William A. Dembski, *No Free Lunch: Why Specified Complexity Cannot be Purchased without Intelligence* (Lanham, Md.: Rowman & Littlefield, 2002), section 4.7.

63. For example, we know that Shakespeare could produce the complex specified information in his sonnets.

64. For example, I think Walter Thorson is right to follow Michael Polanyi in arguing that the functional logic of biochemical structures cannot properly be read through the mechanistic lens of classical physics.

PART II

The Contribution of the Scientific Vocation

4

Science and Christianity

Conflict or Coherence?

HENRY F. SCHAEFER III

Abstract

Drawing from his recent study of Christianity and science,[1] Henry Schaefer debunks the continuing myth that science is in inevitable tension with Christianity. Schaefer shows that while some scientists have viewed their work as pointing to atheism, many have seen Christianity as an essential intellectual foundation for their work. The intelligibility of nature and the origin of modern science as the interpretation of the book of nature both point to God as the guarantor of science as a worthwhile project. What is more, contrary to the assumption that science corrodes faith, there have been great Christian scientists in every century following the inception of modern science. These include intellectual giants such as Michael Faraday, James Clerk Maxwell, and J. J. Thomson. Schaefer shows that a profound Christian understanding has shaped important scientific theorizing and discovery and provides a framework of meaning for science, which cannot be justified by science itself. Faith motivates scientists to do their work well, helps determine the range of applications pursued, raises distinctive questions, and provides a larger context in which the purpose of science can be evaluated independently of purely pragmatic considerations.

Introduction

I first began teaching freshman chemistry at Berkeley in the spring of 1984. The physical sciences lecture hall at Berkeley holds about 550 people. On the first day of class, you could fit in 680 students, which we had on that particular morning. It was a very full auditorium. Those of you who have had freshman chemistry at a large university will know that many have mixed feelings about such courses. I had never addressed a group of 680 people before and was a bit concerned about it. But I had a fantastic demonstration prepared for them.

In this lecture hall the stage is divided into three parts. It rotates, so you can go to your part of the stage and work for two hours before your lecture, getting everything ready. My assistant, Lonny Martin, who still does the undergraduate chemistry demonstrations at Berkeley, was behind the stage in the process of setting up ten moles of a large number of common chemicals: benzene, iron, mercury, ethyl alcohol, water, and so on. At just the right time, at the grand crescendo of this lecture, I was going to press the stage button and Lonny would unexpectedly rotate into view and show the students the ten moles of various items. The students would have a moment of enlightenment as they realized that each displayed quantity of these chemical substances had the same number of molecules, namely, ten times Avogadro's number.

It was going to be wonderful. We got to the critical point in the lecture, and I said, "Lonny, come around and show us the moles." I pressed the button to rotate the stage, but nothing happened. I did not realize that Lonny was overriding my button press because he was not ready with the moles. This was embarrassing. I went out in front of the 680 students and was at a complete loss as to what to say, so I made some unprepared remarks. I said, "While we're waiting for the moles, let me tell you what happened to me in church yesterday morning." I was desperate. There was great silence among those 680 students. They had come with all manner of anticipations about freshman chemistry, but stories about church were not among them!

At least as surprised as the students, I continued, "Let me tell you what my Sunday school teacher said yesterday." The students became quiet. "I was hoping the group at church would give me some support—moral, spiritual, or whatever—for dealing with this large class, but I received none. In fact, the Sunday school teacher first told anecdotes about his own freshman chemistry instructor, who kicked the dog, beat his wife, and so on. Then he asked the class, in honor of me: 'What is the difference between a dead dog lying in the middle of the street and a dead chemistry professor lying in the middle of the street?' "

The class was excited about this and I had not even gotten to the punch line. They roared with laughter. The concept of a dead chemistry professor lying in the middle of the street was hilarious to them. I am sure some of them began to think, "If this guy were to become a dead chemistry professor close to the final exam, we probably wouldn't have to take the final exam. Berkeley would probably give us all passing grades, and this would be wonderful."

Then I told the students that my Sunday school teacher had said that the difference between a dead dog lying in the middle of the road and a dead chemistry professor lying in the middle of the road is that there are skid marks in front of the dead dog. It was a new joke at the time, and the class thought it was outstanding! Just as they settled down, I pressed the button and around came Lonny with the moles. It was an extraordinary beginning to my career as a freshman chemistry lecturer.

About fifty students came down to the front of the auditorium at the end of class. About half had the usual questions, such as "Which dot do I punch out of this registration card?" But the other half of the students wanted to know what I had been doing in church the day before classes started. One student in particular said, "The person I have most admired in my life to date was my high school chemistry teacher last year. He told me with great certainty that it was impossible to be a practicing chemist and a Christian. What do you think about that?" I responded briefly, but we didn't have time for a lengthy discussion. However, some of the other students who were listening asked me if I would give a public lecture on this topic. That was the origin of the present essay.

I gave this talk in Berkeley, at Stanford University, and in the San Francisco Bay area a number of times. The lectures were well attended and mildly controversial. One of the local newspapers ran a substantial story (19 April 1986) on the Stanford lecture, given at an American Scientific Affiliation symposium entitled "God and Modern Science: Who Shapes Whom?" The author of this particular story titled it "Science and Religion: Chemist an Exception." As you will see if you read on, this conclusion was quite the opposite of the picture I had attempted to draw in my lecture. The lecture was also given to a modest audience at Brown University (1985), to a large audience at the University of Canterbury, Christchurch, New Zealand (1986), and to an audience of five brave souls at the University of Kansas (1986; a return trip to the University of Kansas drew an audience of 200 in April 2000).

When I moved to the University of Georgia in late 1987, the level of interest in these lectures increased dramatically. In large part this was because some faculty members complained to the University of Georgia administration. It was an interesting chapter in my life. The *Atlanta Journal and Constitution*, the largest newspaper in the southeastern United States, ran a front-page story on October 23 entitled "UGA Science Prof's Lectures Prove Volatile Brew." These hostile faculty members were of the opinion that it was unconstitutional for anyone to use a vacant university classroom to discuss the relationship between science and religion. A few days later my sister-in-law called from Seattle, saying that she had heard on the radio that I was being fired for preaching in the classroom!

In fact, I had yet to teach my first class at the University of Georgia. Moreover, the university president, Dr. Charles B. Knapp, swiftly came to my defense. Dr. Knapp stated to the press: "This kind of intellectual ferment is good for the place. I think it's an exercise of his freedom of speech." And on Saturday morning, October 31, the *Atlanta Journal and Constitution* published an editorial supporting me: "Fanatics are demanding rigorous control over the dissemination of ideas. . . . University officials have had the good sense—and the courage—to resist. They must continue to do so." The newspapers of Athens, Georgia (a city of 100,000), also came to my defense and a "street poll" conducted by the media indicated that virtually all the students on the University of Georgia campus viewed the issue as a matter of freedom of speech. Lesser headlines followed, the most creative appearing in the January 10, 1988, edition of the *Savannah Morning News/Evening Press*: "Chemistry Prof's Bible Lectures Explosive."

Scientists and Their Gods

A Perspective on the Relationship Between Science and Christianity

Many educated people are of the opinion that there has been a terrible warfare between science and Christianity. Let us attempt to put this question of the relationship between science and Christianity in the broadest, most reasonable perspective possible. We begin by noting that the rapprochement between science and other intellectual pursuits has not always been easy. For example, in their book *Literature through the Eyes of Faith*,[2] Susan Gallagher and Roger Lundin note that great literature often opposed science.

John Keats, the great English romantic poet, did not like Isaac Newton's view of reality. He said it threatened to destroy all the beauty in the universe. Keats feared that a world in which myths and poetic visions had vanished would become a barren and uninviting place. In his poem "Lamia," Keats talks about this destructive power. In this poem, he calls "science" "philosophy," so I will try to replace the word "philosophy" with "science" so as not to confuse the twenty-first century reader:

> Do not all charms fly
> At the mere touch of cold [science]?
> There was an awful rainbow once in heaven
> We knew her woof, her texture.
> She is given in the dull catalog of common things.
> [Science] will clip an angel's wings,
> Conquer all mysteries by rule and line,
> Empty the haunted air and gnomed mine,
> Unweave a rainbow.

My point is that there has been friction among science and virtually every other intellectual endeavor since the appearance of modern science on the scene around 1600. So it would be surprising if there were not some heated exchanges between science and Christianity. What I am describing is called "the new kid on the block" syndrome in colloquial North American English.

Has Science Disproved God?

Nevertheless, the position is commonly stated that "science has disproved God." In the autobiography of his early life, *Surprised by Joy*, C. S. Lewis says that he believed the above statement. He talks about the atheism of his early youth and credits it to science. Lewis writes: "You will understand that my [atheism] was inevitably based on what I believed to be the findings of the sciences; and those findings, not being a scientist, I had to take on trust, in fact, on authority."[3] What Lewis is saying is that somebody told him that science had disproved God and he believed it, though he knew nothing about science.

A more balanced view of this question was given by one of my scientific heroes, Erwin Schrödinger (1887–1961). He was perhaps the most important of the founders of wave mechanics and the originator of what is now the most important equation in science—Schrödinger's Equation. Schrödinger points out that while science gives a lot of factual information and order to our experience, it does not really account for the subjective character of our experience or for aesthetic, ethical, or religious matters. When science does attempt to offer answers in these areas, they are frequently ridiculously inappropriate.[4]

Scientists do tell some interesting stories about religion. This one is from *Chemistry in Britain*, which is something like the *Time* magazine of the chemical profession in England. Talking about the release of a new book on science policy, *Chemistry in Britain* (July 1989) explores an interesting idea:

> If God applied to the government for a research grant
> for the development of a heaven and an earth, He would
> be turned down on the following grounds:

- His project is too ambitious;
- He has no previous track record;
- His only publication is a book, not a paper in a refereed journal;
- He refuses to collaborate with his biggest competitor;
- His proposal for a heaven and an earth is all up in the air.[5]

Some Alternatives to Belief in the Sovereign God of the Universe

I present here examples of two notable atheists. The first is Lev Landau, the most brilliant Soviet physicist of the twentieth century. Landau received the 1962 Nobel Prize in Physics for his research on liquid helium. Moreover, Landau was named a Hero of Socialist Labor by the Soviet government. He was also the author of many famous physics textbooks with his coworker E. M. Lifshitz. I used some of these books as an undergraduate at M.I.T. A story about Landau by his good friend and biographer I. M. Khalatnikov appeared in the May 1989 issue of *Physics Today*. Khalatnikov writes:

> The last time I saw Landau was in 1968 after he had undergone an operation. His health had greatly deteriorated. Lifshitz and I were summoned by the hospital. We were informed that there was practically no chance he could be saved. When I entered his ward, Landau was lying on his side, his face turned to the wall. He heard my steps, turned his head, and said, "Khalat, please save me." Those were the last words I heard from Landau. He died that night.[6]

The second example is Subramanyan Chandrasekhar, the famous astrophysicist who won the Nobel Prize in Physics in 1983. He was a faculty member at the University of Chicago for most of his life. At the back of his biography is an unusual interview. Chandrasekhar begins the dialogue, saying:

> In fact, I consider myself an atheist… But I have a feeling of disappointment because the hope for contentment and a peaceful outlook on life as the result of pursuing a goal has remained largely unfulfilled.

His biographer, K. C. Wali, is astonished and responds:

> What?! I don't understand. You mean, single-minded pursuit of science, understanding parts of nature and comprehending nature with such enormous success still leaves you with a feeling of discontentment?

Chandrasekhar continues in a serious way:

> I don't really have a sense of fulfillment. All I have done seems to not be very much.

The biographer seeks to lighten the discussion a little, saying that everybody has the same sort of feelings. But Chandrasekhar will not let him escape:

> Well it may be. But the fact that other people experience it doesn't change the fact that one is experiencing it. It doesn't become less personal on that account.

And Chandrasekhar's final statement, which I urge every potential young scientist to ponder:

> What is true from my own personal case is that I simply don't have that sense of harmony which I had hoped for when I was young. And I have persevered in science for over fifty years. The time I have devoted to other things is miniscule.[7]

Is It Possible to Be a Scientist and a Christian?

So the question I want to explore is the one I was asked by that young man after my first freshman chemistry class at Berkeley: "Is it possible to be a scientist and a Christian?" The student and his high school chemistry teacher obviously thought it was not possible.

Let me begin from what some might call neutral ground by quoting two people with no particular theistic inclinations. The first individual is C. P. Snow (1905–1980). Snow remains well-known in intellectual circles as the author of an essay titled "The Two Cultures and the Scientific Revolution." C. P. Snow was a physical chemist, actually a spectroscopist, at Cambridge University. He discovered about halfway through his career that he also was a gifted writer, and Snow began writing novels. One in particular about university life at Cambridge or Oxford is called *The Masters*, which I would recommend. Snow became quite comfortable with the royalties from his novels and was able to sit in a unique position between the world of the sciences and the world of literature. From this perspective, Snow claimed that the proportion of scientists who were unbelievers was only slightly greater than in other intellectual disciplines, and he also noted that there were some devout scientists who were Christian, especially among the young.

So is it possible to be a scientist and a Christian? C.P. Snow answered in the affirmative.

Richard Feynman (1918–1988), Nobel Prize winner in Physics in 1965, was a most remarkable person and author of a book of anecdotes, *Surely You're Joking, Mr. Feynman*. He said some nine years before receiving the Nobel prize, "Many scientists *do* believe in both science and God, in a perfectly consistent way."[8] So is it possible to be a scientist and a Christian? Yes, according to Richard Feynman, an outspoken atheist.

A good summary statement in this regard is by Alan Lightman, who has written a well-received book called *Origins: The Lives and Worlds of Modern Cosmologists*[9]. Dr. Lightman is an M.I.T. professor who published this seminal work with Harvard University Press. Lightman points out that until the middle to late 1800s, it was commonplace for scientists to reference God in their professional literature. What is more, the main reasons for the decline of this practice were changes in social and professional convention, not a fundamental shift in underlying worldview.

Now someone could regard such claims as strictly anecdotal. Many Americans like statistics better than anecdotes. So let me present the results of a poll of the members of the scientific professional society Sigma Xi. Three thousand three hundred scientists responded to the survey, so this is certainly beyond statistical uncertainty. The description in the November 7, 1988, issue of *Chemical and Engineering News* reads: "Scientists are anchored in the U. S. mainstream." The article states that half of the scientists polled participate in religious activities regularly. Looking at the poll more carefully, one sees that something like 41 percent of scientists with a doctorate are in church on a typical Sunday. In the general American public, perhaps 42 percent are in church on a typical Sunday. So it is clear that whatever it is that causes people to adopt religious inclinations is unrelated to having an advanced degree in science.

Let us go a little deeper by considering the views of Michael Polanyi (1891–1976), professor of chemistry and later of philosophy at the University of Manchester. His son John Polanyi won the Nobel Prize in Chemistry in 1986. I think that it may be true that when John Polanyi's scientific accomplishments, which have been truly magnificent, have been mostly forgotten, the impact of his father's work will continue.

Michael Polanyi was a great physical chemist at the University of Manchester. About halfway through his career, he switched over to philosophy and particularly the philosophy of science. He was equally distinguished there. His books, the most influential of which is *Personal Knowledge*, are not easy to read but are worthwhile. Polanyi was of Jewish physical descent, raised in Budapest,

Hungary. About the same time that he began the switch from chemistry to philosophy, he joined the Roman Catholic Church. According to Michael Polanyi, the presuppositions underlying science include nothing less than the spiritual foundations of humanity, thus science is a reflection of a much wider set of commitments than is usually recognized.

If you read Polanyi, you will probably come to the same conclusion that I draw. Polanyi points out that the observer is always there in the laboratory. He or she always makes conclusions. He or she is never neutral. Every scientist brings presuppositions to his or her work. A scientist, for example, never questions the basic soundness of the scientific method. This faith of the scientist arose historically from the Christian belief that God the Father created a perfectly orderly universe. Now I must provide some concrete evidence for the latter conclusion.

Why Might a Scientist Become a Christian?

I will ask this question several times during the course of this essay. Physics Nobelist Eugene Wigner (1902–1995) once noted "the unreasonable effectiveness of mathematics" and remarked that "the miracle of the appropriateness of the language of mathematics for the formulation of the laws of physics is a wonderful gift that we neither understand nor deserve."[10] Interestingly, Wigner (like Polanyi) was a man of Jewish origin who found his way into nominal Christendom, in his case Protestantism. Indirectly, Wigner is hinting that the intelligibility of the universe points to a sovereign creator God. Thus mathematical physics can be an answer to the question we pose in this section. The laws of nature look just as if they have been selected as the most simple and elegant principles of intelligible change by a wise creator. Belief in the intelligibility of nature strongly suggests the existence of a cosmic mind who can construct nature in accordance with rational laws. Dr. Keith Ward, Regius Professor at Oxford University, has argued that the mathematical intelligibility of the natural world points to the existence of a creative mind possessing great wisdom and power. Certainly, science seems unable to start if one assumes that the universe is unintelligible chaos. It is not outrageous to suggest that the birth of modern science depended on the Christian assumption of a rational creator who governed His creation through coherent laws.

I need to be clear that it is not only persons with Christian sympathies who acknowledge the remarkable intelligibility of the universe. For example, Sheldon Glashow, who received the Nobel Prize in Physics in 1979, has pointed out that even if scientists are not religious in the normal sense, they nonetheless have a strong faith in the basic simplicity of nature. However, as an unbeliever, Glashow is forced to claim, implausibly, that this assumption of simplicity is quite irrational and without justification.

Science Developed in a Christian Environment

I like to begin with an outrageous claim that always causes reaction. This is the position of British scientist Robert Clark, and it will at least make you think. Clark argues in his book *Christian Belief and Science* that science has only developed in Christian culture. Part of the reason for this, Clark maintains, is that non-Christians typically held that there was something morally wrong in investigating nature. Thus the Greeks have the myth of Prometheus, who is punished for stealing fire from the gods. I would prefer if Dr. Clark had claimed that science has only developed in a sustained fashion in Christian culture. I think he went a little too far here, but his words certainly give people something to cogitate.

A frequent objection to Clark's view is that science made significant progress in the Middle East under Islam during the Middle Ages. This is true, of course, but why did these early scientific contributions fail to be "sustained"? In his important 2002 book, Professor Bernard Lewis of Princeton University has addressed this critical question. Lewis's book is appropriately titled *What Went Wrong? The Clash between Islam and Modernity in the Middle East.* The inability of science to continue under Islam is perhaps best illustrated by the fate of the great observatory built in Galata, Istanbul, in 1577. This observatory gave every promise of being comparable to that of the Danish scientist Tycho Brahe (1546–1601), who revolutionized astronomy. In *What Went Wrong?* Lewis relates that the observatory at Galata was razed to the ground by an elite corps of Turkish troops by order of the sultan on the recommendation of the Chief Mufti (Islamic leader) of Istanbul. For the next 300 years, there was no modern observatory in the Islamic world.

Let us explore the idea involved in the statements that Polanyi, Ward, and Clark made, that is, that modern science grew up in a Christian environment. I was taught in my childhood that Francis Bacon (1561–1626) discovered the scientific method. The higher critics have now gotten into the history of science and some claim that Bacon stole the scientific method from a multitude of others and just popularized it. We must leave that dilemma to the science historians to settle.

One of Francis Bacon's most frequently quoted statements is called the "Two Books" manifesto. These words of Bacon have been highly influential and the subject of a magnificent recent essay by Thomas Lessl. Francis Bacon urged that no one can be too well steeped in either God's Word or the book of nature. Bacon talks about the Bible as the book of God's words and nature as the book of God's works. He is encouraging us to learn as much as possible about both. So right here in the earliest days of the scientific method we have a statement of the compatibility of science with the 66 books of the Bible. I have taken Bacon's advice personally, having read through the Bible a dozen times since I became a Christian in 1973.

Johannes Kepler (1571–1630) was a brilliant mathematician, physicist, and astronomer. Kepler posited the idea of elliptical orbits for planets and is considered the discoverer of the laws of planetary motion. He was a devout Lutheran. When he was asked the question, "Why do you engage in science?" Kepler is reported to have answered that he desired in his scientific research "to obtain a sample test of the delight of the Divine Creator in His work and to partake of His joy."[11] Kepler might be mistakenly considered a Deist based on this first statement alone. But (in a personal creed widely attributed to him), he clarified: "I believe only and alone in the service of Jesus Christ. In him is all refuge and solace."[12]

Blaise Pascal (1623–1662) was a magnificent scientist. He is the father of the mathematical theory of probability and combinatorial analysis. He provided the essential link between the mechanics of fluids and the mechanics of rigid bodies. And he is, in my opinion, the only physical scientist to make profound contributions to Christian thinking. Many of these thoughts are found in the little book the *Pensées*, which I was required to read as a sophomore at M.I.T. They were trying to civilize us geeks, but a few years later M.I.T. decided that it was not working, so current students are not required to take as many humanities courses.

Pascal's theology is centered on the person of Jesus Christ as Savior and based on personal experience. He said that God makes people aware of their wretchedness and that God joins Himself to their soul so they now find humility, joy, confidence, and love with Jesus Christ as the center of everything.

Robert Boyle (1627–1691) was perhaps the first chemist. He gave the first operational definition of an element, demonstrating enormous ingenuity in constructing experiments in support of the atomistic hypothesis. Many of my freshman chemistry students remember Boyle's Law. I typically return to Berkeley for a week or two every year, and every once in a while I will meet one of my former chemistry students on the campus. They typically ask, "Didn't you used to be Professor Schaefer?" I ask them in return, "What do you remember from my freshman chemistry course?" Occasionally they will say, "pV = nRT." Then I know that I was fabulously successful. This, of course, is the ideal gas law, of which Boyle's Law is a critical part.

Boyle was a busy person. He wrote many books, one of which is *The Wisdom of God Manifested in the Works of Creation*. He personally endowed an annual lectureship promoted to the defense of Christianity against indifferentism and atheism. He was a good friend of Richard Baxter, one of the great Puritan theologians. Boyle was also governor of the Corporation for the Spread of the Gospel of Jesus Christ in New England.

Although I disagree, a recent poll concerning the most important person in history gave that honor to Sir Isaac Newton (1642–1727). Newton was a mathematician, physicist, co-discoverer with Leibniz of calculus, and the founder of classical physics. He was the first of the three great theoretical physicists. He also investigated many other subjects. Newton tried hard to do chemistry but was less than successful. He wrote more words about theology than science. Still in print is his book about the return of Jesus Christ, entitled *Observations on the Prophecy of Daniel and the Revelation of St. John*. One of Newton's most frequently quoted statements is: "This most beautiful system of the sun, planets and comets could only proceed from the counsel and dominion of an intelligent and powerful Being."[13]

One might assume from the previous statement that Newton was a Deist (the system of natural religion that affirms God's existence but denies revelation). However, typical Newton statements such as the following show that this is not true: "There are more sure marks of authenticity in the Bible than in any profane history."[14] In fact, one may more reasonably conclude that Newton was a biblical literalist than a Deist. As Edward B. Davis points out, for Newton:

> It was not enough to say that an article of faith could be deduced from scripture: "It must be expresst in the very form of sound words in which it was delivered by the Apostles," for men were apt to "run into partings about deductions. All the old heresies lay in deductions; the true faith was in the [Biblical] text."[15]

Beyond the Eighteenth Century

My favorite among these legendary figures and probably the greatest experimental scientist of all time is Michael Faraday (1791–1867). His two hundredth birthday was celebrated in 1991 at the Royal Institution (the multidisciplinary scientific research laboratory in London, of which Faraday was the director). There was an interesting article published in this context by my friend Sir John Meurig Thomas, who said that if Michael Faraday had lived into the era of the Nobel prize, he would have been worthy of eight. Faraday discovered benzene and electromagnetic induction, invented the generator, and was the main architect of the classical field theory of electromagnetism.

Let me contrast the end of Faraday's life with the end of Lev Landau's life, previously described. As Faraday lay on his deathbed, a friend and well-wisher came by and asked, "Sir Michael, what speculations have you now?" This friend was trying to introduce some cheer into the situation because the passion of Faraday's career had consisted of making speculations about science, then dashing into the laboratory to either prove or disprove them. It was a reasonable thing for a friend to say in a difficult situation and Faraday took the question seriously. He is said to have replied:

> Speculations, man, I have none! I have certainties. I thank God that I don't rest my dying head upon specu-

lations for I know whom I have believed and am persuaded that he is able to keep that which I have committed unto him against that day.[16]

The first time I used this statement in a public setting (nearly
twenty years ago) a bright-eyed and bushy-tailed young person in
the front row of the audience burst out: "I've heard that before,
and I am delighted to know that it was Michael Faraday who first
spoke those words." As gently as possible, I informed him that the
words were first penned by St. Paul some 1,800 years earlier to
express his confidence in Jesus Christ. Michael Faraday had a firm
grasp of the New Testament.

The second of the three great theoretical physicists of
all time would certainly have to be James Clerk Maxwell
(1831–1879). Trevor Williams has summarized Maxwell's career
this way:

> Maxwell possessed all the gifts necessary for revolution-
> ary advances in theoretical physics: a profound grasp of
> physical reality, great mathematical ability, total absence
> of preconceived notions, a creative imagination of the
> highest order. He possessed also the gift to recognize the
> right task for this genius—the mathematical interpreta-
> tion of Faraday's concept of electromagnetic field.
> Maxwell's successful completion of this task, resulting in
> the mathematical [field] equations bearing his name,
> constituted one of the great achievements of the human
> intellect.[17]

Those who have thought deeply about the history and philosophy of science (e.g., Michael Polanyi and Thomas Kuhn) would
disagree with one statement made above. If Maxwell indeed had a
"total absence of preconceived notions," he would have accomplished a total absence of science.

Although Maxwell's Equations are one of the great achievements of the human intellect, as a member of the M.I.T. sopho-

more physics class during the 1963–1964 academic year, I probably would have described them in different language at the time. However, just before our first examination in electromagnetism, one of the members of our class had a brilliant idea. This entrepreneurial wag had 900 T-shirts printed with Maxwell's Equations embossed in large script. The entire class showed up to the first exam dressed in this unusual garb. Maxwell's Equations were plainly visible from every seat in the auditorium. Our class averaged 95 percent on the first exam! Regrettably, the professor was distinctly unhappy. The average on his second exam, despite our awesome T-shirts, was 15 percent. Never mess with a professor.

On June 23, 1864, James Clerk Maxwell wrote:

> Think what God has determined to do to all those who submit themselves to his righteousness and are willing to receive his gift [the gift of eternal life in Jesus Christ]. They are to be conformed to the image of His Son, and when that is fulfilled, and God sees they are conformed to the image of Christ, there can be no more condemnation.[18]

Maxwell and Charles Darwin were contemporaries. Many wondered what a committed Christian such as Maxwell thought of Darwin's ideas. In fact, Maxwell once was invited to attend a meeting on the Italian Riviera in February to discuss new developments in science and the Bible. If you have ever spent time in Cambridge, England, you know it is gloomy in the wintertime. If I had been a member of the Cambridge faculty, I would have taken every opportunity to go to the Italian Riviera at this time of the year. However, Maxwell turned down the invitation, explaining in his letter of declination that because scientific hypotheses change much more quickly than Biblical interpretations, founding the latter on the former might keep a hypothesis in circulation long after it should have been rejected.

This is sage advice. An example of just this is the steady state theory, which was popularized by Fred Hoyle and others. It was for decades one of the two competing theories of the origin of the universe. The steady state hypothesis basically says that what you see is what was always there. It became less tenable in 1965 with the observation by Arnold Penzias and Robert Wilson of the microwave background radiation. There are not many cosmologists left who believe in the steady state hypothesis. But it is amusing to go back to about 1960, find biblical commentaries on the Book of Genesis, and see how an unfortunate few explain how the steady state hypothesis can be reconciled with the first chapter of Genesis. Any reasonable person can see that the Genesis account is describing a creation from nothing (ex nihilo), so it takes a vivid imagination to reconcile a beginning in space, time, and history with the now discredited steady state hypothesis. By the second half of the twenty-first century, should planet Earth still be here, the steady state hypothesis will be dead and nearly forgotten. These commentaries probably still will be available in libraries, but few people will be able to understand them. This is an excellent example of the important point made by James Clerk Maxwell well more than a century ago.

One of my favorite cartoons was published by Sidney Harris a few years ago in The American Scientist. Two distinguished elderly scientists are staring unhappily at an obscure equation on a blackboard. One of them delivers the punch line: "What is most depressing is the realization that everything we believe will be disproved in a few years." I hope that is not true of my students' research in quantum chemistry. I do not think it will be the case, but there is an important element of reality to the fact that science is inherently a tentative activity. As scientists we come to understandings that are always subject, at the least, to further refinements.

Of course, not all biographers of these pioneers of modern physical science spoke positively of their Christian convictions. For example, James Crowther claims in his biography of Faraday and Maxwell that the religious decisions of Faraday and Maxwell evaded the social problems that affect many other gifted scientists of the time.[19] In context, what Crowther is saying is that because they were Christians, Maxwell and Faraday did not become alcoholics, womanizers, or social climbers, to enumerate the disabling sins of a number of gifted scientists of the same era.

I need to insert a little organic chemistry here, so my colleagues on the organic side will know that I paid some attention to them. William Henry Perkin (1838–1907) was perhaps the first great synthetic organic chemist. Perkin was the discoverer of the first synthetic dye, known as Perkin's mauve or aniline purple. Prior to Perkin's discovery, the use of the color purple had been extremely expensive and often limited to persons of royal descent. He is the person for whom an important journal, the Perkin Transactions of the Royal Society of Chemistry (London), is named. In the year 1873, at the age of 35, Perkin sold his highly profitable business and retired to private research and church missionary ventures. One of the more humorous responses to the present lecture was a suggestion from the audience a few years back that I follow William Henry Perkin's example in this particular respect.

Perkin was carrying out research on unsaturated acids three days prior to his death, which was brought on by the sudden onset of appendicitis and double pneumonia. The following account is given in Simon Garfield's 2001 biography of Perkin. On his deathbed, William Henry Perkin stated: "The children are in Sunday School. Give them my love, and tell them always to trust Jesus." He then sang the first verse of the magisterial Isaac Watts hymn "When I Survey the Wondrous Cross." When he reached the last line, which reads "And pour contempt on all my pride," Perkin declared, "Proud? Who could be proud?"[20]

One can find the name of George Stokes (1819–1903) in any issue of the Journal of Chemical Physics, the most prestigious journal in my field. In recent issues, Coherent Anti-Stokes Raman Spectroscopy (CARS) has been a subject of much scholarly investigation. Stokes was one of the great pioneers of spectroscopy, fluorescence, and the study of fluids. He held one of the most distinguished chairs in the academic world for more than fifty years, the Lucasian Professorship of Mathematics at Cambridge University. This was the position held by Sir Isaac Newton and is the chair currently occupied by Stephen Hawking, subject of the second lecture in this series. Stokes was also the president of the Royal Society of London.

Stokes wrote on a range of matters beyond chemistry and physics. Concerning the question of miracles, Stokes argued in his book Natural Theology, published in 1891, that once one allows that a personal God exists, it immediately follows that miracles are possible. If God wills the laws, He can also will their suspension, though in fact we do not even have to suppose that they have been suspended.[21]

William Thomson (1824–1907) was later known as Lord Kelvin. Lord Kelvin was recognized as the leading physical scientist and the greatest science teacher of his time. His early papers on electromagnetism and his papers on heat provide enduring proof of his scientific genius. He was a Christian with a strong faith in God and the Bible. In a speech to University College in 1903, Kelvin stated: "Do not be afraid of being free thinkers. If you think strongly enough, you will be forced by science to the belief in God."[22]

In 1897 J. J. Thomson (1856–1940) identified and characterized the electron, one of the most profound discoveries in the history of science. Thomson was for many years the Cavendish

Professor of Physics at Cambridge University. The old Cavendish Laboratory still sits in the middle of the beautiful Cambridge campus. So many remarkable discoveries were made in the old Cavendish that it has essentially become a museum. A total of something like a dozen Nobel prizes resulted from research done in that laboratory. When the old Cavendish was opened by James Clerk Maxwell in 1874, he had a Latin phrase from Psalm 111 carved over the front door. Perhaps ten years ago, I had my daughter Charlotte, who subsequently graduated from Stanford University in classics, translate this phrase for me. Then we walked out into the Cambridge countryside, where the shiny new Cavendish Laboratory was dedicated in 1973. Placed over the front door is the same phrase, but this time in English: "The works of the Lord are great, sought out of all them that have pleasure therein." Cavendish Professor J. J. Thomson made this statement in *Nature* (a journal in which I have actually published):

> In the distance tower still higher [scientific] peaks which will yield to those who ascend them still wider prospects, and deepen the feeling whose truth is emphasized by every advance in science, that "Great are the works of the Lord."[23]

For the brilliant Thomson, the bottom line in science was that the works of the Lord are magnificent.

Those who know my research will not be surprised that this lecture must include at least one theoretical chemist. Let's make it three in this paragraph. Charles Coulson (1910–1974) was one of the three principal architects of the molecular orbital theory. I had the privilege of meeting Coulson just once, at the Canadian Theoretical Chemistry Conference in Vancouver in 1971. He probably would have received the Nobel prize, but he did not pass the usual first test. This typical first hurdle to receiving the Nobel prize is to live to be 65 years old—a wonderful excuse for those of us comfortably below that threshold who have not made the trip to Stockholm. The second test, far more challenging, is to have done something important when you were 30–40 years old. Coulson indeed did profoundly significant work when he was in his thirties, but he died at 64, thus disqualifying himself from the Nobel prize. Coulson, a professor of mathematics and theoretical chemistry at Oxford University for many years, was also a Methodist lay minister. Norman March (a good friend), successor to the renamed Coulson Chair of Theoretical Chemistry, was also a Methodist lay minister. Alas, upon the retirement of Professor March a few years ago, a suitable Methodist lay minister could not be found for the Coulson Chair at Oxford, so the university settled for an Anglican Christian, Professor Mark Child (also a friend). Charles Coulson was a spokesman for Christians in academic science and the originator of the term "god of the gaps," now widely used in philosophical circles. From the biographical memoirs (1974) of the Royal Society of London, following Charles Coulson's death, we read Coulson's own description of his conversion to faith in Jesus Christ in 1930 as a 20-year-old student at Cambridge University:

> There were some ten of us and together we sought for God and together we found Him. I learned for the first time in my life that God was my friend. God became real to me, utterly real. I knew Him and I could talk with Him as I never imagined it possible before. And these prayers were the most glorious moment of the day. Life had a purpose and that purpose coloured everything.[24]

Coulson's experience was fairly similar to my own, 43 years later, as a young professor at Berkeley. It would be arresting if I could say that there was a thunderclap from heaven, God spoke to me in audible terms, and hence I became a Christian. However, it did not happen that way. The apostle Paul's experience was the exception rather than the rule. But I did (and still do, some 28 years later) experience the same perception that Coulson described. My life has a purpose in Jesus Christ, and that purpose colors everything.

The "Why" Question

Before we move on exclusively to contemporary scientists, let us explore some of the reasons for the observations I have described thus far. Namely, why did sustained scientific development occur first in a Christian environment? The best answers I have seen to this question were recently (2000) formulated by my University of Georgia chemistry colleague Dr. Wesley Allen. His (slightly modified) five answers to this question are as follows:

1. If Christianity is true, the universe is real, not illusory. The universe is thus the product of a God whose character is immutable, at variance with pantheistic notions, which place inherent distrust in sensory experience in a mercurial world.

2. If Christianity is true, the universe, being divinely created, is of inherent value and thus worthy of study. This conclusion supplants any zeitgeist that would view science as a mere intellectual pastime.

3. If Christianity is true, nature itself is not divine, thus humanity may probe it free of fear. This was an important realization in early eras dominated by superstitions about the natural environment. Worship and ultimate reverence is reserved for the Creator, not the creation, nor humans as creatures therein.

4. If Christianity is true, humankind, formed in the image of God, can discover order in the universe by rational interpretation. That is, the codes of nature can be unveiled and read. Without such faith, science might never have developed because it might have appeared impossible in principle.

5. If Christianity is true, the form of nature is not inherent within nature but rather a divine command imposed from outside nature. Thus the details of the world must be uncovered by observation rather than by mere rational musing because God is

free to create according to His own purposes. In this way science was liberated from Aristotelian rationalism, whereby the Creator was subjected to the dictates of reason constructed by humans. Such gnosticism, which transformed speculation into dogma, undermined the open-endedness of science. To be sure, Christianity holds that God is a perfectly rational being who cannot act inconsistently with His character. But this principle only places partial constraints on His creative activity, which science must be free to discover in all its diversity.

Contemporary Scientists

Robert Griffiths (1937–), a member of the U.S. National Academy of Sciences, is the Otto Stern Professor of Physics at Carnegie-Mellon University. He received one of the most coveted awards of the American Physical Society in 1984 for his work on statistical mechanics and thermodynamics. The magazine *Physics Today* reported that Griffiths is an evangelical Christian who is an amateur theologian and who helps teach a course at Carnegie-Mellon on Christianity and science. I find this to be particularly intriguing because for the last five years I have taught a freshman seminar at the University of Georgia on the same subject. Professor Griffiths made the interesting statement: "If we need an atheist for a debate, I go to the philosophy department. The physics department isn't much use."[25]

At the University of California at Berkeley, where I was a professor for 18 years, we had fifty chemistry professors. But for many years there was only one who was willing to publicly identify himself as an atheist, my good friend Robert Harris, with whom I still have occasional discussions about spiritual things, usually during my annual summer week on the Berkeley campus. After one such discussion perhaps twenty years ago, Bob told me he might have to rethink his position and become an agnostic. I thought to myself, "Okay, Bob, one step at a time." But Bob came back to me a week later, firmly reinstalled in the atheist camp. A more recent addition to the Berkeley chemistry faculty is a second open atheist, Richard Saykally. Rich is also a close friend, soundly disproving the notion that disagreements about ultimate questions necessarily lead to personal rancor.

For many years, Richard Bube (1927–) was the chairman of the Department of Materials Science at Stanford University. No less than 56 Stanford graduate students have received their doctoral degrees under Professor Bube's direction. Bube has carried out foundational research in solid state physics concerning semiconductors, the photoelectronic properties of materials, photovoltaic devices (solar cells), and amorphous materials. He seconds Robert Griffiths' above statement, noting that the proportion of atheistic scientists is no different than the proportion of atheistic truck drivers. Richard Bube has long been a spokesman for evangelical Christians in academic life, serving for many years as editor of the journal *Perspectives on Science and the Christian Faith*, published by the American Scientific Affiliation, of which I am a Fellow. Bube currently teaches a second-year undergraduate course at Stanford entitled "Issues in Science and Christianity."

Another member of the U.S. National Academy of Sciences is John Suppe, noted professor of geology at Princeton University. John is an outstanding scholar in the area of plate tectonics, the deformation of the earth's crust. Vaguely aware of his own spiritual needs, he began attending services in the Princeton chapel, then reading the Bible and other Christian books. He eventually committed himself to Christ and, remarkably, had his first real experience of Christian fellowship in Taiwan, where he was on a prestigious Guggenheim Fellowship. I have spoken before the Christian faculty forum at the National Taiwan University in Taipei, so I know personally that they are a good group.

Suppe has argued that the Gospel is no different for scientists than it is for anyone else. In this sense, evolution is really beside the point because it is not where scientists look to discover the meaning of life. For this reason, Suppe maintains that the controversy over evolution is not the best place to engage scientists with Christianity.

My candidate for scientist of the twentieth century is Charles Townes (1915–), who received the 1964 Nobel Prize in Physics for his discovery of the laser. However, I must confess to some possible bias because Professor Townes is the only plausible candidate for scientist of the century that I know personally. But the laser is a discovery that has significantly impacted the life of every person who reads these words. Dr. Townes almost received a second Nobel prize for his observation of the first interstellar molecule. The study of interstellar molecules has subsequently become a major part of astrophysics, affecting even my own research. Charles Townes was the provost at M.I.T. when I was an undergraduate, and he later was a colleague (but in the physics department) during my 18 years on the faculty at Berkeley.

At Berkeley every doctoral oral examination requires four faculty members from the candidate's own department and a fifth committee member from an outside department. In chemical physics, which is actually a part of the chemistry department at Berkeley, the "outside" committee member is almost inevitably a physics faculty member. This puts a significant strain on some of the physics faculty because only a few of them are sufficiently knowledgeable about chemistry to serve on such committees, of which about thirty must be constituted each year. So it was not unusual for this particular subset of the physics faculty to come up with highly original reasons why they were unavailable for such two-hour ordeals. But Charlie Townes was never such a one. He always served the chemistry department cheerfully, though his duties in Washington and elsewhere were legion. And his demeanor on these committees was always gentlemanly. His questions to the chemistry doctoral students were almost inevitably thoughtful and designed to bring out the best in a quaking student.

Charlie has written an autobiography entitled *Making Waves*, a pun referring to the wavelike phenomena that scientifically describe lasers. The book was published in 1995 by the American Institute of Physics, and I recommend it. Charlie makes reference to his church involvement, then provides the statement:

> You may well ask, "Just where does God come into this?" Perhaps my account may give you some answer, but to me that's almost a pointless question. If you believe in God at all, there is no particular 'where.' He's always there—everywhere. He's involved in all of these things. To me, God is personal yet omnipresent—a great source of strength, Who has made an enormous difference to me.[26]

Arthur Schawlow (1921–2000) won the Nobel Prize in Physics in 1981 for his work in laser spectroscopy. Artie Schawlow served until his recent death as a professor at Stanford and was a truly beloved figure in the physics community. He did not hesitate to identify himself as a Protestant Christian. And he makes the unusual claim, which I suspect might only be made by a scientist, that it is fortunate that the New Testament tells us about God in ways accessible to everyone. I know that Arthur Schawlow believed that his experimental studies of molecular spectroscopy were also telling him something about God's creative powers. The contrast with the New Testament accounts of the life of Jesus was that Schawlow did not think that his work was providing information about God in ways accessible to everyone.

John Polkinghorne (1930–) was the chaired professor of mathematical physics at Cambridge University from 1968 to

1979. This is the "other" chair of theoretical physics at Cambridge, in addition to that held by Stephen Hawking. In 1979 Polkinghorne made an abrupt career switch, enrolling in theological studies before becoming an Anglican priest. Then in 1986 Polkinghorne returned to Cambridge, first as dean of Trinity Hall and later becoming president of Queen's College. Queen's College sits next to St. Catherine's College, where I stay in Cambridge during my frequent visits to my longtime scientific collaborator and close friend, theoretical chemistry Professor Nicholas Handy, also an Anglican. Perhaps, needless to say, John Polkinghorne has been outspoken in his commitment to Jesus Christ.

I would like to make one particular point about cosmology as it relates to biology and to a more general question. The world's greatest observational cosmologist is Allan Sandage (1926–), an astronomer at the Carnegie Institution in Pasadena, California. Sandage was called the "Grand Old Man of Cosmology" by the New York Times when he won the highly lucrative 1991 Crafoord Prize, given by the Royal Swedish Academy of Sciences. This prize is given to a cosmologist every sixth year and is viewed by the Swedish Academy as equivalent to the Nobel prize. Allan Sandage was born into a Jewish family and committed his life to Jesus Christ at the age of 50. Dr. Sandage was asked the old question: "Can a person be a scientist and also be a Christian?" Sandage's affirmative response is expected, but he provides a surprising focus: "The world is too complicated in all its parts and interconnections to be due to chance alone. I am convinced that the existence of life with all its order in each of its organisms is simply too well put together."[27]

Sandage is the person responsible for the best current scientific estimate of the (apparent) age of the universe, perhaps 13 billion years. Yet when this brilliant astrophysicist is asked to explain how one can be a scientist and a Christian, he turns not to cosmology but biology. Which brings me full circle to the question I addressed earlier from the perspective of mathematical physics and the intelligibility of the universe: Why might a scientist become a Christian? The answer from biology is that the extraordinary complexity and high information content of even the simplest living thing (the simplest self-replicating biochemical system) points to a sovereign creator God.

As mentioned earlier, a typically important ingredient to receiving the Nobel Prize in chemistry is the attainment of age 65. For example, my good friend John Pople, a serious Methodist, received the prize in quantum chemistry at the age of 73 in 1988. He shared the prize with Walter Kohn, who was 75 at the time. However, the physics Nobel is often given to much younger individuals. William Phillips (1949–) received the Nobel Prize in physics at the age of 48 for the development of methods to cool and trap atoms with laser light. On the announcement date, October 15, 1997, Phillips was participating in a conference on high-powered telescopes in Long Beach, California. At the mandatory press conference William Phillips spoke the words: "God has given us an incredibly fascinating world to live in and explore."

Phillips formed and sings in the gospel choir of the Fairhaven United Methodist Church, a multiracial congregation of about three hundred in Gaithersburg, Maryland. He also teaches Sunday school and leads Bible studies. If you took the time to delve further into the October 1997 media reports, you could find out that on Saturday afternoons, William Phillips and his wife often drive into central Washington, D.C. to pick up a blind, 87-year-old African American woman to take her grocery shopping and to dinner.

Allow me just once more to ask the critical question: Why might a scientist become a Christian? My third answer is the remarkable fine-tuning of the universe. Let me draw a picture by citing three persons with no obvious theistic inclinations. Paul

Davies, an excellent popularizer of science, points out that the way matter is currently arranged depends on a highly "special choice" of initial conditions. Now, if language means anything, a special choice implies that someone or something is doing the choosing. Likewise, Stephen Hawking points out the enormous odds against a universe like ours. And Fred Hoyle has said that the evidence is that there is no such thing as "blind forces" in nature. My own view is that all three of these skeptics, in their own unique ways, are unintentionally supporting the position put forth by St. Paul more than 1,900 years earlier: "For since the creation of the world God's invisible qualities—His eternal power and divine nature—have been clearly seen, being understood from what has been made" (Romans 1:20).

Two Common Questions

Prior to my concluding remarks, I would like to respond to two questions that are frequently raised when I have delivered a version of this essay as a public lecture. The first question is: "Given the evidence you present, why do so many persist in the belief that it is not possible to be a scientist and a Christian?" Although I am about as far from being a conspiracy theorist as possible, I conclude that part of the problem is indeed misrepresentation.

The respected British science historian Colin Russell has described T. H. Huxley's important role in these developments in his scholarly account in the April 1989 issue of *Science and Christian Belief*, the quarterly publication of the Victoria Institute, of which I have been a member for the past fifteen years. Here, rather, I would like to focus on a famous two-volume work published in 1896 entitled *A History of the Warfare of Science with Theology in Christendom*.[28] Of course, given the origins of modern science, such a title sounds silly. The author of this polemic was Andrew Dickson White, the first president of Cornell University and the first North American university founded on purely secular terms. White famously claimed that Calvin had used Psalm 93 to condemn those who denied the geocentric model of the universe. Perhaps, needless to say, this was not making Calvin look good. That was not Andrew Dickson White's intention. However, the truth of this matter has recently been brought forth by Dr. Alister McGrath, the Bampton Lecturer at Oxford University. In his definitive biography of Calvin, McGrath writes:

This assertion [by White] is slavishly repeated by virtually every writer on the theme "religion and science," such as Bertrand Russell in his History of Western Philosophy. Yet it may be stated categorically that Calvin wrote no such words (in his Genesis commentary) and expressed no such sentiments in any of his known writings. The assertion that he did is to be found, characteristically unsubstantiated, in the writings of the nineteenth century Anglican dean of Canterbury, Frederick William Farrar (1831–1903).[29]

The second frequently asked question following this lecture is "Okay, but how does it change your science?" Having first heard this question at Stanford University fifteen years ago, I have had plenty of time to develop a good answer. But I must confess that I cannot qualitatively improve on the answer given by the brilliant Notre Dame historian George Marsden in his book *The Outrageous Idea of Christian Scholarship*.[30] My answer modifies Marsden's only slightly. In science, Christian faith can have a significant bearing on scholarship in at least four ways:

1. One's Christian faith may be a factor in motivating a scientist to do his or her work well. This is not to deny that some atheist or agnostic scholars may be just as motivated to work with just as much integrity. For any particular scholar, however, Christianity may be an important motivator.

2. One's Christian faith may help determine the applications one sees for his or her scholarship. One may carry out

research in anything from materials science to molecular biology with the hope that it may contribute to the well-being of others. Again, the fact that some atheists are also altruistic does not negate the Christian contribution to altruism.

3. Such motives may help shape a subfield, specialty, or the questions a person asks about his or her research. For example, I readily confess that my scientific interest in interstellar molecules was initially inspired by the oft-repeated claims that this field will ultimately explain the origin of life. Ultimate questions tend to be of special interest to Christians.

4. When on occasion the scientist is asked to reflect on the wider implications of his or her scholarship, faith may have an important bearing on how that person sees the field, or its assumptions, fitting into a larger framework of meaning.

Concluding Remarks

My collection of scientists with Christian commitments is far from exhaustive. The publication of this lecture will surely bring me correspondence from near and far with excellent new examples of the genre. Should a second edition be forthcoming, I will be happy to attempt to incorporate new material. Please do send cards and letters. But I should mention now a few others not included above. Among chemists, Professors Andrew Bocarsly (Princeton University) and James Tour (Rice University) have given Christian testimonies that have touched my heart and mind in a special way. Both Andy and Jim were born into Jewish families and gave their lives to Jesus Christ during their undergraduate years. Bocarsly is an inorganic photochemist and Tour a synthetic organic chemist turned materials scientist. Jim Tour's work on fullerenes, bucky tubes, and more generally nanochemistry is definitely on track for a trip to Stockholm some December, perhaps a decade from now.

The present discussion has focused on physics and chemistry for the obvious reason that I am a chemical physicist. This is my professional life. I suspect that it would be possible to make a similar case for the biological sciences. For example, biochemistry Professor David Cole was the steadfast leader of the Christian faculty organization during my years on the Berkeley campus. Francis Collins is one of the most outstanding research biologists of our generation. While a professor at the University of Michigan, Collins discovered the cystic fibrosis gene. For the past five years, Francis Collins has been director of the now successful National Institutes of Health (NIH) Human Genome Project, the largest scientific project ever undertaken. In a 1999 paper, Collins began with the following words:

> Let me begin by saying a brief word about my own spiritual path. I did not come from a strongly Christian home. I was raised in a home where faith was not considered particularly relevant, sent to church to learn music, but instructed that it would be best to avoid the theology. I followed those instructions well and went off to college with only the dimmest idea of what saving faith in Jesus Christ was all about. What little glimmers of faith I might have possessed were quickly destroyed by the penetrating questions of my freshman dorm colleagues who, as one will do at that phase in life, took great delight in destroying any remnants of superstition, which is what they considered faith to be. I became quite an obnoxious atheist with whom you would not have enjoyed having lunch. I too felt it was part of my mission to point out that all that really mattered could be discerned by science, and everything else was irrelevant.

> Fortunately, through the guidance of some very patient people, who tolerated a lot of insolent questions, I was led to read C. S. Lewis and then the Bible, and so was led

to understand many of the concepts that had completely eluded me before, and I gave my life to Christ 20 years ago.[31]

I hope that this essay has given you a flavor of the history of science. Those of you who have taken a freshman chemistry or physics course will surely recognize many of the names of the great scientists described here. In fact, the reason this chapter took its general shape was to present minisketches of the spiritual lives of scientists with whom my Berkeley freshman chemistry students would be familiar. There is a tremendous tradition, past and present, of distinguished scientists who are Christians. It gives me great joy to be a small part of that continuing tradition. And perhaps I have given you sufficient evidence that you will never again believe that it is difficult to be a scientist and a Christian. Finally, following the example of Oxford Professor Charles Coulson in his public lectures on science and the Christian faith, I encourage you to consider the advice of Psalm 34:8: "Taste and see that the Lord is good."

Notes

1. Henry F. Schaefer III, *Science and Christianity: Conflict or Coherence?* (Watkinsville, Ga.: The Apollos Trust, 2003).

2. Susan V. Gallagher and Roger Lundin, *Literature through the Eyes of Faith* (San Francisco: Harper & Row, 1989).

3. C. S. Lewis, *Surprised by Joy: The Shape of My Early Life* (New York: Harcourt Brace, 1956), 174. Lewis actually says "rationalism," not "atheism," but it is clear in context that the kind of rationalism he has in mind is the kind that denies the supernatural, thus is incompatible with any robust notion of theism. To this day, there are "Rationalist" societies that are clearly atheistic—editor.

4. Erwin Schrödinger, *Nature and the Greeks* (Cambridge: Cambridge University Press, 1954).

5. *Chemistry in Britain* 25, no. 7 (July 1989), 663.

6. *Physics Today* 42, no. 5 (May 1989), 41.

7. Kameshwar C. Wali, *Chandra: A Biography of S. Chandrasekhar* (Chicago: University of Chicago Press, 1991), 304–306.

8. Richard Feynman, *The Pleasure of Finding Things Out* (Cambridge, Mass.: Perseus Publishing, 1999), 247. [On the same page, Feynman clarifies that by "God" he means "the kind of personal God . . . to whom you pray and who has something to do with creating the universe and guiding you in morals"—editor.]

9. Alan Lightman and Roberta Brawer, *Origins: The Lives and Worlds of Modern Cosmologists* (Cambridge, Mass.: Harvard University Press, 1990).

10. Eugene Wigner, "The Unreasonable Effectiveness of Mathematics in the Natural Sciences," *Communications in Pure and Applied Mathematics* 13, no. 1 (February 1960). The quotation can be viewed on-line at: www.Dartmouth.edu/~matc/Mathdrama/reading/Wigner.html.

11. The quotation can be found at numerous web-sites, including "Scientific Evidences of Christianity," www.granbychurchofchrist.org/studies/christianevidences/creationscientists.htm.

12. Quoted in J. H. Tiner, *Johannes Kepler—Giant of Faith and Science* (Milford, Mich.: Mott Media, 1977), 193. This statement is frequently attributed to Kepler, although it does not appear in his published writings, according to Peter Barker—editor.

13. Newton, *General Scholium*—editor.

14. Cited in Henry M. Morris, *Men of Science, Men of God* (Green Forest, Ark.: Master Books, 1992), 26.

15. Edward B. Davis, "Newton's Rejection of the 'Newtonian World View': The Role of Divine Will in Newton's Natural Philosophy," *Science and Christian Belief* (October 1991): 103–17 (107).

16. The Faraday quotation is listed in "Quotes from some Scientists," at:http://www.valleypresbyterian.org/curriculum/science/quotes.htm. The content of the quotation is simply a paraphrase of 2 Timothy 1:12.

17. Trevor Williams, entry for James Clerk Maxwell in *The Biographical Dictionary of Scientists* (London: A & C Black, 1982).

18. This quotation can be found in "Quotes from some Scientists," at: http://www.valleypresbyterian.org/curriculum/science/quotes.htm.

19. James Crowther, *Founders of Modern Science* (Westport, Conn.: Greenwood Publishing Group, 1982).

20. Simon Garfield, *Mauve: How One Man Invented a Colour That Changed the World* (New York: Norton, 2001), 137.

21. That miracles do not really "break" the laws of nature is argued by C. S.

Lewis in his *Miracles*, 2nd ed. (New York: Macmillan, 1960), chapter 8—editor.

22. Lord Kelvin made this statement during an address to University College, Dundee, Scotland in 1903. See: http://users.ipfw.edu/isiorho/.

23. *Nature* 81 (1909): 257.

24. *Biographical Memoirs of Fellows of the Royal Society*, vol. 20 (1974), 76-77. According to an archivist at the Royal Society, the quote is from a sermon preached by Coulson in 1931, where he talks of the influence that his membership of a Methodist group had on his faith—editor.

25. Quoted in Hugh Ross, *The Creator and the Cosmos*, second expanded edition (Colorado Springs, Col.: NavPress, 1995), 123.

26. Charles H. Townes, *Making Waves* (New York: Springer Verlag, 1995), 203.

27. Allan Sandage, "A Scientist Reflects on Religious Belief," *Truth*, Vol. 1, (Dallas, Texas: Truth Incorporated, 1985), 54. Available on-line at http://www.leaderu.com/truth/1truth15.html.

28. Andrew Dickson White, *A History of the Warfare of Science with Theology in Christendom* (London: D. Appleton, 1910).

29. Alister McGrath, *A Life of John Calvin: A Study in the Shaping of Western Culture* (Oxford: Blackwell, 1993).

30. George M. Marsden, *The Outrageous Idea of Christian Scholarship* (New York: Oxford University Press, 1997).

31. Francis Collins, "The Human Genome Project: Tool of Atheistic Reductionism or Embodiment of the Christian Mandate to Heal?" *Science and Christian Belief* 11, no. 2 (1999).

5

Astronomy, Providence, and the Lutheran Contribution to Science

PETER BARKER

Abstract

Recent work by Sachiko Kusukawa and Charlotte Methuen attributes slightly different religious significance to the Wittenberg program in natural philosophy and especially astronomy. Methuen believes that Wittenberg students were expected to draw moral lessons from their study of the heavens. Kusukawa, on the other hand, connects Wittenberg scientific activity generally to Philip Melanchthon's vision of a causally ordered providence. I will suggest that, for Melanchthon's followers, moral knowledge and knowledge in the mathematically based exact sciences shared a single divine origin and was accessible through a single mental faculty: the "natural light" of human reason. Thus it was not necessary to derive moral truths from astronomical knowledge, though the study of astronomy showed the existence of a providential, causal order that was divine in origin, a theme that recurs in the work of Erasmus Reinhold, Caspar Peucer, and their successors. Kepler believed he had definitively uncovered this providential order in his 1596 *Mysterium Cosmographicum* and established its causal structure in the 1609 *Astronomia Nova*.

Introduction

Throughout the sixteenth century and as late as 1607, the statutes of the University of Wittenberg began: "Many clear evidences of God are impressed on the things of the natural world, which the Most Benevolent Founder wished to be seen, that we may come to know him."[1] The prominence assigned to the study of natural philosophy, and especially astronomy, in the Wittenberg curriculum goes some way to explain the appearance of this statute. Two recent books have addressed these issues. In her book *Kepler's Tübingen* and related papers, Charlotte Methuen argues that Lutheran students were expected to draw moral lessons from the study of the heavens. In *Phillip Melanchthon: The Transformation of Natural Philosophy*, Sachiko Kusukawa makes a more general case for the significance of the study of natural philosophy, including astronomy, in the Lutheran curriculum. She suggests that natural philosophy, of which astronomy was an important part, played a special role in demonstrating the existence of providential design in the universe, which separately included moral rules.[2]

According to Kusukawa, the fundamental category "law of nature" was understood by Lutheran followers of Melanchthon to cover moral rules in the first instance and also, by extension, the causal laws established for the proper governance of the physical world. The laws of celestial motion, understood as the mathematical regularities defined by Ptolemaic astronomy, were the clearest examples of these. According to Methuen, astronomy was in some sense a source of, or foundation for, moral knowledge. According to Kusukawa, moral knowledge was founded separately but in the same category as knowledge of nature, of which astronomy was the prime example. This seemingly small difference between the two writers may have important consequences. Although Methuen's work appeared after Kusukawa's, she passes over in relative silence Kusukawa's main argument about the providential design of the world, and hence, the main motive for Lutheran pursuit of natural philosophy. If one of these positions is right, it should have important consequences for understanding later Lutheran natural philosophers. Prominent among these are the so-called Wittenberg astronomers, who are responsible for adopting and propagating a special version of Copernicus's views, and the later Lutherans Tycho Brahe and Johannes Kepler. In this essay I will examine the work of the most important Lutheran astronomers, beginning with Erasmus Reinhold and Casper Peucer. This examination will, I believe, generally confirm Kusukawa's providential reading of Lutheran natural philosophy.

Methuen and Kusukawa on Astronomy and Morals

Where Kusukawa examines the whole scope of natural philosophy, with particular attention to Melanchthon's text on physics, and other work in the areas of anatomy and psychology, Methuen confines her attention almost exclusively to astronomy. She suggests that astronomy is unique in Melanchthon's thinking: ". . . recognition of God is the highest knowledge which can be achieved through the mathematical sciences, and it can be achieved only through astronomy."[3] Here Methuen is actually making the same argument as Kusukawa: that study of natural philosophy leads to knowledge of God, though the claim that such knowledge can be achieved only through astronomy is an overstatement. As Methuen herself acknowledges elsewhere, other branches of natural philosophy—especially anatomy, the study of plants, and the subject we would now call psychology—equally reveal God by revealing causal structures established by God.[4] The reason for this mistaken emphasis on astronomy seems to be Methuen's notion that astronomy permits the derivation of moral rules or in some sense provides a foundation for such rules.[5] The whole question of the status of moral rules or laws and corresponding principles of natural philosophy is presented quite differently by Kusukawa.

Sachiko Kusukawa presents a strong case for a specifically Lutheran ideal of natural philosophy. Kusukawa suggests that natural philosophy in the tradition founded by Melanchthon saw the world as governed by a structure of causal laws, established providentially by God. Natural philosophy was, in her felicitous phrase, "providence made visible."[6] Melanchthon and his followers believed the providential plan came in two parts, which we might call the moral law and the physical law. They called both parts natural laws. Although all Lutherans (and more generally all human beings) were believed to be capable of understanding the moral law, the second part of the plan, understanding physical laws, such as the laws governing the motions of the planets, might require special mathematical insight. This called for a person with a special vocation, one whom at least one later Lutheran would describe as a "priest of nature."[7]

Kusukawa connects developments within the history of science proper with developments in general history in an exemplary way. Far too often, historians of science have attempted to treat scientific change as insulated from any important factors connected with issues outside science. One of Kusukawa's central arguments is that Melanchthon's doctrines of providential design grew out of the response to civil disorders in the late 1520s.

The Reformation was a widely based movement with many sources preceding Luther's famous intervention of 1517. However, Luther's rapid rise to prominence, his publication of several books that would today count as best sellers, and his role in politics as well as religion made him a central influence in the Reformation by the early 1520s. In the late 1520s one faction of reformers, called by their detractors the Anabaptists, caused civil unrest throughout Germany. The Anabaptists looked for a time as if they might demolish not only the traditional order of the church but also traditional society. They used force to pursue their aims and were resisted equally violently. For Luther and his followers, including Melanchthon, this was a crucial period. Luther already had established important ties with the temporal authorities in Northern Germany, enjoying the protection of local princes. Now threatened by the disorders, Luther, and his followers such as Melanchthon, sided with established authority against the Anabaptist uprising. This realignment of the Lutheran movement is known technically as the magisterial reform, and it prepared the way for Lutheranism to become a state religion in portions of Germany.[8]

Melanchthon, as well as Luther, played a role in establishing an intellectual foundation for the new Lutheran position. The Anabaptists represented a threat to life and property. From the late 1520s, Melanchthon appealed to the established tradition of "natural law" or innate knowledge of moral rules, to show that the behavior of the Anabaptists was wrong and sinful.[9] What is interesting for historians of science is that from the beginning, Melanchthon linked moral laws with knowledge of nature in the scientific sense. Both the moral laws and the fundamental principles of mathematical natural philosophy were equally part of

God's providential plan. This connection would assume a special importance for later Lutherans, particularly Kepler.

Luther and his followers were initially highly skeptical of the close association between Aristotle and the traditional church, and hence of traditional philosophy. Stimulated by the need to provide an intellectual foundation for the magisterial reform, however, Melanchthon gave new status to philosophy: It was acceptable to the extent that it studied natural causes ordained by God. Any doubts about the legitimacy of particular points could be settled by appealing to a demonstration. And the standards of demonstration were the established standards derived from Aristotle.[10]

In the disputation presented at Wittenberg in 1527, Melanchthon introduced these key points:

> That philosophy is the law of God can also be understood from the fact that it is the knowledge of natural causes and effects, and since these are things arranged by God, it follows that philosophy is the law of God, which is the teaching of that divine order.

> Just as astronomy is the knowledge of the heavenly motions, which are arranged by God, so moral philosophy is the knowledge of the works, that is, of the causes and effects that God has arranged in the mind of man.[11]

In this passage Melanchthon clearly indicates the parity between natural philosophy and moral philosophy. Philosophy, which for Melanchthon means natural philosophy or what we would today call physics, is the general study of causes and effects. In the natural world these causes and effects have been arranged by God. They constitute a divine order in the world, and the celestial motions studied in astronomy are an example. But God has also arranged causes and effects in the mind of humans. This means, for example, connections between good and bad actions and their consequences. Knowledge of these connections constitutes moral philosophy in the same way that knowledge of causal connections in nature constitutes natural philosophy. The importance of both subjects would be reflected in the new curriculum at Wittenberg, in the requirement that students study the Nichomachean ethics, on the one hand, and a series of works on natural philosophy, and especially astronomy, on the other.

Melanchthon distinguishes two categories of innate knowledge on practically every occasion where he mentions this kind of knowledge.[12] One category consists of moral rules that prohibit theft, banditry, and the other things of which the Anabaptists were accused. The other sort of knowledge, usually mentioned at the same time, is knowledge of mathematical truths—for example, that a triangle has three sides. Today we would count knowledge claims in these two categories as completely separate. Melanchthon did not, in large part because he subscribed to a doctrine common throughout the sixteenth and early seventeenth centuries that the human mind possessed a faculty called the "natural light" by means of which it could achieve certain knowledge of mathematical truths and perhaps other things.[13] This knowledge was incorporated in all human souls by God when He created them, and it was there, ready to be brought to mind by the natural light if sin or other distractions did not intervene. The fact that this knowledge was literally inscribed on the soul accounted for its certainty. It was natural for Melanchthon to include the moral principles he wished to defend in the same category and consequently to suggest that they shared the same certainty as mathematical truths. These are "the causes and effects that God has arranged in the mind of man." But not everyone agrees on what the moral rules are. The passage continues:

> Thus we will call philosophy not all the beliefs of everyone, but only that teaching which has demonstrations.

There is only one truth, as the philosophers say, therefore only one philosophy is true, that is the one that
strays least from demonstrations.[14]

Disputes about the content of moral philosophy, or natural
philosophy, could be settled by the use of demonstrations, the
method of the mathematical sciences. So again, uncertainty or
dissent could be eliminated by appealing to mathematics. More
generally, the moral rules inscribed on the soul by God would
ideally bring about a harmonious and just civil society in which
human beings served God's plan by remaining in their proper
station, just as the causal laws revealed in subjects such as astronomy brought about a harmonious structure for the physical
world, in which bodies contributed to the order of the whole system by following the paths ordained for them. Both aspects of
this structure were providential in the sense that they had been
constructed for the good of the human race, and both aspects
contributed to the alignment of Lutheranism with the temporal
powers during the magisterial reform. The moral rules showed
that the actions of Lutheran opponents, for example, Anabaptists,
were evil. The idea of a harmonious structure in the physical
world, for example, in the heavens, reinforced the idea that
human society should also conform to divinely established roles,
undercutting the Anabaptist rejection of civil and church hierar-
chies.

In discussing the providential design of the world,
Melanchthon and his followers repeatedly contrasted their views
with positions in classical philosophy that are incompatible. In
particular, the Epicureans are singled out for special criticism.
Their doctrine that the universe was created by a random combination of atoms is repeatedly criticized as fundamentally incompatible with the evidence of benevolent design and, hence, of a
benevolent designer. Melanchthon and his followers frequently
point to the evidence of the laws of astronomy and the success of

astrology as counter examples. Random chance could not have achieved these regularities. Only the active operation of a designing mind could bring about the order observed in the heavens.

From their first statement in the 1520s, these issues remain a constant theme in Melanchthon's writings and speeches. All the concerns mentioned so far, including the rejection of Epicureanism and similar philosophies in favor of providential design, the linking of the mathematical and the moral, and the status of astronomy as evidence, are succinctly restated in Melanchthon's 1549 address that celebrates the life of his colleague Caspar Cruciger. Melanchthon repeats a saying of Plato: "The joyful rumour of God runs through all the arts" [*Gratam de Deo famam in artibus sparsum esse*]. An example is the provision of specific remedies for specific diseases. However, more generally, this world cannot have flowed together out of chaos (an allusion to the Epicureans). The mathematical order apparent in numbers, the moral order apparent in the discrimination of virtue and vice, and the motions of the heavens are evidence of an eternal, architectonic mind.[15]

In fact, the main concern linking Melanchthon's remarks on astronomy seems to be a demonstration of the providential design of a world. This concern is also apparent in the work of the most important Wittenberg astronomers, supporting Kusukawa's providential reading of Lutheran natural philosophy.

The Wittenberg Program in Astronomy

Melanchthon's influence led to a new emphasis on mathematics and the exact sciences in the curriculum at Wittenberg. In 1536 two new professors were installed to teach mathematics and astronomy. These were Erasmus Reinhold and Georg Rheticus. Rheticus had recently graduated from the university, publicly defending a thesis proposed by Melanchthon, in which he argued that astrology was legitimate and legal just to the extent that it dealt with natural causes.[16] In effect, Rheticus and Melanchthon divide astrological doctrines into two classes: those that can be justified as part of the causal pattern ordained by God for His creation and those that cannot. Only astrological claims that cannot be defended causally need to be legally proscribed.

The chairs to which Reinhold and Rheticus were appointed split the mathematical sciences between them. They were responsible for instructing students in arithmetic and geometry but also in the two main branches of astronomy. The first of these was spherical astronomy—all the astronomical phenomena that could be accommodated in terms of the 24-hour motion of the sky considered as a whole. The corresponding text was a book called a *sphaera*, usually a commentary on the work of Sacrobosco. The second part of the astronomy course, taken by master's students, treated the detailed motions of the planets, including the sun and moon. The corresponding text was called a *theorica*. Advanced students might go on to read Ptolemy's *Almagest* or the *Epitome of the Almagest,* a synopsis and commentary produced by Regiomontanus. Beginning in the 1530s, Melanchthon's network of students and colleagues, some at other universities, set out to provide new versions of these fundamental works for use by Lutheran students.

In August 1531 Melanchthon wrote a prefatory letter for a new edition of Sacrobosco's *sphaera* produced by Simon Grynaeus at Heidelberg.[17] This preface was apparently deemed appropriate as a general introduction to both aspects of the Wittenberg astronomy course because it is also appears in the 1542 and 1553 editions of a new *theorica* prepared by Erasmus Reinhold. Here Melanchthon refers to the pattern of the celestial motions as "fixed computation[s] shown by divine providence" and goes on:

> For it is not possible for the human mind not to conclude that there is a mind that rules and governs every-

thing, if it contemplated these established courses and laws of the great circuits and stars. For no such thing can exist or continue by chance or by another power without a mind.[18]

A few lines later he again attacks the Epicureans, pointing out that "having done away with providence, they have also removed the immortality of the human souls." After specifically praising Peurbach's *theorica*, which would form the basis for Reinhold's work, Melanchthon goes on to give a sustained defense of astrology, recapitulating themes already stated in Rheticus's 1536 defense. Astrology works within the pattern of natural causes—not outside it. Recognizing that the world is providentially ordered does not eliminate the need to understand natural actions and causal roles; providence is simply this divinely ordered pattern. As Melanchthon puts it here: "These things [astrology] do not disagree with Christian doctrine which, although it teaches us that all things are governed by divine providence, nevertheless does not remove the natural actions and import of things."[19] The recipient of the letter, Simon Grynaeus, went on to produce a new Greek edition of Ptolemy's *Almagest* in 1538.[20]

By the 1530s, the most popular introduction to planetary astronomy was the new version of the *theorica* provided by George Peurbach. However, Peurbach's text was brief, and university teachers all over Europe supplemented it with commentaries, expanding on the text, and adding their own ideas. Erasmus Reinhold treated Peurbach's book in just this fashion. In addition to long explanations of Peurbach's cryptic text, Reinhold added many new diagrams, including ingenious volvelles of moving paper that may be used as rough analog computers. He also introduced entirely new material, such as detailed predictions for eclipses of the moon. The book appeared at Wittenberg in 1542 and again in 1553 in a new version with extensive revisions to the section on the sun.[21]

Reinhold was apparently completing the first edition of his book in 1540 and 1541, preparing it for publication in 1542. His work, therefore, coincided with the Lutheran rescue operation for Copernicus. Reinhold's colleague Rheticus had taken a leave in 1538 to visit astronomers in Nuremberg, Tübingen, and Ingolstadt. By 1539, he had decided to visit Copernicus. It was Rheticus who finally persuaded Copernicus to complete the book that we now know as *De Revolutionibus*, and he wrote his own book, the *Narratio prima* to prepare the way for its publication.[22] What is less well-known is the importance of the patronage relationships that Rheticus established at the same time, which would have consequences for his own and for Reinhold's later work.

When Rheticus arrived in Frauenburg, around the end of May 1539, Copernicus had not completed *De Revolutionibus* and there was a serious danger that he never would. He was subject to legal proceedings that could have led to his removal from the church. Rheticus's arrival not only restarted work on *De Revolutionibus* but also provided a way for Copernicus to deflect the wrath of his superior, the bishop of Warmia.

Although the first two-thirds of Rheticus's *Narratio prima* is a nonmathematical exposition of Copernican ideas, the book ends with a lengthy section "In Praise of Prussia" that has nothing directly to say about astronomy. This was an overt, and rapidly successful, attempt by Rheticus to attract the patronage of Duke Albert of Prussia, ruler of the first officially Lutheran province of the Holy Roman Empire. The duke not only accepted Rheticus as a client but also extended his favor to the subject of Rheticus's book. Copernicus was invited to the duke's court and delayed there to frustrate the legal proceedings against him. Further intervention by the duke created an abrupt reversal in the attitude of the bishop toward Copernicus, who now recognizing that he was about to produce an important book, sent to Copernicus a poem, insisting that it be included at the front of the book, where, according to the usual conventions, the poem would have advertised Copernicus's subordinate status in the bishop's patronage network and reflected glory on its donor.[23]

There is no poem by the Bishop of Warmia at the front of *De Revolutionibus*. The reason for this is quite simple: Rheticus returned to Wittenberg while the book was in production and published a separate, much briefer work, in effect just the portion of Book One on spherical triangles. The bishop's poem appears at the beginning of this little volume and, therefore, does not disfigure Copernicus's major work.[24] Instead, through a further set of Lutheran connections established by Rheticus, the reader of *De Revolutionibus* is greeted by an anonymous preface, written by Andreas Osiander, the Nuremberg preacher who had converted the Duke of Prussia to Protestantism.[25]

In his 1542 commentary on Peurbach's *theorica*, Reinhold mentions Copernicus's new model for the moon and makes it clear to the reader that he has high hopes for Copernicus's expected work.[26] However, it should be made clear from the outset that Reinhold is not interested in Copernicus as a radical cosmological alternative to Ptolemy and Aristotle. Rather, he sees Copernicus's work as contributing to an overall effort to reform astronomy along essentially Ptolemaic lines, retaining the earth as the unmoving center of the celestial motions. Reinhold's adoption of Copernican mathematical models, coupled with a rejection of his cosmic scheme, became the basis for the main Wittenberg interpretation of Copernicus.[27]

With Duke Albert's help, Rheticus moved on to a new appointment at the University of Leipzig in 1543, the same year Copernicus's book appeared. Reinhold stayed at Wittenberg, where he began an ambitious program of new publication in the exact sciences, the centerpiece of which was a set of new astronomical tables based on Copernicus's mathematical models. The *Prutenic Tables*, which were published at Tübingen in 1551, are named for and dedicated to Duke Albert ("Prutenic" is an old form of the adjective "Prussian," which identifies the duke's lands).[28]

Reinhold's dedicatory letter begins with a clear statement of Melanchthon's views on the nature of mathematical knowledge and its connection to the providential structure of the world. The human voice, says Reinhold, is not sufficient to praise that admirable wisdom that contains the teaching of numbers, proportions, figures, measurements, and the celestial motions. These arts are "rays of divine wisdom transmitted to the minds of men, and clear and certain evidence of God, and of providence," as well as being necessary for the practical conduct of life.[29] On the next page we find the now conventional attack on the atomists as opponents of a providentially ordered world, which on the evidence considered here can only be the work of an architectonic mind that is eternal, just, and benevolent.[30]

The tables were sufficiently important that Reinhold sought and received an imperial license, which is printed at the front of the first edition. This gave him, in the parts of Europe where the Holy Roman emperor reigned, some of the protections a modern author would receive through copyright. The license was extended to cover not only the current work but also Reinhold's entire proposed output, including the *Prutenic Tables*, a series of related tables that were intended to correct the calendar for church festivals, a new work corresponding to the *Sphere* of Sacrobosco, a new work on optics with obvious connections to astronomy, a commentary on Copernicus's *De Revolutionibus*, and finally a new *theorica* composed specifically to coordinate with the *Prutenic Tables*. The majority of these projects were left unfinished when Reinhold died of the plague in 1553. However, several of them were completed by his successor, Caspar Peucer.

After receiving a master's degree from Wittenberg in 1545, Peucer began teaching in the arts faculty in 1548. He married Melanchthon's daughter Magdalena two years later and became professor of mathematics in 1554, after Reinhold's death. He already had produced *On the Celestial Spheres and Circles*, an elementary textbook on astronomy published in 1551, which was intended as a replacement for Sacrobosco. This book was so successful that its use was mandated in the statutes of the University of Wittenberg.[31]

Like Reinhold, Peucer begins his book with clear statements that the mathematical sciences provide evidence of God and divine providence. The dedication to Augustus, Duke of Saxony, dated June 1551, contains almost identical ideas to Reinhold's at the beginning of the *Prutenic Tables*, though here with additional embellishments. We are told that mankind arose not from a combination of atoms, as Democritus taught, but "from the eternal wonderful wisdom and benevolence in the architectonic mind." Evidence of God is spread throughout the world, and especially in the arts of number, proportion, and motion. Here Peucer repeats Melanchthon's quote from Plato ("The joyful rumour of God runs through all the arts"), using capitals throughout for emphasis. These things stimulate the mind to the knowledge [*agnitionem*] of God and confirm the evidence that the senses give of providence.[32]

Peucer makes the same points in an address on astrology given at Wittenberg, October 23, 1553. God wishes our lives to be governed by teaching, that is, by the rays of His light. At the same time God decrees in law what should be done in the present, shows the future, distinguishes rewards and punishments, and deters us from sin by fear of punishment.[33] Astrology, therefore, has an important moral function, but serves not as the source of knowledge of moral principles but as a warning and guide to the significance of particular events. Peucer goes on to make the usual claims about the application of astrology to medicine and to praise Ptolemy's *Quadripartitum*. In line with Melanchthon's general program of treating astrological influence as a causal process within an overall causal plan, Peucer continues that neither superstition nor the Stoic concept of necessity are needed to account for the effectiveness of astrology, but rather the orderliness of nature, which is clear evidence of the providence of God.[34]

Other Wittenberg faculty make similar claims. Perhaps at the same time as Peucer's address, Sebastian Theodoricus of Winsheim (who became vice rector in 1554) publicly presented a poem that begins: "The world is not a flowing together of minute atoms, as the Epicureans teach us. The shining lights of the beautiful heavens show this."[35] Here again the Epicureans are the antithesis of providential order, and it is the study of the heavens that shows they are wrong and that the world has a providential plan.

In summation, we may say that for Lutheran followers of Melanchthon, astrology and astronomy have important practical uses. The former warns of impending events that may be averted by a suitable change of heart and also has vital applications in medicine, while the latter has important applications in timekeeping. Melanchthon, Reinhold, and Peucer also make use of these subjects as aids to what would today be called apologetics. The study of the heavens is an opportunity to glorify God by showing the beauty of His handiwork. But an equally important function of either discipline is to reveal the causal and providential design of the world. In the letters and prefaces to the most important astronomical books produced by Melanchthon, Reinhold, and Peucer, we find astronomy consistently described not as a source or foundation for moral rules but as the clearest example of the laws by which God governs the world providentially.

The Decline and Fall of the New *Theorica*

Throughout the 1550s and 1560s, the *Prutenic Tables* enjoyed a wide circulation and advertised Copernicus's ideas and the power of Wittenberg mathematicians. But the success of the tables created a problem for the traditional *theorica*. The patterns of circles in the models used by Reinhold in calculating the tables and the corresponding patterns of orbs were different from those in the established *theorica*, which descended from Ptolemy through Peurbach and which Reinhold himself had displayed in his book of 1542. According to the works in the imperial license at the front of the *Prutenic Tables*, Reinhold had intended to remedy this deficiency in a work entitled *Hypotyposes orbium coelestium quas vulgo vocant Theoricas Planetarum* [*Hypotyposes of the Celestial Orbs, Commonly Called Theoricas of the Planets*]. The word *hypotyposis* is unusual. It may mean simply a sketch, a representation known to be incomplete, but to someone with the training in rhetoric received by Melanchthon's students, it would also mean a concrete image of something—in this case the celestial orbs—presented with the intent of showing how things really are in the heavens.[36] How much of it was completed before Reinhold's death in 1553 we do not know, but it seems that Peucer made a significant contribution to the finished product. Judging by the time it took to complete, Peucer's efforts may be the major contribution. The *Hypotyposes orbium coelestium* finally appeared in at least three different forms: an anonymous edition at Strassbourg in 1568, with exactly the title proposed by Reinhold; the same text with a shorter title, and a clear attribution to Peucer, at Wittenberg in 1571; and again at Cologne in 1573, with yet a third variation on the title.[37]

This brings us to the most famous Lutheran astronomer of the sixteenth century, Tycho Brahe. During his education and early career, there was no single generally accepted answer to the question of which combination of circles and corresponding combination of orbs the heavens actually contained. Copernicus's work had destabilized the traditional answer when it was adopted by Reinhold. The possibility of redrawing Copernican models to fit a geocentric framework led many different people to experiment with systems in which the planets moved around the sun, which in turn moved around a stationary earth.[38] However, Brahe's version of the system was arguably superior to the others. He used realistic distances derived from Copernicus and consequently realized that the orbs for the sun and Mars intersected. His ultimate solution was to abandon orbs in favor of a fluid heavens, under the influence of Stoic doctrines that he had adopted from Christopher Rothmann. This innovation was reinforced by his largely successful attempt to establish himself as the preeminent authority on observational evidence, which he used to support the claims of his system against all rivals. He was also the only early geo-heliocentrist to calculate precise positions for celestial objects (though this was largely left to his successors such as Longomontanus), which together with the accuracy of his data made his claims to priority almost unassailable. In effect, then, Brahe resolved the main theoretical dispute in the Wittenberg program by adopting a particular combination of earth-centered circles to represent planetary motion. Interestingly, he, too, uses the word *hypotyposis* to label his best-known diagram.[39] Rather than writing a new *theorica* to display the corresponding orbs, Brahe simply abandoned the Aristotelian and Ptolemaic account of the physical construction of the heavens.

Brahe's astronomical work is framed by research questions generated by other Lutherans. However, it is probably a mistake, and certainly a simplification, to regard him only as an astronomer. Alchemy was central to his thought, which extended also to medical theory and practice, astrology, and meteorology. Brahe's overall approach reflects the providential view of natural philosophy developed by Melanchthon and his students.[40] An example is the exchange with Rothmann in which Brahe computes the size of the gap between Saturn and the fixed stars on the basis of his own observations, then rejects the Copernican universe because of all the wasted space.[41] Brahe's criticisms of Rothmann and Copernicus, as well as his own positive proposals, may be read as a Lutheran making reasonable claims about the providential plan. Religious concerns also appear directly in the work of his most important Lutheran successor, Johannes Kepler.

In 1596 Kepler published a book with an ingenious construction that explained both the number and spacing of the planetary orbs.[42] God had used each of the Platonic solids exactly once in the construction of the world. Five regular solids allowed Him to inscribe and circumscribe six orbs, and the spacing created by this construction showed that the basic plan was Copernican, not Ptolemaic. Given the evidence so far presented that Lutheran astronomers generally saw their subject as the study of God's providential plan, it should be obvious that Kepler's scheme in the 1596 *Mysterium Cosmographicum* is simply an ambitious new version. What is surprising is that Kepler's clear statements to this effect have attracted almost no attention. Even before the main text begins, Kepler's greeting to readers announces that they will learn "what the world is like, that is, God's cause and plan for creating it."[43] It should be clear that Kepler's mention of God's cause and plan connects directly with Melanchthon's vision of a cosmos providentially ordered by causal principles. If further confirmation is needed, after his initial exposition of the evidence for Copernicanism, Kepler tells the reader, in chapter four: "I think that from the love of God towards mankind many causes of things in the world may be deduced."[44] And Kepler's fundamentally religious orientation is restated in the final lines of the book:

And now at last with the divine Copernicus it pleases [me] to cry out: Certainly such is the divine handiwork of the Good and Great [God]; and with Pliny: The immense world is sacred.[45]

I believe it is not overstating the case to say that in his own terms Kepler quite reasonably believes he has completed Melanchthon's program by finding a single unique structure that is God's physical plan for the world.[46] This also explains Kepler's lifelong commitment to the results of his first book, which he maintained foreshadowed all his later successes.[47]

Kepler's *Mysterium* gave the spacing of the planets but not the details, or the causes, of their motions. These he provided in the *Astronomia Nova* (1609), the work in which he introduced the earliest concept of a planetary orbit, and formulated what are now regarded as the first two laws of planetary motion. Again, from the beginning of the book, it is clear that Kepler's ambitions are to describe a providentially ordered cosmos that satisfies Melanchthon's ideals. The title page tells us the new astronomy will be *aitiologetos*, based on causes, unlike the superstitious divination that Melanchthon followed Ptolemy in condemning as *anaitiologetos*, not based on causes, and, therefore, not acceptable in natural philosophy. Indeed, Kepler's title continues by stating that the new astronomy will deserve the name "physics of the heavens."[48]

To vindicate the claims made on the title page, and particularly to establish novel causal regularities, Kepler draws on Melanchthon's ideas about providential order from another source. There is a pattern of argument called "exemplum" that reasons from particulars to particulars, rather than from general terms to particulars as in conventional deductive logic. Although the pattern is accepted as legitimate by Aristotle, its status remained controversial throughout the sixteenth and into the seventeenth century. Today we would simply call it a fallacy. But

Melanchthon, in his book on dialectic, differentiated valid and invalid "exemplum" inferences by appeal to the underlying causal regularities of the providential plan. Successful "exemplum" arguments, according to Melancthon, serve as reminders of some universal rule or law, which converts the apparent fallacy into a valid argument by providing a missing general premise.[49] The examples he gives all employ moral rules that are otherwise instances of "natural laws," in other words, that part of the providential plan intended to regulate human conduct.

Kepler takes the same idea and applies it to the nonhuman part of the providential plan. From the success of an "exemplum" argument about, for example, forces, Kepler concludes not that some general law is true, which would be fallacious, but more subtly that a genus exists of which the "exemplum" argument gives one instance or species. This genus plays a role in God's plan for the world. In this fashion Kepler reasons from the nature of light and the physical behavior of magnets that the providential plan includes as a genus "powers that diminish with distance" and that the motive power by which the sun moves the planets is another species of the same genus.[50] Kepler employs this "power" to establish the distance-velocity law in chapter 40 of the *Astronomia Nova*. Later in the book this result is rederived for the case of an elliptical path, the result we would today call Kepler's second law of planetary motion. Here, Melanchthon's idea of the providential plan contributed directly to establishing some of the central results of modern science.

Was Melanchthonian Astronomy Lutheran?

This brings us finally to the disputed question of whether these ideas and achievements deserve to be labeled Lutheran. Methuen is frankly skeptical:

It seems doubtful, however, that Melanchthon's approach can really be categorized as specifically "Lutheran," especially since other Lutherans—including Luther—take a completely different attitude towards natural philosophy.[51]

Hal Cook is also skeptical in his review of an earlier essay on the Lutheran response to Copernicus:

> Many of the arguments also fail to show that religion "caused" one or another scientific outlook. Barker, for instance, fails to convince this reviewer that Lutheranism and Copernicanism went together because of something in Lutheran theology or outlook, rather than because of the historical accident that Melanchthon was friendly to it, encouraging new astronomical teachings in Lutheran schools like Wittenberg.[52]

Here I would offer three considerations. First, if any religious doctrine or practice was introduced by Melanchthon, then it is Lutheran by definition. This is also true for purposes of understanding historical causation, even if Melanchthon's later version of Lutheranism was written out of the official record. As David Bloor put it recently in the postscript to the new edition of *Knowledge and Social Imagery*, the history of theology has been written by the victors.[53] It may well be that contemporary theological writing is not a reliable indication of the historical situation in the sixteenth century.

Second, and more important, Kusukawa has presented a quite general historical argument that the Lutheran attitude to nature developed from historical causes specific to Lutheranism, not to other confessions. As described by Kusukawa, the key episode here is Melanchthon's use of the doctrine of natural law to provide intellectual justification for the magisterial reform of Lutheranism. This led to an account of providence in which God ordained moral laws to regulate the human world and mathematical laws to regulate the heavens. To this I would add that the doctrine of the natural light, another old idea pressed into new service by Melanchthon, provided an epistemological basis for claims to knowledge that would inevitably privilege the mathematical sciences as examples of certain knowledge. Astronomy was important because it offered the clearest *undisputable* examples of the laws that constituted the providential design of the world. The explicit statements of Melanchthon, and especially the statements of the astronomers who worked for and with him, show that their main interest in astronomy was as a particularly clear instance of the providential architecture of the world.

Methuen fails to recognize the contribution to natural theology by Melanchthon and his followers as distinctively Lutheran, in part because she misidentifies the role of astronomy in their thought as a source of, or foundation for, moral knowledge. She misses the point that moral rules have an independent and equal status and neither require nor are capable of derivation from astronomy or any other mathematical discipline. Although Methuen comes close to acknowledging Kusukawa's argument about the significance of natural philosophy for the magisterial reform of Lutheranism,[54] she fails to recognize that if correct, this argument establishes that the Lutheran attitude to nature developed from historical causes that occurred uniquely in the development of Lutheranism, not of other confessions. With all due respect for Cook, it may be a historical accident that Melanchthon was a Lutheran (what if he had refused the job at Wittenberg?), but once he became a Lutheran it is paradoxical to deny that label to doctrines with a clear religious dimension introduced by Melanchthon. The doctrines of natural law and natural light may have been used by other people and other confessions, but after their appropriation by Melanchthon as part of his account of divine providence, they became elements in a

Lutheran religious view of the world, which was developed and changed by and through Lutherans.

Let us conclude with a third general consideration. For Melanchthon and his followers, the providential architecture of the cosmos is causal, a doctrine that both establishes connections between Melanchthon's concept of providence and traditional natural philosophy and also between that concept and the received concept of demonstration, which is inherently causal.[55] However, Melanchthon and his Lutheran followers' preoccupation with understanding causal regularities points to an unusual feature of their astronomy that perhaps deserves recognition as distinctively Lutheran. Today we consider causal theories in astronomy to be standard, but Kepler thought it enough of a novelty that he put it on the title page of his book. What was the status of causal theories in astronomy during the early reception of Copernicus's work?

I suggested above that we can distinguish at least three strands in the reception of Copernicanism by Lutherans. The first strand is the Wittenberg interpretation maintained by Reinhold, Peucer, Rothmann in his early days, and many others. Tycho Brahe develops a second strand, which keeps the earth central but locates the sun as the center of the planetary motions and breaks decisively with the Ptolemaic tradition. But there is a third, tiny minority: Those astronomers who accept Copernicus's system as a true causal account of the world.[56] In other writings these people are called "radical Copernicans."[57] It is, I think, particularly significant that they emphasize causal arguments in their defense of Copernicus. Kepler is among the most prominent, and perhaps the most successful, of the group. What is curious, and requires illumination, is why anyone should have been concerned with understanding astronomy in terms of causes at all. As the work of Pierre Duhem shows, it is all too easy to read the history of astronomy, and particularly the history of the sixteenth century, in terms of a general abandonment of causal explanation in favor of mere instrumentalist calculations.[58] But Lutherans, following Melanchthon, were supposed to be concerned with the causal structure of the providential plan. Thus, perhaps Reinhold and his contemporaries were moved to consider the consequences of adopting Copernicus's new calculational techniques for their overall picture of the world, even if this meant for a time that there was no agreed answer to the question of the constitution of the heavens. Tycho Brahe introduced his novel system precisely because he could no longer defend the Aristotelian or Ptolemaic world system as a causal account.

Finally, Kepler's proclamation of a causal astronomy must be seen as the descendant of an intellectual tradition in which the question of the causal structure of the world plays a special role. All these figures chose among varied options for cosmic schemes and planetary models, rejecting not only the traditional answers to physical questions about the world but also each other's answers. They felt called to endorse and defend new cosmic schemes in part from their conviction that there was only one right answer, only one providential plan.[59] This led, in turn, to the rejection of Ptolemy, to Tycho Brahe's brilliant compromise position, to Kepler's novel defense of Copernicanism, and to Kepler's discovery of the laws of planetary motion that we still accept today. Even if Melanchthon's followers lost in the internal warfare with the anti-Calvinists, the scientific vocation of Reinhold, Peucer, Brahe, and Kepler is surely a legacy for Lutherans to recall with pride.[60]

Notes

1. E.g. *Leges Academiae Witebergensis de Studiis et Moribus Auditorum* (Wittenberg: George Rhaw, 1562). A2r: *Academiae Witebergensis leges de studiis et moribus auditorem, quae bis quotannis recitantur. Prima Lex. Testimonia de Deo multa & illustria universae naturae rerum impressa sunt, quae optimus conditor uult aspici, ut agnoscamus eum.*

2. Charlotte Methuen, *Kepler's Tübingen: Stimulus to a Theological Mathematics* (Brookfield, Vt.: Ashgate, 1998); "The Role of the Heavens in the Thought of Philip Melanchthon," *Journal of the History of Ideas* 57:3 (1996): 385–403. Sachiko Kusukawa, *The Transformation of Natural Philosophy: The Case of Philip Melanchthon* (Cambridge: Cambridge University Press, 1995). Both books build on earlier doctoral dissertations: Charlotte Methuen, *Kepler's Tübingen: Stimulus to a Theological Mathematics*, University of Edinburgh, 1995; Sachiko Kusukawa, *Providence Made Visible: The Creation and Establishment of Lutheran Natural Philosophy*, University of Cambridge, 1991.

3. Methuen, *Kepler's Tübingen*, 74.

4. Methuen, *Kepler's Tübingen*, 84.

5. Methuen, *Kepler's Tübingen*, 73–78; cf. Methuen "Role of the Heavens," 393–95. "For Melanchthon, in contrast, it is precisely astronomy's capability to interpret the natural world and to decode the motions of the heavens that gives it its value, for in doing so it is able to show the will of God" (394). "It is because the heavens reveal God that they may be—and should be—read as a message from God to the world which tells how life should ideally be lived" (395).

6. For the origin of this phrase, see n 2.

7. See the discussion of Kepler by Harrison elsewhere in this volume.

8. Kusukawa, *Transformation of Natural Philosophy*, esp. 49–74.

9. Kusukawa, *Transformation of Natural Philosophy*, 70ff.

10. Kusukawa, *Transformation of Natural Philosophy*, 72–73.

11. Philip Melanchthon, *Orations on Philosophy and Education*, ed. Sachiko Kusukawa, trans. Christine F. Salazar (Cambridge: Cambridge University Press, 1999), 24. Philip Melanchthon, *Corpus reformatorum*, ed. C. G. Bretschneider (Frankfurt am Main: Minerva, 1834–1900; reprint, New York: Johnson, 1963–1964), 12:689–91. Subsequently referred to as *CR*.

12. See for example, the oration on Caspar Cruciger (n 15) and the discussion in *De anima* described by Kusukawa, *Transformation of Natural Philosophy*, 94ff.

13. Melanchthon subscribed to this doctrine even before he joined Luther at Wittenberg; see, for example, the discussion of his 1517 Tübingen oration *De artibus liberalibus* in J. R. Schneider, *Philip Melanchthon's Rhetorical Construal of Biblical Authority* (Lewiston, N.Y.: E. Mellen Press, 1990), 38–43. On the later employment of the same doctrine by Kepler, see Peter Barker, "Kepler's Epistemology," in *Method and Order in Renaissance Philosophy of Nature: The Aristotle Commentary Tradition*, eds. Daniel A. Di Liscia, Eckhard Kessler, and Charlotte Methuen

(Aldershot: Ashgate, 1997), 355–68, and Peter Barker and Bernard R. Goldstein, "Theological Foundations of Kepler's Astronomy," in eds. John Hedley Brooke, Margaret J. Osler, and Jitse van der Meer, *Osiris* 16 (2001): 88–113.

14. Melanchthon, *Orations*, 24.

15. Philip Melanchthon, "De Casper Crucigero," *CR*, XI:833–41, esp. 838: *Ac talis cum esset, vestigia Dei in natura etiam libenter considerabat, ac saepe dictum Plutonis repetebat, gratam de Deo famam in artibus sparsam esse. . . . Convinci etiam homines dicebat, ne casu existiment hunc mundum ex chao temere confluxisse: quia ordo in numeris, in discrimine honestorum et turpium, in motibus coelstibus, in vicibus temporum testaretur mentem aeternam architectatricem esse.*

16. Melanchthon, *Orations*, 120–25.

17. Simon Grynaeus, *Liber Iohannis de Sacro Busto, de Sphaera, Addita est praefatio in eundem librum Philippi Mel. Ad Simonem Grynaeum* (Wittenberg: Klug, 1531).

18. Melanchthon, *Orations*, 106.

19. Melanchthon, *Orations*, 109.

20. Simon Grynaeus, *Claudii Ptolemaei Magnae Constructionis, perfectae coelestium motuum pertractationis lib. XIII. Theonis Alexandrini in eosdem commentariorum* (Basel: Walderus, 1538).

21. Erasmus Reinhold, *Theoricae novae planetarum*, 2nd ed. (Wittenberg: Lufft, 1542; 2nd ed., 1553). The complete revision of the book was prevented by Reinhold's untimely death, and the second edition was actually completed by his successor Caspar Peucer.

22. Georg Joachim Rheticus, *Narratio prima* (Gdansk: F. Rhodus, 1540). English translation in E. Rosen, ed. and tr., *Three Copernican Treatises* (New York: Octagon, 1971).

23. This paragraph summarizes the documentary evidence presented in M. Biskup, *Regesta Copernicana (Studia Copernicana VII)* (Warsaw: Polish Academy of Sciences, 1973), esp. 185–205. For a more detailed study see Peter Barker and Bernard R. Goldstein, Patronage and the Prodution of *De Revolutionibus," Journal for the History of Astronomy* 34 (2003): 346–68.

24. Nicolas Copernicus, *De lateribvs et angvlis triangulorum* (Wittenberg: Johannes Lufft, 1542). Dantiscus's poem appears at [AiV].

25. On the contents of Osiander's preface, see Peter Barker and Bernard R. Goldstein,"Realism and Instrumentalism in Sixteenth Century Astronomy: A Reappraisal," *Perspectives on Science* 6:3 (1998): 232–58.

26. Erasmus Reinhold, *Theoricae novae planetarum* (Wittenberg: Lufft, 1542), [CviiR] and [ciiiR].

27. Robert S. Westman, "The Melanchthon Circle, Rheticus and the Wittenberg Interpretation of the Copernican Theory," *Isis* 85 (1974): 79–115. See also Barker and Goldstein "Realism and Instrumentalism."

28. Erasmus Reinhold, *Prutenicae tabulae coelestium motuum* (Tübingen: Ulricus Morhardus, 1551).

29. Reinhold, *Prutenicae tabulae*, "3R: Dedication to Albert of Brandenberg, Duke of Prussia, etc.: *Quanquam haec admiranda sapientia, quam doctrina de numeris, proportionibus, figuris, mensuris, et motibus coelestibus continet, nulla humana voce satis laudari potest, . . . vident eas [=has artes] esse & sapientiae divinae radios transusos in hominum mentes, et illustria ac firma testimonia de Deo, et de providentia, & necessaria vitae adminicula.*"

30. Reinhold, *Prutenicae tabulae*, 3V: " . . . sed architectatricem esse mentem aeternam, iustam, et beneficam."

31. *Leges Academiae Witebergensis de Studiis et Moribus Auditorum* (Wittenberg: George Rhaw, 1562). A3V: "*Et priuatim & publice prima aetas diligenter discat grammaticen latinam, dialecticen, elementa Rhetorices, & summam doctrinae Christianae. Publice uero omnes qui uersantur in studiis philosophicis, audiant hus praelectiones, in quibus traduntur Elementa doctrinae circulis coelestibus, collecta a Iohannede Sacro Busto, seu a Peucero, Arithmetica, Physica, liber de anima, secundiis liber Plinii, & Aristotelis Ethica.*" The 1573 statutes contain exactly the same wording as above on A3R–V.

32. Caspar Peucer, *Elementa doctrinae de circulis coelestibus* (Wittenberg: J. Crato, 1569), fol.)(4R. [Note: the printer appears to have used ")(" to simulate an *X—editor.*]

33. *Scriptorum publice propositorum a gubernatoribus studiorum in Academia Witebergensi, t.II, complectens annum 1553 et tres sequentes* (Wittenberg: George Rhaw, 1562). Caspar Peucer's address on astrology begins (F1R–F2V): *Vult Deus hominum vitam doctrina, hoc est, suae lucis radiis gubernari, ac in lege simul sancit quid in praesentia agendum sit, et futura monstrat, et mentione praemiorum et poenarum discernat honestes et turpes actiones, et simul metu poenarum deterreat homines a sceleribus.*

34. *Scriptorum publice propositorum*, t.II, F1V: *Nec vero hac doctrina ad superstitiones et ad Stoicam necessitatem studiosos aducimus, sed volumus eos naturae ordinem considerare, qui est illustre testimonium de providentia Dei.*

35. *Scriptorum publice propositorum*, t.II, [E7V–E8R] :
Ex Atomis mundum non confluxisse minutis,
Ceu tua vana fides, nos Epicure docet.
Ostendunt pulchri rutilantia lumina coeli.

36. Barker and Goldstein, "Realism and Instrumentalism," 236–37.

37. *Hypotyposes orbium coelestium, quas apellant theoricas planetarum con-gruentes cum tabulis Alphonsinis et Copernici, seu etiam tabulis Prutenicis* (Strassbourg: Rihelius, 1568); Caspar Peucer, *Hypotheses astronomicae, seu theoriae planetarum, ex Ptolemaei et aliorum veterum doctrina ad observationes Nicolai Copernici, et canones motuum ab eo conditos accommodatae* (Wittenberg: 1571); *Absolutissimae orbium coelestium hypotyposes, quas planetarum theoricas vocant* (Cologne: 1573). Konrad Dasypodius, in the preface to the Strassbourg edition, suggests that the book was a work of Reinhold's completed by Peucer.

38. Christine Jones Schofield, *Tychonic and Semi-Tychonic World Systems* (New York: Arno, 1981); Owen Gingerich and Robert S. Westman, *The Wittich Connection: Conflict and Priority in Late Sixteenth-Century Cosmology, Transactions of the American Philosophical Society*, 78:7 (Philadelphia: American Philosophical Society, 1988).

39. "Nova mundani systematis hypotyposis." See Tycho Brahe, *Tychonis Brahe Dani Opera omnia*, ed. J. L. E. Dreyer (Copenhagen: Libraria Gyldendaliana, 1913–1929), 4.1.158, corresponding to *De mundi aetherei recentioribus phaenomenis* (Uraniborg: 1588), 189.

40. For the importance of alchemy in Brahe's research, see Jole Shackelford, "Tycho Brahe, Laboratory Design, and the Aim of Science: Reading Plans in Context," *Isis* 84 (1993): 211–30. On the connection to providential natural philosophy, see Jole Shackelford, "Providence, Power and Cosmic Causality in Early Modern Astronomy: The Case of Tycho Brahe and Petrus Severinus," in *Tycho Brahe and Prague: Crossroads of European Science*, eds. J. R. Christianson, A. Hadravova, P. Hadrava, and M. Solc, *Acta Historica Astronomiae* 16 (Frankfurt am Main: Wissenschaftlicher Verlag Harri Deutsch, 2002). The latter extends and corrects remarks made on Brahe in Peter Barker, "Stoic Contributions to Early Modern Science," in *Atoms, Pneuma and Tranquillity: Epicurean and Stoic Themes in European Thought*, ed. M. J. Osler (Cambridge: Cambridge University Press, 1991), 135–54.

41. Brahe to Rothmann, 24 November 1589. Brahe's large and, therefore, accurate instruments showed that the fixed stars had to be at least 700 times further away than Saturn. Taking this as the radius of the sphere of fixed stars, then, would lead to a universe containing one unit of occupied volume in an otherwise empty sphere of 343 million units of the same volume. Tycho Brahe, *Tychonis Brahe Dani Opera omnia*, ed. J. L. E. Dreyer (Copenhagen: Libraria Gyldendaliana, 1913–1929), 6:197.

42. *Prodromus dissertationem cosmographicarum, continens mysterium cosmographicum* (Tübingen: Gruppenbach, 1596), now usually referred to as *Mysterium cosmographicum*; translated as A. M. Duncan, *Johannes Kepler—Mysterium Cosmographicum: The Secret of the Universe* (Norwalk, Conn.: Abaris, 1981).

43. Kepler, *Mysterium cosmographicum*, fol. A1V: "*Quid mundus, quae causa Deo, ratioque creandi*"; cf. Duncan, *Secret of the Universe*, 48.

44. Kepler, *Mysterium cosmographicum*, 27; cf. Duncan, *Secret of the Universe*, 106.

45. Kepler, *Mysterium cosmographicum*, 82; cf. Duncan, *Secret of the Universe*, 223. The passage ends: ". . . and with Pliny: The immense world is sacred, the whole considered as a whole, yea verily itself the whole, finite and resembling the infinite."

46. P. Barker and B. R. Goldstein, "Theological Foundations of Kepler's Astronomy," in eds. John Hedley Brooke, Margaret J. Osler, and Jitse van der Meer, *Osiris* 16, 88–113, esp. section 6.

47. On Kepler's religious orientation, see especially Jürgen Hübner, *Die Theologie Johannes Keplers zwischen Orthodoxie und Naturwissenschaft* (Tübingen: Mohr, 1975); Methuen, *Kepler's Tübingen*, esp. chapter 6; and the essay by Harrison, elsewhere in this present volume.

48. *Astronomia nova AITIOΛΟΓΗΤΟΣ [AITIOLOGETOS], sev physica coelestis* (Heidelberg: Voegelinus, 1609); translated as William H. Donahue, *Johannes Kepler—New Astronomy* (Cambridge: Cambridge University Press, 1992). For the word *anaitiologetos*, see Melanchthon, *Orations*, 122.

49. *Erotemata Dialectices* in Melanchthon, *CR*, 13:621–24, col. 622: "*Sunt igitur exempla commonefactiones* [i.e., reminders] *de aliqua universali regula seu lege, quae complectitur similia*." See also Barker and Goldstein, "Theological Foundations," section 7.

50. Kepler, *Astronomia Nova*, 172–73; cf. Donahue, *New Astronomy*, 383–86. For an extended discussion, see Barker and Goldstein, "Theological Foundations," section 8.

51. Methuen, "Role of the Heavens," 385.

52. Harold J. Cook, "Review of *Rethinking the Scientific Revolution*, Edited by Margaret J. Osler," *Perspectives in Biology and Medicine* 44.2 (2001): 309–13, (312); commenting on Peter Barker, "The Role of Religion in the Lutheran Response to Copernicus," in *Rethinking the Scientific Revolution*, ed. M. J. Osler (Cambridge: Cambridge University Press, 2000), 59–88.

53. David Bloor, *Knowledge and Social Imagery*, 2nd ed. (Chicago: University of Chicago Press, 1991).

54. Methuen, *Kepler's Tübingen*, 73; cf. 70.

55. Barker and Goldstein, "Realism and Instrumentalism," 243–52; Barker, "Lutheran Response to Copernicus," 72–86.

56. "Between 1543 and 1600, I can find no more than ten thinkers who chose to adopt the main claims of heliocentric theory" (Robert S. West-

man, "The Astronomer's Role in the Sixteenth Century: A Preliminary Study," *History of Science* 28 [1980]: 105–47, 106).

57. Barker, "Lutheran response to Copernicus."

58. Barker and Goldstein, "Realism and Instrumentalism."

59. On the possible connections between the view that there was a unitary providential plan and the sixteenth century conviction that there was one right answer in cosmology, which perhaps had yet to be found, see Barker "Kepler's Epistemology," 367–68; Barker and Goldstein "Realism and Instrumentalism"; and Methuen, *Kepler's Tübingen*, 216–19.

60. I would like to thank Charlotte Appel, Bernard R. Goldstein, Angus Menuge, Knut Ottosen, and Katherine S. Tredwell for help and criticism. This work was supported by a sabbatical leave from the University of Oklahoma. I would also like to express my gratitude for the support of the Danish Institute for Advanced Studies in the Humanities and Danmarks Nationalbank during 2002. A version of this essay was presented at the University of Aarhus, in Spring 2002 and I would like to thank the faculty of the History of Science department for their hospitality.

6

Science as Christian Vocation[1]

The Case of Robert Boyle

EDWARD B. DAVIS

Abstract

Robert Boyle is an outstanding example of a Christian scientist whose faith interacted fundamentally with his work. His remarkable piety was the driving force behind his interest in science, and his Christian character shaped the ways in which he conducted his scientific life. A deep love for Scripture, coupled, ironically, with a lifelong struggle of religious doubt, led him to write several important books relating scientific and religious knowledge. Ultimately, Boyle was attracted to the mechanical philosophy because he thought it was theologically superior to traditional Aristotelian natural philosophy: By denying the existence of a quasi-divine "Nature" that functioned as an intermediary between God and the world, it more clearly preserved God's sovereignty and more powerfully motivated people to worship their creator.

⌒

Most people today know Robert Boyle as the person who published "Boyle's Law," the inverse relation between the pressure and volume of what we now call gases, that is a standard part of a high school chemistry course. Because of his many important scientific discoveries, we typically think of Boyle as "the father of chemistry and brother of the Earl of Cork," to borrow an old witticism. What is absent from this popular image, however, is the deeply religious man who wrote as much about the nature of God as he did about the nature of air.

This is hardly news to anyone who has explored the life and writings of this important early scientist. The depth, extent, and sincerity of Boyle's Christian beliefs and spirituality are well known and unchallenged features of his biography. Nevertheless, they deserve to be better known and more fully appreciated, especially by those who share his view of science as a Christian vocation. Having devoted many years of my own life to learning about his, I am delighted to be invited to reflect on this particular aspect of Robert Boyle. This is not a scholarly essay. It breaks no new ground, introduces just a smattering of new information, and says nothing that would surprise anyone with a good working knowledge of Boyle's life. I offer no apology, however, for putting forth Robert Boyle as an outstanding example of a Christian scientist whose faith interacted fundamentally with his science in ways that all Christian scientists might profitably emulate.

Why Boyle Is Important for Us:
Some Thoughts on the Integration
of Faith and Learning

Modern science, technology, and medicine raise many tough ethical problems, not to mention a number of specific intellectual issues that are often perceived to challenge Christian faith. Although I will not deal with any of these ethical or intellectual issues extensively here (my assignment is quite different), I want to provide some historical reflections that may be helpful to scientists who are Christian (and students of science) who want to develop a theology of science adequate for dealing with tough questions and designed to encourage a deeply Christian spirituality. Our own development as individual persons of faith cries out for the thoughtful integration of science and faith. As lovers of the unity of truth, as Boyle was, we should not tolerate what amounts to intellectual schizophrenia—the separation of two parts of our brains, one for faith and the other for science, one for Sundays and the other for the rest of the week.

The integrative task is especially important for those of us who teach at religious colleges, where we serve as mentors for other Christians who seek to answer their own personal questions about science and faith. But Christian faculty at secular institutions also need to openly discuss their faith in relation to science. They, too, can mentor Christian students—students who otherwise will assume that they must ignore or even contradict their faith when thinking about science. All Christian scientists, inside and outside the academy, at all sorts of institutions, should seek to model the transforming power of Christian thinking about science and everything else. We can in this way offer nonreligious students and colleagues a witness to the wholeness of Christian thinking and living in an environment filled with the need to narrowly specialize and the fragmentation of the mind that often accompanies this. We need to challenge the modern secular view of science as "truth" and theology as "nonsense" and to demonstrate that this is not the only way of understanding how scientific knowledge relates to other forms of knowledge. If we Christians do not take it upon ourselves to demonstrate this, then who will? Our students, our colleagues, and even the general public will benefit from our witness: The whole culture needs the whole Gospel. With all these reasons, as we shall see, Boyle would have agreed.

The fundamental problem is not simply that people in the modern West often find religion irrelevant to science; if that were the main sentiment, it would not be nearly as difficult to promote a conversation. Many scientists, including a number of highly vocal prominent scientists, hold the view that Christianity and science have been engaged in open conflict for centuries, with science winning the war for cultural and epistemic territory. My own discipline, the history of science, has been instrumental in debunking this myth, which has specific ideological roots in the eighteenth and nineteenth centuries and actually tells us more about the people who believe it than about the history it purports to relate.[2] In fact, Christianity has often provided a powerful motivation for the practice of science and medicine, and it has helped to mold science into the highly successful empirical enterprise that it has become in the last three centuries. Both of these points are well illustrated in Boyle, as we shall see.

No less important, much recent scholarship in the history of science "demythologizes" the common image of science as purely objective knowledge and faith as purely subjective belief, from which the warfare view easily follows. We now know that scientific knowledge is determined not simply by observations and experiments but also by the outcome of debates about how to interpret observations and experiments. These are influenced by a variety of factors—philosophical, religious, sociological, political, and personal. It is now possible as never before to see both science and religion as containing deeply held, rationally structured beliefs, some of them not directly testable. It is even possible for us to see how, for many in the modern world, science itself wears the mantle of religion: It provides a value-laden creation myth, reveals our true human nature, proclaims the promise of material and cultural salvation, gives us every good and perfect gift, offers eschatological hope, and functions as the ultimate arbiter of truth.

For Boyle, too, science performed a religious function, so much so that he thought of himself as a "priest of nature."[3] By detailing the intricate constructions of marvelous creatures, it called attention to their creator in a manner that could not be equaled by other means. In his last major work, *The Christian Virtuoso*, Boyle not only developed this line at length, he also introduced an entirely different line of thinking that elegantly linked the character of the Christian scientist (the "virtuoso") with the actual practice of science. The Christian virtuoso, said Boyle, was to be known for the following traits: placing the pursuit of truth over personal gain; openness and generosity over secrecy; the virtue of having "a great and ingenuous modesty of mind"[4]; personal honor and trustworthiness; devotion to one's work as a divinely ordained vocation, even a religious duty; and reliance on the visible testimony of nature, not human opinion. Boyle especially stressed the cultivation of humility because "the higher degree of knowledge" that the scientist attains "seems more likely to puff him up, than to make him humble."[5] Scientists are human beings like everyone else, subject to the same foibles and heirs of the same fallen nature. The proper response to this is indeed humility, not arrogance. Although it is important to aim toward the establishment of truth, none of us can be certain that we have actually achieved it.

Humility, and the intellectual openness that accompany it, are also the most important attitudes to bring to the task of putting science and faith together. In practice, this means that no one particular way of relating Christianity and science is going to answer all the important questions satisfactorily. We must expect to encounter difficulties that have no clear solutions, and we must be careful not to hitch our theological wagons too tightly to any particular scientific or philosophical horses—while at the same time we must recognize that, without particular horses, we can only stand still. Above all, we must retain that combination of mystery and faith that breathes life into the dry bones of human existence. Once again, we shall see that the diffident, eclectic, and scrupulously honest Robert Boyle has gone before us.

Who Was Robert Boyle?

Bombarded by deafening claps of thunder in the dead of night, an adolescent boy awoke suddenly from a deep sleep, terrified by the loud darkness, punctuated by staccato flashes of light so frequent and dazzling that he imagined himself amid the fire that would someday consume the world on the Day of Judgment. Trembling at the hideous thought of being unprepared to face the awesome finality of that dreadful day, he solemnly resolved to live more piously henceforth. Robert Boyle kept that vow with remarkable consistency and dated his conversion from that awful night.

Within months, however, Boyle's faith came under attack. During a casual visit to the original Carthusian abbey of Grande Chartreuse in "those Wild Mountaines" near Grenoble, as Boyle described them in a memoir he wrote in his early 20s, he became deeply depressed. There "the Devil taking advantage of that deepe, raving Melancholy, [and] so sad a Place," combined with "the strange storys & Pictures he found there of [Saint] Bruno the Father Patriark of that order; suggested such strange &

hideous thoughts, & such distracting Doubts of some of the Fundamentals of Christianity" that Boyle even contemplated suicide. Only "the Forbiddenesse of Selfe-dispatch" prevented him from taking that fatal step. "But after a tedious languishment of many months in this tedious perplexity," he reflected, "at last it pleas'd God one Day he had receiv'd the Sacrament, to restore unto him the withdrawne sence of his Favor." Although the youthful Boyle saw "those impious suggestions, rather as Temptations to be suppress't then Doubts to be resolved; yet never after did these fleeting Clouds, cease now & then to darken the clearest serenity of his quiet."[6] "Of my own Private, & generally unheeded doubts," he wrote just a few years later, "I could exhibit no short Catalogue."[7]

Religious doubt remained a defining characteristic of Boyle's personality. Many of his mature works can be seen as parts of a lifelong conversation with his own soul, and the quality of his thoughts in most of those works proves that doubt played a positive role in the construction of his faith. Boyle's approach to doubt—the other side of the coin of faith—was frankly precocious. Not long after his twentieth birthday, he wrote, "He whose Faith never Doubted, may justly doubt of his Faith." Immediately before this, he had written, "The Dialect of Faith runs much upon the First Persen[;] or True Faith speakes always in the First Persen."[8] Boyle understood both intuitively and cognitively a crucial fact about religious faith: It is a highly personal matter, and only those who take steps to examine their own beliefs can really lay claim to them and live accordingly. I take this point to heart in my teaching, especially in courses about Christianity and science. What I aim to achieve is not indoctrination in any sense but the creation of a supportive environment in which students are helped to form their own conclusions and to evaluate the assumptions that accompany their faith so the faith they have at the end of the course will truly be their own.[9]

Boyle's faith was indeed his own, a product of thoughtful reflection as well as religious experience. "I am not a *Christian* because it is the Religion of my Countrey, and my Friends," he confessed at one point. "I admit no mans Opinions in the whole lump, and have not scrupled, on occasion, to own dissents from the generality of learned men, whether Philosophers or Divines: And when I choose to travel in the beaten Road, 'tis not because I find 'tis the Road, but because I judge 'tis the Way."[10] Precisely what Boyle meant by this is best seen in a highly interesting unpublished treatise "On the Diversity of Religions" that survives among his papers. "[N]ot only do far fewer religions differ fundamentally than men perceive," he observed,

> but far fewer men follow any of those religions of their own choice than some believe. For it is one thing for a man to profess this or that religion, but another thing entirely for him to choose the best. For the latter cannot be done save by one who has seriously and carefully examined the religion he has embraced in preference to others, and has compared it with them. But unless this serious and deliberate choice has taken place, one cannot legitimately conclude from the number of men adhering to that religion that it is the best. . . . Thus, when all things are duly considered, we may readily note that there are few who choose a given religion, even though there are many that follow it, for the rest all behave passively, so to speak, each man professing his religion more by chance than by judicious choice.

Not surprisingly, Boyle's overall conclusion was "that a wise Christian should not be disturbed by the number and diversity of religions."[11]

Nevertheless, Boyle knew more than most Englishmen about religions other than Christianity, and he was well read in the doctrinal controversies among Christians—especially those related to Socinianism, which he regarded as a dangerous heresy.

He knew and respected the great Amsterdam rabbi Manasseh ben Israel, studied Hebrew under a Jewish scholar in London, and even tried learning Arabic before weakening eyesight forced him to abandon the project. Boyle actively sought conversation with Jewish scholars, regarding such "Fundamental Controversys" as "both more Necessary & more Worthy a Wise mans Study, then most of those, comparatively Trifling ones, that at present so miserably (not to say so causelessly) distract Christendome."[12]

Having taken full ownership of his faith, Boyle cultivated an active piety that friends noticed and admired—above all in his strict habit of honoring God's name. Before he turned 21, he wrote two essays on the spiritual damage done by swearing that were published after his death. Nor was Boyle the least bit hypocritical in writing them. His confidant, Bishop Gilbert Burnet, remarked on this decades later in his funeral oration, stating that Boyle "had the profoundest Veneration for the great *God of Heaven and Earth*, that I have ever observed in any Person. The very name of God was never mentioned by him without a Pause and a visible stop in his Discourse." So careful was Boyle's adherence to this practice that longtime friends could not recall him ever failing in it.[13] Sir Peter Pett once asked Boyle about this, only to be told that "not to have an awe upon us when the name of God is spoken of in Company, is a sign of want of Grace."[14]

Boyle approached the Bible with a similar reverence, so much so that he gently reproved anyone who would use the words of Scripture in jest. As Pett recalled: "He inculcated the sinfulness of mens diminishing thereby the constant awe that the Scriptures should have on their thoughts: and minded the company of the Words of Isaiah to him will I look, who is of contrite heart & trembles at my word."[15]

Morning devotions were a standard part of Boyle's daily routine, despite his poor eyes.[16] Judging from the number of times he cited it, one of his favorite verses was 1 Peter 1:12. In keeping with this verse, Boyle hoped for a "dayly encrease" in the number of those "who have such a desire as St. *Peter* tells the Angels themselves cherish, to look into the Mysteries of Religion, and are qualified with elevated and comprehensive Intellects to apprehend them in some measure."[17] This is precisely what Boyle tried to do himself: to develop a serious interest in biblical scholarship, a trend apparently dating to his youthful trip to the Continent. According to Burnet, in Florence Boyle met a Jewish refugee from Spanish persecution, a man with whom he "had many discourses about the Scriptures," and "this led him first to enquire into them." Several years later his father's close friend, the great biblical scholar Archbishop James Ussher (the same man famous for calculating the date of creation), reproached him for being ignorant of Greek, so "he studied it and read the N[ew] T[estament] in that Language so much that he could have quoted it as readily in Greek as in English."[18] As his eyes dimmed, he had to give up studying Hebrew, which none of his servants could read, but he was able to receive help reading Greek.[19] Nevertheless, Pett claimed that Boyle "alwaies had in his hand" in church a copy of the Bible in the original languages, which he liked to compare with the reading of the chapters assigned for that Sunday, "wondring to heare our English translation so different" from the original.[20]

Boyle's love for God found further expression in love for his fellow human beings, starting with the tenants of his estate at Stalbridge, the poorest of whom annually received a cash gift at Christmas; he also instructed his bailiff not to oppress them with onerous rents. On other occasions, money would accompany medicines Boyle had made in his own laboratory for sick paupers.[21] Many people felt the gentle hand of his love, freely given and gratefully accepted. "His Charity to those that were in Want," Burnet reminded Boyle's friends at his funeral, was "so very extraordinary, and so many did partake of them, that I may spend little time on this Article. Great Summs went easily from him, without the Partialities of Sect, Country, or Relations; for he considered himself as part of the Humane Nature, as a Debtor to the whole Race of Men." Burnet knew of what he spoke: He had served often as an intermediary in Boyle's giving, helping to keep Boyle's identity secret. The donations he could vouch for sometimes exceeded £1000 per year, a significant sum at the time.[22] Boyle also supported expensive projects to translate the Bible into Welsh, Irish, Turkish, Malayan, and the language of the Indians in Massachusetts, as well as Edward Pococke's Arabic translation of Hugo Grotius's important treatise, *On the Truth of the Christian Religion.*

Christian love is also seen in Boyle's attitude toward individual persons in ordinary discourse. As Burnet said: "When he differed from any, he expressed himself in so humble and so obliging a way, that he never treated Things or Persons with neglect, and I never heard that he offended any one Person in his whole Life by any part of his Deportment."[23] Boyle's approach to intellectual opponents was identical, going out of his way on several occasions to treat their positions fairly and their persons graciously, avoiding gratuitous *ad hominem* comments. "I love to speak of Persons with Civility, though of Things with Freedom," he announced in one of his first books. "I think such a quarrelsome and injurious way of writing does very much mis-become both a Philosopher and a Christian."[24] Elsewhere I have shown the extent to which Boyle consistently kept this policy.[25] Overall, Boyle left a truly remarkable legacy on this score. Although he was constantly in the public eye, often writing on controversial subjects and speaking with a wide range of people, Boyle seems to have had no real enemies—with the sole exception of philosopher Thomas Hobbes, a truly disagreeable man who had few friends and managed to alienate many leading English thinkers of the time.

Boyle exhibited a similar charity in matters of conscience, proving more ecumenical than many of his countrymen. Although he always supported the established church, as Stalbridge rector Thomas Dent duly noted, he "was for moderation to those, who dissented from us, & not to force Tender consciences–for which he seem'd to expresse great aversen[ess]."[26] According to Burnet, "He had a most peculiar zeal against all Severities and Persecutions upon the account of Religion. I have seldom observ'd him to speak with more Heat and Indignation, than when that came in his way." Boyle not only considered religious persecution "immoral," he also "loved no Practice" that "occasioned Divisions amongst Christians." He tried to foster a "pure and disinteressed Christianity" and "was much troubled at the Disputes and Divisions which had arisen about some lesser Matters, while the Great and the most Important, as well as the most universally acknowledged Truths were by all sides almost as generally neglected as they were confessed."[27] The ecumenical attitude evident here (and elsewhere) has long made me suspicious of several scholarly works that present Boyle as an anti-Catholic thinker and writer, based on the widely accepted assumption that Boyle wrote an anonymous controversialist tract called *Reasons Why a Protestant Should Not Turn Papist*. Upon deeper investigation several years ago, primarily motivated by the generous picture of Boyle I have presented, I discovered that he did not write it. The real author was the Scottish physician David Abercromby, a former Jesuit who had become a Protestant and who worked for Boyle in the 1680s.[28]

It was most likely his profound love for God and humanity that drove Boyle to become a scientist in the first place—but his family background did not point him clearly in this direction. Born in January 1627, he was the seventh son and fourteenth child of the second wife of Richard Boyle, the first Earl of Cork, an unscrupulous man who took advantage of English colonialism in Ireland to become one of the wealthiest men in all the realm. Young "Robyn" (or "Robin"), as Boyle was called, watched as his thirteen older brothers and sisters became pawns in a game of power, the boys given titles and lands and the girls married off to the sons of other powerful men—who usually had more ardor for their houses and horses than for their wives. Robyn's sister Katherine, Viscountess Ranelagh, married at 15 to a drunken brute, lived apart from her husband for many years before his timely death gave her two decades of blessed widowhood. His brother Francis, all of 16 years of age himself, was torn from his 17-year-old wife, Elizabeth, a servant to Queen Henrietta Maria, four days after their wedding at the Royal Chapel of Whitehall and sent with Robyn on the Grand Tour for two-and-one-half years. Elizabeth went on to fame as "Black Betty," a mistress who bore Charles II a daughter. With such examples (and others I have not mentioned) close at hand, it is little wonder that he took a dim view of courtly mores and declined the offer of a title at the Restoration, when three of his brothers became peers.

The youthful Boyle narrowly avoided an arranged marriage himself and later dodged the well-intended effort of his good friend John Wallis (the great Oxford mathematician) to match him up with an eligible woman from a wealthy family. Years later he told Burnet that he had "abstained from purposes of marriage at first out of Policy afterwards more Philosophically."[29] He held these attitudes from an early age. In his first published book, which extolled "the Joyes of *Seraphick Love*" over merely human romance, he commented more fully: "I am no such enemy to Matrimony, as some (for want of understanding the Raillery, I have sometimes us'd in ordinary discourse) are pleased to think me." Without skipping a breath, he added, "Yet I have observed so few Happy Matches, and so many Unfortunate ones; and have so rarely seen men love their wives at the rate they did, whilst they were their Mistresses, that I wonder not, that Legislators thought it necessary to make marriages Indissoluble, to make them Lasting." Comparing marriage to a lottery, he noted that both offered a chance for success, "but in both Lotteries, there lye a pretty store of Blancks for every Prize."[30] Having seen many women try to make the best of bad marriages, Boyle advised the woman who wanted to be a good wife "to deliberate much upon a Choice she can probably make but once; and not needlesly venture to embarque herself on a Sea so infamous for frequent Shipwracks, only because she is offer'd a fine Ship to make the long Voyage with."[31] Boyle remained not only unmarried but also celibate his entire life.

Although she was 12 years older, the unhappily married Katherine became Robyn's closest confidant. A brilliant woman, she convened a salon for important intellectuals, including John Milton, Samuel Hartlib, and several members of Parliament. Her brother lived in her London house for much of his adult life. She was also deeply pious and well versed in theology, traits she shared with their sister Mary Rich, who unexpectedly became Countess of Warwick when her husband's elder brother died without a male heir in 1659. Having experienced a religious conversion in her early 20s, brought on partly by the influence of her sister and brother, the previously worldly Mary kept a book in which she jotted well-chosen proverbs that she often shared with others. Some of her sayings can be described only as profound; others were more practical but no less wise, such as her advice that "the best shield against slanderers is to live so that none may believe them." In a diary she also kept, Mary noted how Robyn, Katherine, and she would sometimes have "holy discourse" together or "good and profitable discourse of things wherewith we might edify one another."[32]

Boyle's earliest writings, dating from around his 20th birthday though not published (if at all) until many years afterward, reflect the intensity of his own intimate relationship with God.

These include the essays on swearing; an ethical treatise influenced by Aristotle; and various essays, reflections, and romances on moral and religious subjects. One of the latter, *The Martyrdom of Theodora and of Didymus*, became the basis for Handel's opera *Theodora*. Another work begun at this time and dedicated to Katherine, *Occasional Reflections upon Several Subjects*, was popular with Puritans and remained in print for almost two hundred years. After reading it, Richard Baxter told Boyle that "your pious Meditations & Reflextions, do call to me for greater Reverence in the reading of them, & make me put off my hatt, as if I were in the Church" and "your special way of *Occasionall Meditation* I take to be exceeding usefull!"[33] Isaac Watts based a four-line hymn on one section, which was later set to music by the great colonial American composer William Billings as part of his anthem *Creation*.[34] The following passage is typical for its tone and content: "We must never venture to wander far from God, upon the Presumption that Death is far enough from us, but rather in the very height of our Jollities, we should endeavour to remember, that they who feast themselves to-day, may themselves prove Feasts for the Worms tomorrow."[35] Here Boyle expresses not a morbid interest in death but an appropriate Christian recognition that a sense of our mortality is the foundation of morality.

It was only after writing many of these works, at some point in his twenty-third year, that Boyle embarked on serious scientific study.[36] As far as we can tell, his motivation was primarily religious, and it took two specific forms. One impulse was a strong desire to improve the human condition and to ameliorate suffering, particularly through the application of chemical knowledge to medicine. To some extent, Boyle's interest in medicine reflected some unfortunate encounters with unhelpful physicians and his own generally poor health—his friend John Evelyn described him as "rather talle & slender of stature" but "pale & much Emaciated," and his diet as "extreamely Temperate & plaine."[37] Yet it is clear that Boyle deeply felt that physicians had a religious duty to be more forthcoming with effective remedies and to provide them even to those who could not afford to pay. The title of his first published essay shows this well: "Invitation to a free and generous Communication of Secrets and Receits in Physick"—in other words, a call for physicians and apothecaries to throw off the veil of secrecy and to make known the recipes for medicinal substances.[38] Boyle further developed this theme in other early essays that later became part of his longest book, *Some Considerations Touching the Usefulnesse of Experimental Naturall Philosophy*. This included a number of recipes for medicines thought to be effective to make them more widely available, especially among the poor. In the last few years of his life, Boyle published a much larger collection of recipes for this purpose, just as John Wesley did in the following century.

The second motive for Boyle's increasing interest in science was equally religious. He became profoundly convicted that the investigation of nature was a fundamentally religious enterprise, even that nature was the third great divine book in the human library—the other two being Scripture and conscience. He stressed this in one of the early essays just mentioned, "Of the Study of the Booke of Nature," which he originally intended to include with the homilies and meditations comprising *Occasional Reflections*—further evidence of the intimate connection Boyle saw between his religious life and his new interest in science. Although he would later try carefully to maintain a formal public distinction between his "philosophical" (i.e., scientific) and "theological" writings, partly because religion and politics were supposed to be kept out of Royal Society business, the interplay between scientific and religious ideas would henceforth be one of the most prominent features of his thought.

Once Boyle had begun the investigation of nature he never slackened, and he found his Christian character ideally suited to his new activities. The highly competitive aspect of modern science sometimes hides the fact that science is a fundamentally cooperative enterprise in which groups of people work toward common goals. Boyle's unquestioned honesty, unfailing charity, and genuine interest in the public welfare helped him gain the respect and friendship of an important community of "gentlemen" who met regularly in Oxford to view experiments and to discuss the latest scientific discoveries and ideas. In 1660 Boyle joined with many other "gentlemen" to found the Royal Society, the first scientific organization in the English-speaking world.

The next dozen years were the most productive of Boyle's life, earning him a worldwide reputation as the outstanding experimental scientist of his generation. His most famous contributions involved the use of an air pump, expertly made for him by Robert Hooke, a brilliant Oxford student who went on to become a great scientist himself. With this apparatus, Boyle demonstrated several properties of air, confirming in clear and clever ways the hypothesis of Blaise Pascal and others that the atmosphere is a vast fluid like the ocean. Just as water pressure increases with depth, so air pressure depends on the height of the atmosphere. Several other experiments involving insects and small mammals clarified the connections among respiration, combustion, and various components of air. He also published weighty tomes of observations on colors and cold, drawing in part on his extensive collection of reports from experienced travelers to the northernmost parts of the globe and treatises on good experimental practice and scientific reasoning. Boyle's interest in travel literature was typical for the period. Although the precise contents of his library are not known, his situation was probably not much different from that of Isaac Newton and Robert Hooke, who both owned many books by navigators and other travelers.

In the same period, Boyle wrote most of his subtle book on the doctrine of creation, *A Free Enquiry into the Vulgarly Receiv'd Notion of Nature*, which illustrates some of the reasons why he found the new science of his day so attractive theologically. The book opposed the prevailing "vulgar" (or popular) concept of nature, ultimately derived from the Greek scientist Aristotle and the Roman physician Galen. Adherents of this view tended to personify nature, saying (for example) that "nature abhors a vacuum" or that "nature does nothing in vain." Boyle considered this idolatrous because it effectively placed an intelligent, purposive agent, "much like a kind of *Goddess*," between God and the world God had made. Noting that the Old Testament contained no "word that properly signifies *Nature*, in the sense we take it in," Boyle argued for the theological superiority of what he elsewhere called the "mechanical philosophy," which explains natural phenomena from the purely "mechanical" properties and powers given to unintelligent matter by God at the creation. Such an approach, he believed, more clearly underscored the sovereignty of God and located purpose where it properly belonged: in the creator's mind, not in some imaginary "Nature."[39]

In keeping with his view that the mechanical philosophy was a powerful ally for religion, Boyle was an outspoken advocate of the design argument. Indeed he had a strong interest in apologetics generally, reflecting the lifelong conversation he had with his own religious doubts. He wrote extensively on apologetic themes, and in his will he established a lectureship for "proveing the Christian Religion against notorious Infidels (*viz*) Atheists, Theists [that is, Deists], Pagans, Jews and Mahometans, not descending lower to any Controversies that are among Christians themselves."[40] Although he often targeted "atheists" in his writings, he realized that genuine philosophical atheism was rare in his day. Boyle was actually more concerned with what he once called "practical Atheists," those "baptised infidels" who lived as if there were no God to judge them—and here he thought the design argument had its greatest value.[41] As he stated in *A Disquisition about the Final Causes of Natural Things*, he desired "that my Reader should not barely observe the Wisdom of God, but be in some measure Affectively Convinc'd of it." There was no better way, in Boyle's opinion, to "give us so great a wonder and veneration for it" than "by Knowing and Considering the Admirable Contrivance of the Particular Productions of that Immense Wisdom," by which he mainly meant the exquisitely fashioned parts of animals both great and small. Thereby, Boyle believed, "Men may be brought, upon the same account, both to *acknowledge* God, to *admire* Him, and to *thank* Him."[42] A pious and humble man, Boyle always sought to cultivate the same attitude in others.

Robert Boyle died in his sister's house shortly after midnight on the final day of 1691. She had died herself just eight days before, and it is probably true that grief hastened his passing, though he was never robust and had been in declining health for several years. Laid to rest close to her in the chancel of their parish church, St. Martin-in-the-Fields, the precise location of his grave is no longer known. The humility suggested by this fate is entirely fitting to the character of one of the greatest scientists who has ever lived.

Notes

1. The first version of this essay was given at the Massachusetts Institute of Technology on January 9, 1998, in the series, "The Faith of Great Scientists," organized by Ian Hutchinson. A second version was presented as part of a series on "Science and Vocation" at Concordia University, Mequon, September 26, 2001. A shorter version was recently published as, "A Priest Serving in Nature's Temple," *Christian History* 21:76 (November 2002): 20–32.

2. For a comprehensive treatment of the "conflict" thesis and its deleterious influence on decades of scholarship, see James R. Moore, *The Post-Darwinian Controversies: A Study of the Protestant Struggle to Come to Terms with Darwin in Great Britain and America, 1870–1900* (New York: Cambridge University Press, 1979). John Hedley Brooke shows the value

of rejecting this approach in *Science and Religion: Some Historical Perspectives* (New York: Cambridge University Press, 1991). Other excellent studies are Colin A. Russell, "Some Approaches to the History of Science," in *The "Conflict Thesis" and Cosmology*, by Russell et al (Milton Keynes: Open University Press, 1974), 5–50; and two essays by David C. Lindberg and Ronald L. Numbers, "Beyond War and Peace: A Reappraisal of the Encounter between Christianity and Science," *Perspectives on Science and Christian Faith* 39 (1987): 140–49, and the introduction to their edited collection, *God and Nature: Historical Essays on the Encounter between Christianity and Science* (Berkeley: University of California Press, 1986), 1–18.

3. *Christian Virtuoso, II*, in *The Works of Robert Boyle*, ed. Michael Hunter and Edward B. Davis, 14 vols. (London: Pickering & Chatto, 1999–2000), xii, 490. Henceforth, all quotations from Boyle (unless otherwise indicated) are from this edition.

4. Boyle, *Christian Virtuoso, I*; *Works* xi, 322.

5. Boyle, *Christian Virtuoso, II*; *Works* xii, 490.

6. "An Account of Philaretus during His Minority," in *Robert Boyle: By Himself and His Friends*, ed. Michael Hunter (London: Pickering & Chatto, 1994), 17. In *Occasional Reflections*, much of which was also written early in his life, Boyle compares "Prophane or Atheistical wits" to "the black Clouds that then over-cast the Sky," accompanied by "affrighting Thunder, and hurtful Storms" (*Works* v, 37–8).

7. Quoting the unpublished "Essay of the Holy Scriptures," *Works* xiii, 180.

8. "Diurnall Observations, Thoughts, & Collections," a diary begun in April 1647 (Royal Society, Boyle Papers, vol. 44, fol. 95). Michael Hunter has recently made this available at http://www.bbk.ac.uk/boyle/workdiaries/wdframeindex.html.

9. For more on this, see http://www.messiah.edu/HPAGES/FACSTAFF/TDAVIS/course.html.

10. *Reason and Religion; Works* viii, 241.

11. "On the Diversity of Religions," as translated in *Works* xiv, 237–64, quoting 255–56 and 237.

12. "Essay of the Holy Scriptures," *Works* xiii, 217.

13. Burnet, *A Sermon Preached at the Funeral of the Honourable Robert Boyle* (London, 1692), in *Robert Boyle: By Himself and His Friends*, 48.

14. "Sir Peter Pett's Notes on Boyle," in *Robert Boyle: By Himself and His Friends*, 67.

15. "Sir Peter Pett's Notes on Boyle," in *Robert Boyle: By Himself and His Friends*, 66, quoting Isaiah 66:2.

16. "John Evelyn's letter to William Wotton," in *Robert Boyle: By Himself and His Friends*, 88.

17. *Style of the Scriptures*; *Works* ii, 401.

18. "Burnet Memorandum," in *Robert Boyle: By Himself and His Friends*, 27–28.

19. Burnet, *Sermon*, 47.

20. "Sir Peter Pett's Notes," 65.

21. "Thomas Dent's letter to William Wotton," in *Robert Boyle: By Himself and His Friends*, 105.

22. Burnet, *Sermon*, 52.

23. Burnet, *Sermon*, 50–51.

24. *Certain Physiological Essays*; *Works* ii, 26.

25. See my essay, " 'Parcere nominibus': Boyle, Hooke, and the Rhetorical Interpretation of Descartes," in *Robert Boyle Reconsidered*, ed. Michael Hunter (Cambridge: Cambridge University Press, 1994), 157–75.

26. "Thomas Dent's letter," 105.

27. Burnet, *Sermon*, 48–49; and "Burnet Memorandum," 28.

28. See my article, "The Anonymous Works of Robert Boyle and the *Reasons Why a Protestant Should not Turn Papist* (1687)," *Journal of the History of Ideas* 55 (1994): 611–29.

29. "Burnet Memorandum," 27.

30. *Seraphic Love*; *Works* i, 80–82.

31. *Martyrdom of Theodora*; *Works* xi, 32.

32. Anthony Walker, *Memoir of Lady Warwick: Also her diary, from A.D. 1666 to 1672, now first published: to which are added, extracts from her other writings* (London: Religious Tract Society, 1847), 38, 91, and 102. Mary Rich's life receives an interesting analysis in Sara Heller Mendelson, *The Mental World of Stuart Women: Three Studies* (Amherst: University of Massachusetts Press, 1987), 62–115.

33. Michael Hunter, Antonio Clericuzio, and Lawrence M. Principe, ed., *The Correspondence of Robert Boyle*, 6 vols. (London: Pickering & Chatto, 2001), ii, 473 and 476.

34. For more on this, see my, "Robert Boyle as the Source of an Isaac Watts Text Set for a William Billings Anthem," *The Hymn: A Journal of Congregational Song* 53:1 (January 2002): 46–47.

35. *Works*, v, 153.

36. I am relying on the lucid account by Michael Hunter, "How Boyle Became a Scientist," *History of Science* 33 (1995): 59–103.

37. "John Evelyn's letter," 88–89.

38. For the text of this essay, see *Works*, i, 1–9.

39. *Notion of Nature*; *Works* x, 456 and 459. Boyle coined the term "mechanical philosophy" in 1661 in "Certain Physiological Essays," *Works* vii, 87.

40. The relevant part of Boyle's will is printed in R. E. W. Maddison, *The Life of the Honourable Robert Boyle F.R.S.* (London: Taylor & Francis, 1969), 274.

41. *Christian Virtuoso, II*; *Works* xii, 482. The term "practical Atheists," found in the original manuscript version, was deleted in the final version of this posthumous work, which Henry Miles compiled from Boyle's papers in the early 1740s.

42. *Final Causes*; *Works* xi, 145 and 95.

7

The Christian as Biologist

PAUL R. BOEHLKE

Abstract

It the Christian is a biologist, what are the implications for faith/life? How will a Christian serve in this vocation? God blesses us through science. However, science is a human activity and subject to human limitations, sin, and abuse. Modern science also includes many assumptions, some of which can challenge faith. Some content and conclusions are also objectionable. Nevertheless, history shows that the Lutheran faith has never been antagonistic toward the process of doing science. This vocation is both natural and necessary to protect our environment and to help and benefit our neighbor. Science requires careful and honest work. Furthermore, the Lutheran will communicate awe and wonder at the complexity in nature's design—giving credit to the Creator—indicating that science is not the only way of knowing. When an answer generates more questions, we should be reminded to be humble. There are things that are too wonderful for us. The Lutheran will also naturally demonstrate a fearful respect for life at all stages and for ecology. The Christian is free but not free to do malice. The Christian biologist is called to be an example in word and action. As we imitate Christ and He lives in us, we are asking people to figure us out. What drives us? What informs us? Faith will show. If the Word is allowed to work, it will show in the laboratory and in fieldwork. Others will see that our hope is in the Lord.

⌒

God tells us a wonderful story in Scripture. A young Hebrew girl had been captured by the armies of the king of Aram. She became a servant in a foreign land, a slave in the house of Naaman, commander of the army. However, her master suffered from an incurable illness. She heard of this and had every reason to stay quiet. Nevertheless, she could not help but speak up out of love and sympathy. She told his wife, "If only my master would see the prophet who is in Samaria! He would cure him of his leprosy." Because of the presence of this believer, Naaman heard and went to see the prophet (2 Kings 5).

This unnamed girl is a model for us. Believers in Christ, like the Hebrew girl, will often find themselves working in places where others do not know the power and love of God. It is inherent in our faith to share our knowledge with others. We cannot be quiet when we know that others will suffer eternally because they do not know Jesus as Savior. We are citizens of two kingdoms. The first is heaven, which is to come. The second is earth, which is now. In both kingdoms we show love for God and cannot ignore either kingdom. The Lord rules both.[1]

In a Foreign Land

Yet the earthly kingdom seems foreign. We are *in* it but not *of* it. We are saved but still sin. In particular, Christians who are biologists often feel as if they are outsiders. They should feel tension. Science has its own way of looking at nature. Biology has its own way of looking at life.

Thomas Kuhn identified this phenomenon in science as the *paradigm*. He claimed that science is not as straightforward as previously thought. The paradigm controls the way scientists see and do their work. This is like having a pair of glasses that selects what can be viewed. The paradigm is a matrix that includes all the content that has been previously accepted. It interweaves assumptions, definitions, methods, and truth-claims that are unique to science. The paradigm indicates what questions to ask and what experiments to attempt.[2]

Even the scope of science is restricted to perceptions of objects and events in which *universal agreement* by the community of scientists is possible.[3] Accordingly, some things are not included as subject matter for science. For example, Lutherans believe that the bread and wine taken in Communion are also the body and blood of Christ. This fact is seen only through the eyes of faith, which trust the Word of God. However, this truth of our faith will not count as science because it is inaccessible to a competent but unbelieving scientist. Paradigms do not guarantee truth; they guarantee consensus.

It follows that the results and interpretations of scientific observations and experiments are expected to conform to the paradigm that is currently held by the community of scientists. Failure by an investigator to fit knowledge claims to the paradigm can call into question a person's legitimacy as a scientist. Puzzle-solving in science has rules that dictate acceptable techniques and conclusions. If Kuhn was right in his analysis, it is incorrect to think that science is a logically straightforward and open-minded process.[4]

I hold that the shared presuppositions that are embedded in scientific paradigms are absolutely critical in determining conclusions. Presuppositions are what we suppose before we suppose. They are fundamental assumptions that often are not articulated. Some color the very meanings of observational and theoretical terms.

Study James Watson's personal account of the *discovery* of the structure of DNA and decide if the structure of the molecule was discovered—or invented. James Watson and Francis Crick were driven to fit known data into a structure and were influenced by the deeply held assumption that DNA would be beautiful.[5] They saw the beauty in a helical model as a mark of truth. Their inherent "beauty in nature" presupposition is an old one, stemming from the scriptural knowledge that if God created it, it would be good. This recognition of goodness of design in nature is part of the natural knowledge of God's general qualities "which leave no excuse" for claiming unbelief (Romans 1:18–20). Neither Watson nor Crick has indicated belief in God. Theologically, they stopped short, but the idea of beauty in nature was still assumed by them and had power over the direction of their inventive science.[6]

Likewise, under the influence of presuppositions, concepts such as fields, force, gravity, atoms, and genes are all scientifically constructed in response to perceived problems in nature. These concepts may work well enough for us as observational explanations, but when we reach heaven, God may have to break it to us gently that our world is not His world.[7] Our knowledge is likely to be superficial or even wrong at times. For example, consider that we do not really know how gravity is produced. We describe it as associated with mass but wonder if it has wave properties. The invention of the concept of universal gravity was driven by the assumption that there can be no force on an object without a physical connection: "no action at a distance."[8] One has the feeling that we really do not know much about gravity at all.

Some of these basic assumptions are innocent enough, but some challenge our faith. Many are also quite hidden—hidden in the sense that fish would be the last ones to discover water, someone has said. These ideas are taken as granted and permeate the process of doing science. Harold Schilling has identified an extensive list of such presuppositions that are built into the fabric of our science. Here are a few samples from his work:

1. Nature is real.

2. Nature exhibits orderliness and regularity.

3. Nature is intelligible.

4. There is no reality aside from the physical.

5. No physical event occurs without a prior physical cause.[9]

One can see that a Christian framework supports the first two presuppositions in science.[10] The third one is optimistic. The fourth and fifth are contrary to Christian faith because the fourth rules out God and the fifth does not allow that God can do miraculous, supernatural events.

Note that when a biologist assumes that all physical events occur with a prior physical cause, the investigator has no choice but to explain everything in terms of some form of evolutionary process. This leaves the Creator without purpose.

One can see where this leads. If there are only natural causes, there is no purpose or meaning in life. There was no divine planning for any of the adaptations that can be observed.[11] The creature does not have the adaptations to survive; it survives because it has the adaptations. God did not give gifts to His creatures; the environment selected them. Finally, the very existence of humankind is viewed as a fortunate accident that would most likely not reoccur if evolution could somehow go back and repeat the process.[12]

Then why are people religious? Evolutionary psychologists, also known as sociobiologists, explain religion as one of many adaptive devices of the past. It is seen as an evolving cultural unit, called a meme, that played a role in survival. The concept of a god or of many gods is then seen as having been useful in explaining the unknown. God functioned as a "god of the gaps" in knowledge. It is usually implied that humanity has progressed beyond this device and should discard what is becoming an artifact. Furthermore, researchers in cognition will often state that there is no soul and that our awareness is only a function of the firing of neurons. Today we hear that God is no longer needed.

Accordingly, some outspoken biologists have no time or toleration for any form of Creationism or for any mention of God. Even the use of certain words such as *creature* or *design* in a scientific setting can cause a reaction. The content and conclusions of biology can challenge faith. Our special place in creation is questioned: Some feel that other creatures have equal status and that we are just another type of animal.

Science is moving into the position of being the only acceptable source for determining reality. On the surface, science appears able to determine truth objectively. However, in practice, according to Richard Lewontin, "science, like the Church before it, is a supremely social institution, reflecting and reinforcing the dominant values and views of society."[13]

Experiences

One would like to say that a person with faith would be safer on the streets than in the laboratory, but the devil works everywhere. Nevertheless, there is data to indicate that the sciences, and particularly the science of biology, are quite hostile to faith in a personal God. In 1998 Edward Larson and Larry Witham reported in *Nature* that 60.7 percent of scientists in the United States do not believe in God.[14] Interestingly, the same study was narrowed to look only at the subgroup of scientists who held membership in the National Academy of Science.[15] These individuals were judged to be at the top of their fields. With this select group, the survey showed disbelief at 72.2 percent, doubt or agnosticism at 20.8 percent, and belief at a mere 7 percent. Belief was highest among mathematicians at 14.3 percent. Biological scientists were lowest at 5.5 percent. This suggests that a Christian with the vocation of biologist will be surrounded mainly by people with a different worldview.

Response to the presence of a Christian in science obviously will vary. The following examples, collected for this essay, represent some of the experiences of Lutherans who are biologists or who work in closely related scientific fields.[16]

One biologist noticed that other Christians in the scientific community often gladly identify themselves when they recognize another with Christian faith. Christians will feel their hearts fill with joy when they recognize another member of the invisible church.

A Christian chemist agreed and recalled that it was in informal interactions where faith-sharing occurs. He also felt that he could not work in areas where the assumptions directly confronted Scripture. He did not see how a Christian would be able to publish in macroevolutionary biology or in geology.

A Lutheran biologist reported that his article on teaching "form and function" in anatomy and physiology had been rejected in peer review. The presupposition he focused on was that form controls function and that function calls for proper form. This idea that the anatomy reflects the physiology and vice versa is a major assumption in biology. In the introduction to his article he had noted that everything on King Solomon's list of things that were "too amazing" involved the association of form and function (Proverbs 30:18–19). The editor initially welcomed the article and set it up for publication. After review by committee, the only criticism given was that the Bible reference was inappropriate for the journal. The editor still liked the article and suggested that the Bible reference could be dropped, then the article could be published. However, the reviewers were not forgiving and did not wish to see the article again.

One Lutheran molecular biologist reported that he was generally tolerated in the lab, and no one found it impossible to work with him. He did recall one person who raised an eyebrow and directly expressed disbelief that a person with a doctorate in biology could believe in the creation.

A Lutheran biochemist recalled his graduate work at a large university as not being that difficult spiritually. He added, however, that he was not studying in an area that directly confronted Scripture. He reflected:

> It became well known that I was a Christian. . . . While the climate of most universities is generally anti-Christian, the university population is slow to ridicule outright on a personal level. To most, I was an interesting novelty to be occasionally poked to elicit a response. The liberal university climate is one of nauseating tolerance . . . with two exceptions, my intolerance and my "unscientific faith." [My intolerance of sin] was seen as something that could not be tolerated. The more pertinent issue was the questioning of my scientific merit . . . [my holding] so firmly to an "unscientific" idea cast doubt upon my scientific ability as a whole.

A biologist recalled hearing a keynote speaker on bioengineering at an annual meeting of the Association of College and University Biology Educators. The speaker claimed that biologists could now boldly stand up and take a bite from the "apple" of the Tree of the Knowledge of Good and Evil. "We no longer need the crutch of religion," the speaker claimed. Furthermore, he exhorted the audience especially to encourage students to reject all supernatural belief systems. The Lutheran biologist reacted:

> At first I wanted to stand up and argue the point but then had very mixed feelings. I felt like an outsider and

was uncomfortable. It wasn't the forum; it would have been a spiritual argument. Later, when I was talking with others, I found strong divisions on the presentation ranging from approval to rejection. It is difficult. One fellow came over and said, "I have to talk with you." He was interested in why I would be a scientist and also believe in God. To my disappointment, his interest turned out to be only academic. To him I was a rare specimen which needed to be studied.

Still another Christian reported on his undergraduate years at a secular college: "It is interesting that an in-house study was done at my college in 1986 which revealed that student retention was related to faith. It turned out that [at this college] the more religious you were, the more likely you were to leave the campus." While more often than not there is toleration, modern science is done in a foreign land. Christians are outsiders.

One Lutheran biologist reported that a faculty member refused to serve on his committee when he was finishing his doctorate. The faculty member felt that anyone who believed in creation should not receive a doctorate. However, he added that this was a personal bias of his and that he would not take the matter any further. He wished the candidate success, but he would not be a part of it.

After passing his comprehensive exams and defending his thesis, another Lutheran biologist found out later that his committee had considered failing him. The committee debated if they could award him an advanced degree because of his faith in the creation. Fortunately, the biologist's adviser argued successfully on behalf of his candidate, pointing out that the candidate knew biology and *understood* the theory of evolution. The committee conceded that *belief* in macroevolution could not be required.

Martin Sponholz, now a professor at Martin Luther College in New Ulm, Minnesota, recalled that working in science can be spiritually difficult. Sponholz did extensive research on the atmosphere in the Antarctic, risking his life in the cold conditions. Other teams of scientists had drilled deep into the ice of Antarctica to remove core samples to study seasonal changes.[17] They assumed that the ice had been formed by compressed snow; hence the ice had trapped air bubbles in it. The deeper the ice, the more compressed the air became because of the weight of the ice. Placing such ice into a drink produced a wonderful fizz. However, at a core depth of approximately three thousand feet all compressed air bubbles disappeared. This was also found to be true in samples taken in Greenland. What could be the cause of the missing air bubbles?[18]

Sponholz was a participant at the ISAGE Symposium meeting at Dartmouth University when the data was presented. He volunteered that the cause might be that the water was from a source other than snow. A Christian from his youth, it occurred to him that the deep ice could be frozen flood waters from the time of Noah. When pressed about this at the meeting, Sponholz shared this thought. "Mad hysteria ensued! It was the joke of the convention," he writes. They did not think he could be serious.[19]

The point of retelling this episode is not to examine additional support for the Genesis flood.[20] Rather, it is to show from the reaction that scientists hold deep, fundamental, shared assumptions that quickly rule out all supernatural events and causes even when there are no alternative explanations. Sponholz's explanation could not be entertained seriously in this community of scientists. The paradigm controls the questions and the answers.

A professor in the area of natural resources shared the feeling that his scientific vocation truly belonged to him. However, he also felt as if he was being "dispossessed" by others working in the same area. In connection with Larson and Witham's study of belief in God, Peter Atkins commented: "You clearly can be a scientist and have religious beliefs. But I don't think you can be a real scientist in the deepest sense of the word because they are such alien categories of knowledge."[21]

The differences are deep. The differences are at the presuppositional level. Returning to our Bible story, when Naaman was told to wash himself in the Jordan River, his initial reaction was that doing so was unreasonable. He, like so many of today's scientists, had certain expectations in mind that were not met. He had to be urged by others to get past the assumptions he had made (1 Kings 5:11–13). This is the challenge for biologists.

The basic assumptions prevalent in science are a major barrier. They are fundamental to the foreignness in today's biology. Everyone needs to recognize that God's ways are not our ways. As Scripture proclaims about the patriarchs: "All these people were still living by faith when they died. They did not receive the things promised; they only saw them and welcomed them from a distance. And they admitted that they were aliens and strangers on earth" (Hebrews 11:13). That is the position in which today's Christian biologists find themselves.

Christians as Salt

On the other hand, the Lutheran faith has never historically been antagonistic toward the process of doing science. History lists many outstanding Lutheran scientists, including Tycho Brahe (who observed a supernova and disproved the Greek idea of planets traveling in solid crystalline spheres), Johannes Kepler (who discovered elliptical orbits), Immanuel Kant (who proposed the nebular hypothesis for the formation of planets), Johannes Schefferus (author of the first anthropological monograph on a single culture), Olof Celsius (inventor of the thermometer scale), and Carl Linnaeus (creator of the binomial classification system). While some of these may have had thoughts that were counter to complete orthodoxy, they were able to flourish within Lutheran culture. Kepler's famous statement was that he wished "to think God's thoughts after Him." He wanted to find out how God had created things and decided that God would have used the perfect solids of the Greeks to space the planets.[22] Furthermore, Linnaeus tried to catalog the biblical "kinds" of creatures that God had created. Clearly, the paradigm was different from today. Faith and scholarship mixed.

Culture has changed, but our Lutheran colleges still continue to prepare young people in the vocation of science. However, as we have seen, "God's thoughts" are no longer part of the paradigm. How will Christians function? What are the implications for their faith-life?

Christians ought to be involved in all the sciences. God has created us as rational creatures and blesses us through scientific discoveries. Medical discoveries can enable the practice of "Godly cooking" to offset some of the damage of sin to creation.[23] For example, because of the fall childbirth is painful. Nevertheless, we do not stand aside and allow women in labor to bear children without every effort to help them and to reduce pain. Again, the risk of polio, an epidemic in the mid-1950s, was reduced to rarity by the vaccines developed by Jonas Salk and Albert Sabin. Finally, without the discovery of penicillin in the middle of the last century and its use against bacteria, this chapter would have been written by someone else. Christians will recognize these activities as wonderful blessings and naturally have desires to help others in similar ways. As Christ was moved to heal people, His followers will also be moved to enter the fields of medicine and biological research.

The study of biology in the medical areas can be a great blessing. Here we show concern for the health and well-being of our neighbor. Even if our understanding of these things is superficial, we can marvel. Plus, if we are wise enough to know our limitations in understanding, we can marvel all the more and gain humility when confronted with nature's complexity. There are things in nature and in God's dealing with us that are "too wonderful."[24]

At every turn science causes the Christian to have a greater awe of God. Even simple daily activities reveal their complexity through scientific study. What a wonder it is to know how the myosin protein in muscle fibers attaches to the actin protein, then how a chemical reaction produces a surge of power that pulls the proteins past each other, causing the muscle to contract. The designs generate wonder in all who study nature. Answers generate more questions. We probe further and further into God's engineering. Einstein's search for a grand unification theory that would explain the ultimate structure of everything is an example of this passion of the mind that drives science.[25]

Furthermore, the study of natural resources and ecology are absolutely essential for the Christian in view of God's command to us to be stewards (caretakers) of His creation (Genesis 1:18). How can we care for His planet if we do not know how it works? If we love God, it follows that we will respect His handiwork. Second, if we love our neighbor, we will not want to damage the environment in which all must live. To show this concern we must study nature and humanity's effects on it.

A Lutheran scientist working in natural resources reported for this essay that out in the field God's glory is seen in the wonder of an intricate ecosystem:

> Near Casper, Wyoming, there is a grassland area that has been intensely mined for bentonite and coal. To most people it is a desolate spot, and they may not appreciate it. But wherever water occurs in stock ponds formed by earthen dams or in holes from mining, you can see that everything flocks to it. There are elk, antelope, and mule deer in the area. It is a spiritual experience to realize how God has made everything for us and how everything is

connected. The more that is learned about the ecological relationships, the more one praises God.

This becomes a call to stewardship. Two extreme viewpoints exist regarding the use of nature. There are those who would lock it up and forbid any use. There are those who would use everything up and cut it all down. The Christian knows that nature is to be used but also sustained. The Christian ecologist will respect the creation if only because it is God's artwork. The Christian ecologist will also be aware that in order to show love of neighbor, we must not damage the world in which we live. Yes, we are bound for a better place, but we have obligations while we are here.

A Lutheran organic chemist interviewed for this study shared his wonder for his lab work:

When God lets you unlock how a particular synthesis works, it is very humbling. Discovery is not easy in a fallen world. God does not give up His secrets easily. It is a thrill and at the same time it is very humbling if you are the first to make a particular compound. One senses the inherent order of things. Someone is in charge, holding things together (Colossians 1:16–17). It is faith building. One can see that things do not occur by chance.

This is a turning point that is mentioned in Scripture. The wonder not only drives scientific inquiry, the experience leaves no excuse. One should try to find out who the Designer is (Romans 1:20). Unfortunately, modern science points people the other way.

We can see how this happened. As modern science continued to develop, it limited itself to the discovery of natural causes. It became clear that the supernatural was not something that could be studied using scientific methods. Furthermore, when Christians look at nature through the eyes of modern science, they, too, are obligated as part of the discipline to look for natural causes in their work.

Increasingly, however, many people began to believe that science is the only way of knowing. Because God was placed outside of scientific inquiry, many also concluded that He was not necessary and did not exist. The assumption of natural cause, the complexity of nature, and our knowledge of natural processes brought evolutionists to another step. They concluded that all that we see came slowly from natural events over billions of years. This was the end result of the presuppositions that are built into science. A fellow student at the University of Iowa once wrote quite fairly, "The creationist view may well be absolute truth, but this is not within the realm of science to determine."[26] After this was published, he was asked to present a special seminar on evolution. Many of us concluded that it was to make sure that he "understood" evolution. During the same time I had often been told that if I studied more evolution, I would come to accept it. Many in science cannot entertain the idea that any worthwhile knowledge exists outside of science. Nevertheless, the student was right. The scientific community has moved to the position *of not being able* to discover God even though He does exist. The limiting presuppositions on reality and cause are producing the blindness to the Creator referred to in Romans 1:21.

Accordingly, Martin Sponholz has pointed out that the naturalist is more likely to retain the thought there must be a Designer. This is because the naturalist makes fewer assumptions than the scientist does. Those with a less formal education are not as likely to become bound by the scientific paradigm and do not have to deal directly with a scientific community. Sponholz views the naturalist as being the layperson who enjoys identification of creatures and observation of migration and habits. An example of a naturalist would be a birdwatcher or someone who notes the color changes in fall. They find much wonder in creation without knowledge of the constraints of the paradigm.[27] "When nature is viewed as it is, nature truly testifies of God."[28]

Science is reasonable if it is anything, but reasoning is impossible without assumptions. So when some scientists look at Genesis, they find the story impossible. To try to save the day, some well-meaning Christians try to reinterpret the six days of creation as six periods of millions of years to somehow allow the science of natural causes to work. Their reason urges them to try to make science and the Scriptures compatible.

It is interesting to go back to an ancient church father and see a different assumption. St. Augustine (A.D. 354–430) thought that a six-day creation was also illogical. He thought (and also had apocryphal texts to support him) that God, who was almighty, would surely create everything in an instant. After all, the Almighty God did not need to take a week to make Earth and the heavens. Ah, but then why the story of six days? Perhaps it was to impress and educate the angels that were watching that God was an organized God who did things systematically.[29] Augustine's problem was not that creation was too quick but that it wasn't quick enough. Different assumptions were operating. Augustine concluded that the creation was both six days and instantaneous. He also concluded that this was beyond human understanding.

We need to let Scripture be Scripture. We dare not apply science to it. We must trust what Scripture tells us. Christians cannot be bound by the macroevolutionary paradigm prevalent throughout scientific circles. By faith, one might understand our "First Cause" to be God if we understand this to be a God that orders the world in such a way that He is properly our Father. The problem with sin is that we lose the true First Cause through severing that fatherly relationship and fleeing into rebellion and the camp of Satan. Human reason has its place, but that place is neither to define God nor to replace Him because such a god can be neither Father nor Savior.[30]

On the other hand, there are no theological problems with accepting microevolution for even the most conservative Christians. Microevolution includes the changes that can occur in a population by natural selection. In fact, it is possible to view microevolution as part of God's preservation. Gene frequency in a population can certainly change in response to a shifting environment. For example, populations of small freshwater organisms called *Daphnia* (water fleas) will show an increase in the frequency of individuals that have protective spikes if predators are in the area. There is no deep mystery in the fact that predators will prefer *Daphnia* without spikes and allow those with the spikes to produce the next generation.

By analogy, as Christians we know that we grow and change spiritually under the influence of the Holy Spirit. We are becoming what we will be in heaven.[31] So it follows that God may well have made populations of His creatures flexible enough to be able to better fit changing conditions. The reader may still feel free to reject microevolution, but not on theological grounds. The point is that efforts are often made to convince Christians of macroevolution by using examples of microevolution. Examples of microevolution can just as well support the idea of a loving Creator who willed to preserve His creatures. There are many examples of this flexibility in creatures.[32]

On the other hand, this process carried out over long periods of time did not cause us to be on the planet. Macroevolution as the reason for our existence cannot be proven or disproven by science. The available evidence is circumstantial and theory laden. The fossil record is lacking. The supporting facts are selected and do not speak for themselves—they are always interpreted. Again, presuppositions are the key to what will be accepted by individuals. Ernst Mayr, the biologist largely responsible for the modern understanding of evolution, recently pointed out that when it comes to macroevolution, "there seems to be an astonishing conflict between theory and observation."[33] Christians need to remember that we know our origin by faith (Hebrews 11:3).

The role of the Christian in science is not to pick and choose bits of science with which to defend Scripture. We dare not confound Scripture with human science. Science is not sure enough. We might bet our life on human understandings but not our soul. History shows that science can change. Phlogiston theory, caloric theory, N-rays, and many other ideas are now discarded debris from the science of the past. The process of doing science is subject to everything that is human. What will happen to a person's belief if some well-meaning scientific supports are removed by new scientific insights? Science changes but Scripture remains without our help. We need to go to the Word.[34]

Dietrich Bonhoeffer was a German pastor who was executed in 1945 at the end of World War II for his part in an assassination attempt on Adolph Hitler. In explaining creation, Bonhoeffer said that we find ourselves in the middle trying to figure out the edges: the beginning and the ending of things. In his discussion he turns toward Christ who came into the middle to show us who God is: "Indeed it is because we know of the resurrection that we know of God's creation in the beginning."[35] This is what we need to do for those who are troubled by questions about the beginning or the ending. We need to go to the center of our faith and present Jesus. No one can come to God except through Him. We need to move from the human scientific arguments at the edge of our faith and focus on the center of Scripture: Jesus.

Characteristics

In this manner the Christian in the laboratory needs to say, "Let me tell you about Jesus." This is expressed in how we speak and in how we live. The Christian biologist is called to be an example in word and action. As we imitate Christ and He lives in us, we are asking people to figure us out. What drives us? What informs us? Faith will show. If the Word is allowed to work, it will show in laboratory and in fieldwork. Others will see that our hope is in the Lord.

Sometimes we speak the loudest without words. Lutheran artist Wendysue Fluegge composed a song that expresses how we should act, how we can be used as God's instruments:[36]

> Gentleness Godliness
> Patience and kindness and peace
> Holiness faithfulness
> Loving in truth and in deed
> Living a life that reflects who you are
> So that God's voice will be heard
> Sometimes you can speak the loudest
> Without a word
>
> Words may be hard to find
> But your light still will shine
> If you let your actions show your faith
> The world will see anyway

The following is an attempt to identify such scriptural characteristics that will appear especially in the Christian biologist. Like all Christians, these biologists will be at various places in their faith life but will be growing in Christ—becoming what they will be in heaven.[37]

Especially in scientific vocations the growing Christian shows gentleness. Love for others means that we do not ridicule them. Too often this happens in exchanges between Christians and non-Christians.[38] Mocking the intelligence of educated men and women will not help to bring them to faith. Respect for them will be returned. St. Paul approached the philosophers on Mars

Hill with a compliment about their care in religious matters (Acts 19:22). He did not deride them. To ridicule evolution, as often occurs in creationist literature, is not showing love and is likely to close off discussion and cause a backlash. Consider how the evolutionist will react to the following.

Commenting on the evolutionary explanation that humans once moved on all fours, a creationist writes: "The thought . . . is *laughable*." The author suggests that the reader try walking on all fours to prove that it is ridiculous.[39] The reasoning used by the creationist is a stretch. How does our present condition disprove a previous one? On the other hand, the insult is clear. The message is that whoever thought that humans could have walked on all fours is not using his or her intellect. Just the opposite is true. It is important that the Christian be gentle and careful. Personally insulting attacks on evolutionists do not invite them to a conversation.

Another creationist wrote: "In actual fact, it is . . . the evolutionists who *so blissfully fail to recognize* the significance of these very same data."[40] Apparently, the evolutionists are bad at doing science.

Some educators also are apparently spineless. A creationist publication stated: "[Teachers of evolution are] *intimidated* by the prevailing evolutionary establishment in science education—not to mention the biased legal system, media, A.C.L.U., etc."[41]

A creationist wrote: "Somehow students know that evolution isn't true. Even students from secular backgrounds *are not silly enough* to believe their ancestors were fish."[42]

Many creationists sympathize with logical positivism and seem to believe that the facts in nature speak for themselves. Hence they jump to accuse scientists of deliberately doing poor science. Creationists often claim that their science is true. To the contrary, the interpretive nature of facts, the role of presuppositions, and finally the effect of paradigms cannot be escaped by anyone. Even if science agrees with Scripture, it can be wrong. Science is a human activity subject to every human limitation. One also has the feeling that the creationist arguments are for the church members, not really for the unbelieving scientists to consider. If they were meant to reach out to evolutionists, why are they so often insulting?

Galatians 5:19ff. warns against behaviors that are common in academic circles, such as discord, jealousy, fits of rage, selfish ambition, dissensions, factions, and envy. Instead, the Christian biologist will be moved by the Spirit to show love, joy, peace, patience, kindness, goodness, faithfulness, gentleness, and self-control. These behaviors will speak to others. These behaviors will allow us to speak at the proper time and will move us out of the way so the Holy Spirit can work when the Word is spoken. Insults and ridicule concerning vocation are not good evangelism tools.

Accordingly, it is important that Christians in science do their work faithfully and live a life that reflects the hope that is in them. We can infer that the Hebrew slave girl in the story of Naaman must have gained the respect of her master by how she lived. Why else would she have risen to working in the household, even having the position of a handmaid to his wife? Why else would his wife have listened to the girl, then carried the information to her husband? Joseph, who saved many by being a good administrator, gives another example. And it is difficult to imagine that St. Paul did not make good tents. Finally, it was Christ who made a better wine at the wedding at Cana. Learning comes much easier from one whom you respect. Christians are called to be faithful and to aim at excellence. How we bear the cross of our vocation is important.[43] We should be on our way to what we will be in heaven; we should be growing.

Faithfulness in vocation is important for the Christian. The Christian biologist is under a microscope. Faithfulness leads to credibility. Credibility is important in science but will also influence how any conversation is received. There is no room to misapply science in daily work or in an attempt to support Scripture.

Christian credibility requires more than mere verbal defense of the truth. Truth must be lived.[44] The world will judge us; it will look at what we do. The hearts of others will question if we really are Jesus' disciples. When Elisha's servant in our Bible story decides to "get something" from Naaman, it calls everything that had been done before into question (2 Kings 5:20). His actions spoke. Others should want to know why we try to do our work well. Our faith life should reflect our hope and concern for others.

It is important that the Christian doing science is humble. The history of science shows that our human understanding changes. History shows that Kepler was too confident. His life-long efforts to show how God used the perfect solids to space the planets in the solar system have been discarded.[45] The use of selected science to support Scripture is well meaning but hazardous. We do not have all the answers to the questions that can be asked. The science may change or be badly understood, then faith may be at risk if the two are mixed. If we send our children off to the secular university armed with knowledge of the second law of thermodynamics to combat the theory of evolution, they are set up to fail. If we are armed with any selected arguments from science alone, there are always faster minds that can out-reason us. The Gospels do not tell us that the Holy Spirit will come and make us the smartest scientists on the planet. Furthermore, even if someone would yield to a creationist's persuasive reasoning, they still do not *believe* in creation. Faith comes only through Scripture.[46]

Some maintain that it takes more faith to believe in macroevolution than to believe in God. The implication is that macroevolution is less reasonable and is the foolish choice. The test for this is to ask which of these choices we can accept by ourselves. Evidently, humankind is quite capable of accepting the macroevolution rationale. However, our faith in Christ is not by our doing. The fact is, as we confess in Martin Luther's explanation of the Third Article of the Apostles' Creed, we are not capable of coming to Christ "by our own reason and strength."[47]

We have the most important answer from Scripture. It is Christ that comes to us through the Word. The Holy Spirit causes faith in us. We do not reason our own way to salvation. Faith comes by hearing. Reason, then, is guided by faith. Consequently, as believers we see that everything falls into place.

Jesus cited the creation story without question or qualification. In preaching about the coming of the end of the world, Jesus said, "Those will be days of distress unequaled from the beginning, *when God created the world*" (Mark 13:18). Again He said, "At the beginning *the Creator made them* male and female"(Matthew 19:4). Jesus spoke with authority about the creation because He was there.

If and when apologetics are needed, the Christian in the laboratory should not select peripheral arguments but rather go to the heart of the matter. The history of science shows that most scientists of the sixteenth century assumed creation had occurred. However, as modern science continued to develop, God's actions were excluded. They were considered to be outside the realm of scientific study. Science could deal only with natural events and natural causes. Because God is not bound by nature and because we cannot apply our science to His work, scientists wisely limited their subject matter to natural events and natural causes. Later, however, many began to view science as the only way of knowing. They began to believe that the only causes were natural ones. Today, the Christian can be faced with the bold claim that science does not need God as an explanation for anything. We can point at the basic assumptions of science: the presuppositions.

C. S. Lewis addressed this issue and pointed out that knowledge claims depend on the assumptions that are made by a person. Assumptions are basic to reasoning and determine the conclusion. If the individual assumes from the outset that miracles are impossible, reason will interpret the data and conclude that there are no miracles. If the individual assumes from the outset that all natural events have natural causes, reason will determine that there was no Genesis creation, no flood, and no Creator.[48]

Creation was a miracle. The flood was a miracle. The death and resurrection of Jesus was a miracle. Our human understanding and reason cannot explain these events. Our physics, our chemistry, our biology, and our mathematics cannot be used on any of these events. They do not apply. However, being outside the realm of science does not mean that these events did not happen. God is not bound by nature; He can do anything.

The Christian can do much to help others by reminding them of the limiting assumptions prevalent in science. Out of love we need to remind others that if one assumes that the only reality is nature, then all supernatural phenomena are likely to be rejected. If all natural phenomena can have only natural causes, no matter what is said, the conclusion will be that there is no God. We cannot think without assumptions, but they must be kept on the table. They must be subject to discussion and to questioning.

Confronting Sin

There is some science that cannot be done. A young graduate in biology from a Lutheran college, a member of The Lutheran Church—Missouri Synod, was hired to work as a lab assistant in a medical research facility. She was candid at her interview, volunteering that she valued human life and would not work with human embryonic stem cells. The interviewer saw no problem because such work was not being done in the institution at that time. Within a year, however, her lab received a grant to work with such cells. She then reminded the supervisor of her belief. She was told that she would be able to work on other projects. Even so, the young Christian sought advice, wondering if she could even continue to work at the lab.

We are part of this sin-filled world and cannot be isolated from it. Sin also remains in us. We are all in the mud. If the graduate stayed, her presence in the lab and continued refusal to join in the project would testify to her concerns. Clearly, her stand might eventually cause her to lose her position, but she did not need to leave. Now with the present situation, her co-workers are likely to ask about her faith, and she will be ready with an answer.

Lutheran theology encourages individuals to be involved in the earthly realm: to speak when the world needs to hear it. Love for our neighbor requires it. While the church as a whole is restrained from taking direct action in the earthly realm, it expects that its members will not be silent.[49] Scientists do not need to hear human arguments that amount to what Luther would call mere "foam on beer." The Hebrew girl, as a faithful servant, could not help but give the right advice: Go to where the Word is. Likewise, the Christian, as biologist, must be ready to direct others to Scripture by both word and deed.[50]

Notes

1. Gene Edward Veith, *The Spirituality of the Cross* (St. Louis: Concordia, 1999), 91.

2. Thomas Kuhn, *The Structure of Scientific Revolutions*. Vol II, 2 *International Encyclopedia of Unified Science*, edited by Otto Neurath (Chicago: University of Chicago Press, 1962).

3. Norman Campbell, *What Is Science?* (New York: Dover, 1932), 27–36. The literal meaning of "common sense" is meant here: that all see the same thing. The community of scientists agrees that they are having the same experience with the phenomenon.

4. Thomas Kuhn, *The Structure of Scientific Revolutions*. Anyone studying

the nature of science must deal with the ideas put forth by Kuhn. His thesis was that scientists see nature through a shared paradigm (worldview) that consists of presuppositions, model solutions, acceptable methods, and previously accepted content, laws, and theories. The result is that scientists tend to select their facts and expect particular results even before they see them. The shared paradigm results in social factors that determine who is viewed as a credible investigator. Doing "normal" science involves articulation of the paradigm. Science, then, is analogous to fitting jigsaw puzzle pieces together. A change in the paradigm constitutes a revolution in science, a new way of viewing nature. An example would be when Nicolaus Copernicus decided to view the Earth as moving in a sun-centered system rather than having our planet stationary in an Earth-centered system.

5. James D. Watson, *The Double Helix: A Personal Account of the Discovery of the Structure of DNA*, ed. Gunther S. Stint (New York: Norton, Critical Edition, 1980), 25, 110, and 120.

6. Watson indicated in *Double Helix*, 62, that he regarded Christmas gift-giving as an artifact. Crick wrote in *What Mad Pursuit* (New York: Basic Books, 1988), 11, that he lost his faith because scientific knowledge made certain religious beliefs untenable for him.

7. Paul R. Boehlke, "Should the Teaching of Science Encourage Active Consideration of Discarded or Rival Explanations?" a position paper presented at The University of Iowa, 1979, 5. The position was that discarded explanations gave insight into the nature of doing all science.

8. Harold K. Schilling, *Concerning the Nature of Science and Religion: A Study of Presuppositions* (Iowa City: University of Iowa, School of Religion, 1958), 4–6.

9. Schilling, *Concerning the Nature of Science and Religion*, 6.

10. Many historians believe that Christianity caused Western science to begin and flourish. Creation by an orderly and unchanging God was fundamental for most early scientists.

11. James G. Lennox, "Teleology," in *Keywords in Evolutionary Biology*, ed. Evelyn Fox Keller and Elisabeth A. Lloyd. (Cambridge: Harvard University Press, 1992), 324ff.

12. Stephen Jay Gould, *Wonderful Life: The Burgess Shale and the Nature of History* (New York: Norton, 1989), 319. Gould repeated this statement in several places.

13. Richard C. Lewontin, *Biology as Ideology* (New York: Harper Perennial, 1991), 9.

14. Edward J. Larson and Larry Witham, "Leading Scientists Still Reject God," *Nature* 392 (23 July 1998): 313.

15. Election to the Academy is considered one of the highest honors that can be accorded a scientist or engineer. The Academy membership is comprised of approximately 1,900 members and 300 foreign associates, of whom more than 170 have won Nobel Prizes. The Academy advises the federal government.

16. The majority of the anecdotes were gathered by interviews conducted at the time of writing. The stem cell situation was reported to the author in 2002 and is used with permission. The case of possible failure during a comprehensive exam for an advanced degree in biology was reported to the author as having happened to his co-worker in the Biology Department at Martin Luther College in New Ulm in 1975. Martin Sponholz's experience is published, and he also furnished further details to the author.

17. Richard B. Alley and Michael L. Bender, "Greenland Ice Cores: Frozen in Time," *Scientific American* 278:2 (February 1998): 80–85.

18. Martin P. Sponholz, "The Fluid Ice," presented at the Creation Science Seminar at Wisconsin Lutheran College, Milwaukee, Wisconsin, 21 March 1981. Sponholz cites Gow et al. and Dansgaard, who presented data on the core samples at the ISAGE Symposium, Dartmouth University, Hanover, New Hampshire, September 3–7, 1968.

19. Sponholz, "Fluid Ice," 186–87.

20. The accepted explanation has come to be that the increasing pressure on the gasses causes them to dissolve, then dissipate throughout the ice. This was not known at the time, but one can appreciate how the presupposition of natural cause would favor this explanation instead of a supernatural one. Gas dissolving into a solid can be compared to a bottle of pop in which a gas is dissolved and dispersed within a liquid. Sponholz relates his experience in his autobiography. Sponholz also communicated additional information to the author.

21. Larson and Witham, "Leading Scientists Still Reject God," 313.

22. Paul R. Boehlke, "Johannes Kepler," in Vol. 3, *Biographical Encyclopedia of Scientists* (New York: Marshall Cavendish, 1998), 739–42.

23. Max L. Stackhouse, "Godly Cooking? Theological Ethics and Technological Society," *First Things* 13 (May 1991): 22–29.

24. The reference is to Job's humility when he realizes that there is much in experience that is beyond his human understanding. When Job questioned why evil came into his life, God used scientific examples to show that there are mysteries. (Cf. Job 42:3: "Surely I spoke of things I did not understand, things too wonderful for me to know.")

25. Lincoln Barnett, *The Universe and Dr. Einstein* (New York: W. Sloane Associates, 1948), 108–9.

26. William C. Kyle, "Should 'Scientific' Creationism and the Science of Evolution Be Taught with Equal Emphasis?" *The Journal of Research in Science Teaching* 17:6 (1980): 519–27.

27. Jeanette C. Boehlke and I had the pleasure of visiting with the naturalist Emil E. Liers on July 28, 1968. He lived in the Winona hills on the Minnesota side of the Mississippi. Liers kept and bred land or river otters (*Lontra canadensis*) and supplied them for the 1950 award-winning Walt Disney nature movie *Beaver Valley*, where they are seen sliding down a snow-covered hill to music. Liers served as a technical adviser for several nature films. His extensive knowledge of Mississippi River animals was the result of personal study, and biologist J. Scott Shannon has respectfully referred to Liers as a "lay expert." Liers told us that after he had written several popular books for Viking Press that told about the lives of animals, reviewers criticized him for using anthropomorphism. There is a presupposition in zoology that one should not infer that animals think like humans. Liers felt that this had caused a loss of interest by Viking in further publications. Liers seemed bitter about this judgment. It was clear that he refused to (or could not) think and tell about the animals with this scientific presupposition as a limitation. He had not been trained to view nature in this way.

28. Martin P. Sponholz, "The Naturalist and the Scientist," *The Lutheran Educator* 27:4 (May 1978): 10–12.

29. Saint Augustine, *The Literal Meaning of Genesis, Volume 1, Books 1–6*, trans. John Hammond Taylor (New York: Newman, 1982), 126–35, 143–45.

30. LW 34:133–45.

31. Martin Galstad, "Being and Becoming," in *Findings: Exploration in Christian Life and Learning* (Winter Haven, Fla.: Haven Books, 1984), 72–74.

32. Another example that is becoming familiar happens when a population of bacteria is exposed to an antibiotic. The drug kills the bacteria without resistance and allows those with resistance to multiply. This is selection that favors individuals having a gene for resistance to the particular antibiotic. As the survivors with resistance multiply, the whole population then becomes more resistant and is undergoing microevolution. Increasing resistance in populations of pests to insecticides is another example. Still another example is the increase in drab guppies as predators tend to remove colorful ones. The genetic makeup of individuals in a population will vary. If the environment favors particular genes, the frequency of these genes will increase in the population when those without them fail to reproduce as many offspring.

33. Ernst Mayr, *What Evolution Is* (New York: Basic Books, 2001), 189.

34. Siegbert W. Becker, *The Foolishness of God: The Place of Reason in the Theology of Martin Luther* (Milwaukee: Northwestern, 1982), 233–40. This is Becker's finest work. It was based on his doctoral dissertation.

35. Dietrich Bonhoeffer, *Creation and Fall: A Theological Exposition of Genesis 1–3*. Vol. 3, *Dietrich Bonhoeffer Works*, trans. Martin Ruter and Ilse Todt (Minneapolis: Fortress, 1997), 35.

36. Wendysue Fluegge, a member of St. John's Lutheran Church, Lannon, Wisc., is a talented composer and performer of many contemporary Christian songs. This verse is based on 1 John 3:18; Galatians 5:22; and Matthew 5:16.

37. Martin Galstad, "Being and Becoming," 72.

38. Don Stoner, *A New Look at an Old Earth* (Paramount, Calif.: Schroeder, 1985), 17.

39. John D. Morris, "Do Back Problems in Humans Prove Evolution from the Animals?" *Acts and Facts* 27:12 (December 1998): d.

40. Margaret Helder, "Evolution: The Secret behind the Propaganda," *Acts and Facts* 31:9 (September 2002): iv.

41. Henry M. Morris, "Inquiring Skeptics Want to Know," *Acts and Facts* 31:6 (June 2002): c.

42. John D. Morris, "Can Children Benefit from Creation Thinking?" *Acts and Facts* 30:4 (April 2001): d.

43. Veith, *Spirituality of the Cross*, 57ff.

44. Francis A. Schaeffer, *The Francis A. Schaeffer Trilogy: The God Who Is There, Escape from Reason, He Is There and He Is Not Silent* (Wheaton: Crossway, 1990), 165–67.

45. Arthur Koestler, *The Watershed* (New York: Macmillan, 1960), 64.

46. Roland Hoenecke, Arnold Koelpin, Gerald Heckmann, and Ralph Swantz, "Questions Concerning Creation." Presented at the Minnesota District State Lutheran Teachers' Conference, 18–19 October 1973, 11. Professor Hoenecke stated: "Perhaps they yielded to a creationist's persuasiveness or to the argumentation of a periodical like *Bible-Science Newsletter*. . . . For them creationism actually is but a theory. Were a more reasonable theory to pop up, like a chameleon, such would find no problem in forsaking creationism and adapting to another view."

47. Martin Luther, "The Third Article," in *A Short Explanation of Dr. Martin Luther's Small Catechism* (St. Louis: Concordia, 1943), 11.

48. C. S. Lewis, *Miracles* (New York: Touchstone, 1947), 9–11.

49. Angus Menuge, "Niebuhr's Christ and Culture Reexamined," in *Christ and Culture in Dialogue*, ed. Angus Menuge et al (St. Louis: Concordia Academic Press, 1999), 46–47.

50. The author wishes to acknowledge several members of the Wisconsin Lutheran College biology and chemistry departments who generously reflected on their experiences for the author of this chapter: Dr. Robert Anderson, Dr. Keith Beyer, Dr. Dan Ebeling, Dr. Jarrod Erbe, Dr. Kevin Glaeske, and Dr. Nick Schmal.

I am also grateful to Amy Hagen, a senior biology major at Wisconsin Lutheran College, who edited, researched, interviewed, and encouraged the completion of this chapter. Responsibility for any errors remains with the author.

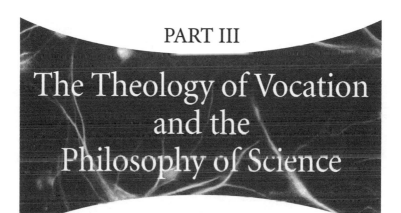

PART III

The Theology of Vocation and the Philosophy of Science

8

Scientists Called to Be Like God

NATHAN R. JASTRAM

Abstract

Two biblical teachings are important for this essay: that man is created in the image of God and that God calls man to participate in His work. In the interplay between these two doctrines, man discovers who he is and what he is to do. Scientists who work with the genetic code of living cells work with the very code of life itself and participate in the work of God, the Creator of life. Their work encourages or even compels scientists to be like God in some ways but also tempts them to "play God" in ways that deny God. Martin Luther's doctrine of vocation as the "masks" of God will be considered in view of the biblical teaching that man is made to be like God and encouraged to imitate his Creator but that, at the same time, man is not God.

Introduction

The relationship between science and theology has often included some tension. Our public schools are battlefields in which lawsuits determine whether creation or evolution or both should be taught. Our government is a battlefield in which fierce debates between scientists and theologians help set national policy with respect to stem-cell research, cloning, and abortion. Some scientists see theologians as ignorant yet pompous irritants who try to impose their own beliefs and fears on others, causing needless delays and restrictions on valuable scientific work. Some theologians see scientists as reckless innovators with deficient moral sensibilities who race to do what *can* be done before deliberating whether or not it *should* be done.

For both sides, the title of this chapter may be unsettling. To affirm that scientists are called to be like God is to awaken a deep fear in theologians, the specter of the scientist who acts as if he were God and cares nothing about the one true God or His laws of right and wrong. On the other hand, to affirm that scientists are called to be like God is unsettling to some scientists because it affirms that there is a God, that He is in control of the universe, and that He has called some of His servants to be scientists. Theological affirmations such as these awaken a deep fear in scientists, the specter of the theologian who presumes to decree what is true or false on the basis of faith rather than on the basis of experiment and observation, thus using theology to smother science.

Unsettling though it may be, to affirm that scientists are called to be like God simply synthesizes two doctrines taught in Scripture, the doctrine of creation in the image of God and the doctrine of vocation. Then this affirmation applies these two doctrines specifically to scientists. It is another way of saying that God created all people, including scientists, in His image, and that God uses many offices, including that of scientist, to carry out His work in the world, and that He fills those offices with people whom He calls (Latin *vocare*, from which comes the word *vocation*).

The following essay, then, will support these claims and suggest some implications. Among the implications is that God, not man, is the center of the universe. After all, it is God who calls man to fulfill His purposes, not vice versa. If God, not man, is in charge of the universe, then the weight of the universe does not rest on the shoulders of scientists—they are freed from the necessity of understanding and eventually controlling all things. On the other hand, scientists are empowered not only to *discover* what God has created but also to *participate* as God's "hands" in His further creative activity. This gives them more freedom of action than they would have under some philosophies.

God Makes Scientists in His Image

The Image of God Is Universal in Application
Creation of Adam and Eve

The doctrine of creation in the image of God is taught first and most clearly in the account of the creation of Adam and Eve:

> Then God said, "Let Us make man in Our image, in Our likeness, and let them rule over the fish of the sea and the birds of the air, over the livestock, over all the earth, and over all the creatures that move along the ground." So God created man in His own image, in the image of God He created him; male and female He created them. God blessed them and said to them, "Be fruitful and increase in number; fill the earth and subdue it. Rule over the fish of the sea and the birds of the air and over every living creature that moves on the ground." (Genesis 1:26–28)

These words help mankind answer that fundamental question, "Who am I?" The components of the answer given here are that human beings are a unity ("man") with distinctions ("male and female") that are in relationship with God and each other. In this way, human beings are like God because the Triune God is also a unity (one God) with distinctions (three Persons) that are in relationship with each other and with mankind. Human beings are like God not only in who they *are* but also in what they *do*: They rule over the world as God's representatives and participate in His work of creating new life through their fruitfulness.

Continuing Creation of All People

The Book of Genesis adds more troubling components to its definition of mankind in the following chapter as it records the fall of man. When man fell, he fell away from God; he became *unlike* God with respect to righteousness. Because man's fall into sin affects his identity so completely, many theologians question whether it is still accurate to claim that all human beings, even after the fall, are created in the image of God. If the image of God is defined narrowly as the ability to know God properly and to live in righteousness and holiness, then the image of God was lost in the fall. Christians can partially regain that image through Baptism but will fully regain it only in heaven after the resurrection. The following passages are often used to support this definition of the image of God, including the loss and restoration of the image:

> When Adam had lived 130 years, he had a son in his own likeness [lit. *in his likeness*], in his own image [lit. *in his image*]; and he named him Seth. (Genesis 5:3)

> You were taught, with regard to your former way of life, to put off your old self [lit. *man*], which is being corrupted by its deceitful desires; to be made new in the attitude of your minds; and to put on the new self [lit.

man], created to be like God [lit. *created after God*] in true righteousness and holiness. (Ephesians 4:22–24)

Do not lie to each other, since you have taken off your old self [lit. *man*] with its practices and have put on the new self [lit. *the new*], which is being renewed in knowledge in the image of its Creator. (Colossians 3:9–10)

On the other hand, the creation account at the beginning of Genesis does not restrict the definition of the image of God to divine knowledge and righteous living. Moreover, the following two passages in Scripture show that, even after the fall, all people are created in the image and likeness of God:

Whoever sheds the blood of man, by man shall his blood be shed; for in the image of God has God made man. (Genesis 9:6)

With the tongue we praise our Lord and Father, and with it we curse men, who have been made in God's likeness. (James 3:9)

These two passages apply to all people, male and female, believers and unbelievers alike. In the first, God tells Noah that no human being should be murdered, and in the second, James shows how incongruous it is for Christians to curse any human being. Both statements depend on the fact that all human beings, even after the fall, are made in the image and likeness of God. In view of these passages, faithful theologians must acknowledge that even scientists who fight against the Christian faith have been made in God's image and likeness, that is, they are like God in various ways.

The Image of God Is Very Broad in Scope
Definition: "To Be Like God"

The best definition of the image of God is that it means to be like God. God made Adam and Eve to be like Himself in various ways. Different passages of Scripture speak of different ways in which people can be like God: in knowledge, in holiness, in dominion, in participating in His work of creating new life, and so forth. Although this definition is broad, it is the one definition that agrees with the common meaning of the words, with the biblical context in which the words are found, and with all the relevant passages in Scripture. It is also the one definition that synthesizes what many influential theologians throughout the ages have said about the image of God.

Is the definition too broad? For instance, would it not lead to the conclusion that all of creation is made in the image of God because every created thing is like its Creator in one way or another? Indeed it would, and probably should, lead to that conclusion. It is true that the Bible uses the term "image of God" specifically of people rather than of the rest of the natural world. Yet the Bible also teaches that the natural world is like God in various ways and thus reveals various attributes of God. According to the Bible, then, the likenesses of God (His shadows, traces, vestiges, or footprints) are found in the entire natural world, but they are found to the greatest extent in human beings. The following two quotations from Thomas Aquinas illustrate both aspects of the image and likeness of God:

> Because His goodness could not be adequately represented by one creature alone, He produced many and diverse creatures, that what was wanting to one in the representation of the divine goodness might be supplied by another. For goodness, which in God is simple and uniform, in creatures is manifold and divided; and hence the whole universe together participates in the divine goodness more perfectly, and represents it better than any single creature whatever.[1]

> Some things are like God first and most commonly because they exist; secondly, because they live; and thirdly because they know or understand; and these last,

as Augustine says (QQ. LXXXIII; qu. 51); "approach so near to God in likeness, that among all creatures nothing comes nearer to Him." It is clear, therefore, that intellectual creatures alone, properly speaking, are made to God's image.[2]

Three Components of Godlikeness

The image of God, then, is broad, including many and various ways in which God's creatures are like Him. Specifically, people can be like God with respect to *being created with certain capabilities*. For instance, all human beings are created with souls and have spiritual capabilities. In this way they are like God because "God is spirit" (John 4:24). People can also be like God with respect to *using their abilities*, so Scripture can say that kings and others who exercise authority over others are "gods" (John 10:34–36; and elsewhere) or "like God" (Zechariah 12:8) because "God is the King of all the earth" (Psalm 47:7). Finally, people can be like God with respect to *being righteous*. Speaking to those who are children of God and have had their sins removed by Jesus, John says: "He who does what is right is righteous, just as He [God] is righteous" (1 John 3:7), thereby reaffirming Daniel's teaching: "The LORD our God is righteous in everything He does" (Daniel 9:14).

It is this last way of being like God that is the most important for the eternal destiny of mankind and, therefore, has been emphasized in traditional Lutheran descriptions of the image of God. Righteousness is the likeness that was lost in the fall and is regained in Baptism and will be perfected in heaven. But the other ways of being like God are also taught in Scripture and are legitimate components of the image of God. Some of these likenesses define who a person is, while others define what a person does. Some likenesses are stable, such as having a soul, while others can change depending on time or circumstance, such as exercising authority over others.

Simul Similis et Dissimilis

It is because people can be like or unlike God in different ways that the Bible can make statements that appear to be contradictory but actually are complementary. The Bible can affirm and deny that the same groups of people are the image of God in different contexts. Some passages affirm that all human beings are created in the image of God (Genesis 9:6; James 3:9), yet other passages teach that Christ is the image of God in a sense that others are not (Colossians 1:15; 2 Corinthians 4:4),[3] that saints in heaven are the image of God in a sense that saints on earth are not (1 Corinthians 15:49; Philippians 3:20–21), that man is the image of God in a sense that woman is not (1 Corinthians 11:7), and that Christians are the image of God in a sense that non-Christians are not (Ephesians 4:22–24; Colossians 3:9–10).

It is tempting to evaluate these passages as contradictory, and some modern biblical scholars have occupied themselves with tracing the development of such contradictory statements in the historical evolution of biblical theology. This modern approach denies that the Bible is God's Word, truthful in everything it teaches. It also fails to appreciate how often the Bible makes statements that are *apparently,* but not *actually,* contradictory.

At the outset of his masterful study on the *Proper Distinction between Law and Gospel,* C. F. W. Walther declares: "no book is apparently so full of contradictions as the Bible, and that, not only in minor points, but in the principal matter, in the doctrine how we may come to God and be saved."[4] Yet as his study progresses, Walther shows that many apparently contradictory statements of the Bible can be resolved through the proper distinction between Law and Gospel. In much the same way, Martin Luther studies the apparently contradictory statements of the Bible about the holiness and sinfulness of believers and concludes: "Therefore, whoever is justified is still a sinner; and yet he is considered fully and perfectly righteous by God who pardons and is merciful."[5] The Latin phrase used for this concept is *simul justus et peccator,* "at the same time justified and a sinner".

To coin a corresponding Latin phrase about the image of God, each person is *simul similis et dissimilis* to God. This phrase, meaning "at the same time similar and dissimilar," resolves the apparently contradictory statements of the Bible about people being the image of God. When the Bible teaches that the same people are and are not the image of God in different ways, it teaches *simul similis et dissimilis,* "at the same time similar and dissimilar". Both Christians and non-Christians are like God in having intellects that distinguish them from animals, but only Christians are like God in having true knowledge of God. Both Christians and non-Christians are like God in being able to make moral choices, but only Christians are like God in having righteousness and holiness. Men and women together are like God in having dominion over the earth, but only men are like God in being the head of the family. Both Christians on earth and Christians in heaven are like God spiritually, but only Christians in heaven are like God in being immortal and free from any stain of sin. Both Christians and Christ are like God in many ways, but only Christ is like Him in such a way that He is true God Himself.

The Image of God Is the Template of the Scientist

In what way, then, is the scientist the image of God? How does the doctrine of creation in the image of God affect the scientist? Clearly the scientist has certain capabilities and acts in certain ways that reflect the Creator. His intelligence allows him, and his thirst for more knowledge compels him, to explore various elements of God's creation. His compassion for other people motivates him to find solutions for some problems. He is not restricted to *discovery* alone, as if nature were a god that must not be tampered with. On the contrary, the scientist also participates with God in *creative activity,* forming new compounds, inventing new devices, and improving natural processes.[6]

When the range of activities is this large, it is helpful to have a guide to point out the direction in which to travel. One such guide is the doctrine of being created in the image of God. An image may often be likened to a shadow of something else, receiving its basic form and outline from another reality.

As I write this, the heavy clouds outside have diffused the sunlight so evenly that no shadows are visible. The light is as bright on one side of a tree as on the other, and the grass covers the courtyard in one monochrome carpet. Judging from the light alone, it would be difficult to tell whether it is morning or afternoon, or whether there are any boundaries separating the grass in one area from that in another. But this day has not always been so overcast. Twice, for less than a minute each time, the clouds broke and let the strong sunlight shine directly on the scene. What a transformation there was! The colors became brilliant, but what I noticed even more was that shadows sprang out of nowhere and staked out boundaries in the grass, boundaries that bore the image of trees. The grass and the trees and the courtyard had not changed into something different, but my perception of them was radically affected. The relationships among them had suddenly been clarified in the bright light of the sun.

The scientist who is the image of God is one shadow of God, seeking to discover other, perhaps fainter, shadows of God. The scientist-shadow is not free to assume any shape he wants, but is shaped and guided by God Himself. Theology provides the tools to break through the clouds of sin and theological ignorance and to correct for other "atmospheric distortions" that prevent shadows from being accurately seen on the grass.

God Calls Scientists to Participate in His Work

Vocations Are More Than Jobs

The doctrine that human beings have been made in the image of God is a broad doctrine that encompasses human capacity (including knowledge and spiritual life), activity (including ruling and procreating), and moral standing (righteousness). The doctrine of vocation—that God calls human beings to fill certain offices through which He works in the world—is a narrower doctrine that deals with human activity. When one asks, "Who am I?" the answer is, "The image of God." When one asks, "What am I to do?" the answer is, "Whatever God has called you to do." Both answers direct attention away from the individual back to God as the source and pattern for human life.

Luther speaks of vocation as the "masks of God":

What else is all our work to God—whether in the fields, in the garden, in the city, in the house, in war, or in government . . . ? These are the masks of God, behind which He wants to remain concealed and do all things. Had Gideon done nothing but take the field against Midian, the Midianites would not have been beaten; and God could certainly have beaten them without Gideon. He could give children without using men and women. But He does not want to do this. Instead, He joins man and woman so that it appears to be the work of man and woman, and yet He does it under the cover of such masks. We have the saying: "God gives every good thing, but not just by waving a wand." God gives all good gifts; but you must lend a hand and take the bull by the horns; that is, you must work and thus give God good cause and a mask.[7]

As "masks of God," vocations are God's method of working in the world. Luther's comments above clarify that it is God Himself who does the good work—"These are the masks of God, behind which He wants to remain concealed and do all things. . . . God gives every good thing . . . God gives all good gifts."

The word *vocation* is used in a theological sense primarily with reference to Christians, who alone know the one true God and willingly follow His calling. However, God uses all people, Christian and non-Christian alike, to accomplish His good purposes. "The goodness of God comes to us, among other ways, through other people, who are 'God's masks' whether or not they have faith."[8] Christians participate in God's works willingly as His servants, while non-Christians participate in God's works against their will or for purposes that are different from God's purposes. For instance, God's commands to avoid sexual immorality and to love one another apply to all people, Christian and non-Christian alike, teaching them how to live a God-pleasing life. Only the Christian, however, fulfills the commandments as God's willing servant; even when the non-Christian avoids adultery and performs loving actions, he does so without faith, and the Bible says, "Without faith it is impossible to please God" (Hebrews 11:6).

It is intriguing how closely related vocations are to the image of God. As images of God, people are like God in many different ways at the same time. They can be powerful, compassionate, creative, holy, intelligent, spiritual, and so on, reflecting many different attributes of God. Likewise in their vocations, "every Christian occupies a multitude of offices at the same time."[9] One can be a scientist, mother, wife, daughter, and citizen, all at the same time, with different duties and responsibilities in each vocation. Ethical decisions about what should or should not be done must not ignore the demands of one vocation in favor of another but must weigh competing claims carefully.

Second, as an image of God, each person is *simul similis et dissimilis,* "at the same time similar and dissimilar" to God. For instance, a ruler is the image of God by virtue of his ruling. But God teaches that rulers are both similar and dissimilar to Him when He says to them, "I said, 'You are "gods"; you are all sons of the Most High.' But you will die like mere men; you will fall like every other ruler" (Psalm 82:6–7). Although rulers are like God by virtue of their ruling, they are unlike Him by virtue of their mortality. From a vocational perspective, it is God who exercises His authority over the earth through the rulers He has called. "What the office does is not part of man's account, but of God's."[10] As Jesus taught Pilate, "You would have no power over Me if it were not given to you from above" (John 19:11). And as Paul taught the Romans: "The authorities that exist have been established by God. . . . [The ruler] is God's servant to do you good. . . . He is God's servant, an agent of wrath to bring punishment on the wrongdoer" (Romans 13:1–4). Because it is God Himself who rules through rulers, Luther says, "He who is in authority is an incarnate god, so to speak."[11] This is a strong statement indeed, but Luther is careful to include the phrase "so to speak" in the statement. Although it is God who performs His work of ruling through rulers, using them as His hands, so to speak, the rulers never become God—they remain God's "masks," His human instruments. It is God's work that is done, but God works through means, through vocations, through people who have been called to do His work, through people who are capable of doing God's work because they have been created in God's image.

Another way in which vocations are related to the image of God is that some vocations are more stable, depending on biological orders or familial relationships (being father or mother, husband or wife, child, etc.), while others are more changeable, depending on occupations (being ruler, judge, teacher, etc.). This is similar to the different ways in which people can be like God as His images. The likenesses can be stable, such as having spiritual capabilities, or they can be changeable, such as exercising authority in certain circumstances. People who see themselves as shadows and masks of God, made in His image and called to do His work, seek to do the work God has given them in a way that most closely reflects God's character and will. The godly judge prays for wisdom and skill in making judgments in which justice is tempered with mercy. The godly laborer prays for strength and skill and faithfulness. The godly scientist prays for the ability to make new discoveries and inventions and for the ability to make moral decisions so his discoveries and inventions serve to make the world a better place.

The Vocation of Scientist

The Bible never uses the words *science* or *scientist*. Therefore, to talk about the vocation of scientist may sound like the verbal equivalent of building castles in the sky. What is the foundation for calling the work of a scientist a "vocation," a calling from God? Is everything people do a vocation?

Clearly, God does not call people to work against Him and His will. Satan's work in opposing God cannot be considered a vocation. God does not call Satan to oppose Him. A thief has no grounds for claiming that he has been called by God to steal what belongs to other people. True, God uses the activities of Satan and the thief to accomplish good things, but God does not commission the sins themselves.

God does, on the other hand, command all to love one another. That basic command is the foundation for all true callings, all just vocations, "such as are ordained by God or those whose existence is not contrary to God's will."[12] Although God has not specifically ordained the vocation of scientist in the Bible, it is an honorable vocation, an existence that is not contrary to

God's will. The vocation of science is filled by people who love knowledge and search for wisdom, two attributes often praised in the Bible. Solomon urges, "Get wisdom, get understanding" (Proverbs 4:5), and rhapsodizes, "How much better to get wisdom than gold, to choose understanding rather than silver!" (Proverbs 16:16). The wisdom that is extolled so highly begins with the fear of the Lord: "The fear of the LORD is the beginning of wisdom" (Proverbs 9:10). It continues with the intricacies of creation: "By wisdom the LORD laid the earth's foundations, by understanding He set the heavens in place; by His knowledge the deeps were divided, and the clouds let drop the dew" (Proverbs 3:19–20). Before the fall into sin, Adam exercised his godly wisdom by engaging in the scientific activity of naming animals (Genesis 2:19–20).

Discovering How the World Works

When Adam fell into sin, his relationships with Eve, God, and the earth became marked by disharmony, misunderstanding, and adversity. In some mysterious way, the earth itself was affected. "Cursed is the ground because of you" (Genesis 3:17). The apostle Paul writes: "The creation was subjected to frustration, not by its own choice, but by the will of the one who subjected it, in hope that the creation itself will be liberated from its bondage to decay and brought into the glorious freedom of the children of God. We know that the whole creation has been groaning as in the pains of childbirth right up to the present time" (Romans 8:20–22). The vocation of scientist is a calling through which God restores understanding of the world so man can discover how it works and promote greater harmony and less adversity, thus more properly fulfilling the God-given purpose to "rule over . . . all the earth" (Genesis 1:26). In recent times, it has become possible for scientists to work with the code of life itself as they experiment with DNA. This is a heady development that

allows scientists to participate in the creative activity of God
Himself, who is the author and designer of all life.

Participating in the Creative Activity of God

As Christian scientists work with the code of life, they do so
with respect for all life but especially for human life. God took
special care in creating Adam; after deliberating about creating
man in God's image, He "formed man from the dust of the
ground and breathed into his nostrils the breath of life, and man
became a living being" (Genesis 2:7). God continues to be actively
involved in creating human life, so Elihu can teach Job: "The
Spirit of God has made me; the breath of the Almighty gives me
life" (Job 33:4). Elihu does not deny that he had human parents
who conceived and bore him in the normal manner, but he
insists that when his parents gave him life, it was God who
worked through them. Elihu's parents participated in the creative
activity of God Himself.

One of the biblical teachings about the image of God is that
human life is fundamentally different from animal life. After the
great flood, God gave Noah permission to kill every animal for
food, but He specifically forbade Noah to kill man, saying, "Whoever sheds the blood of man, by man shall his blood be shed; for
in the image of God has God made man" (Genesis 9:6). This
means that God alone has the right to take human life. Human
beings have sufficient authority for taking away the life of animals, though such actions are regulated by moral constraints
against malice and cruelty. In the case of human life, however, it is
only God who has the authority to take away life, even when He
uses a human executioner or other means to do so. The executioner has the right to kill by virtue of his office and on God's
behalf, not by virtue of his humanity or on his own behalf.[13]

This is the theological basis for the distinction made by theologians between the genetic research performed on animals and

that performed on human beings. The consistent Darwinist may feel constrained to treat all life similarly because human beings are considered to be merely another category of animals. The scientist who is a Christian has biblical warrant for differentiating between research performed on animals and research performed on human beings. One can justify performing legitimate research on animals even when the research is fatal because God has given people permission to kill animals for good purposes. One cannot justify performing similar research on human beings; their lives belong to God. As David says, "You are my God. My times are in Your hands" (Psalm 31:14–15).

The vocation of scientist, then, does not include the right to destroy human life. This precludes any research or technique that is fatal to human embryos. It also precludes activities that hurt or harm one's neighbor. What Luther says about craftsmen applies as well to scientists:

> If you are a manual laborer, you find that the Bible has been put into your workshop, into your hand, into your heart. It teaches and preaches how you should treat your neighbor. . . . You have as many preachers as you have transactions, goods, tools, and other equipment in your house and home. All this is continually crying out to you, "Friend, use me in your relations with your neighbor just as you would want your neighbor to use his property in his relations with you."[14]

On the positive side, the scientist is an image of God who is called by God to do His work in the world. This gives the scientist tremendous freedom and possibilities for work. The scientist who works with the code of life is like the Creator who developed the code of life. If the scientist fulfills his vocation properly, he will also be like the Redeemer who conquered sin and reversed its effects in the lives of people he touched. Whatever leads toward death is an effect of sin because "the wages of sin is death"

(Romans 6:23). When the scientist fights against disease, then, he is like Christ with respect to ameliorating an effect of sin in people's lives. The fight against disease may take the form of lessening its potency, completely eliminating it, or preventing it from happening in the first place. Whether the scientist fights disease through standard medical procedures or through genetic therapies is immaterial from a theological perspective. In any case, when working with the code of life like the Creator or when reversing some effect of sin like the Redeemer, the faithful scientist does not set himself up as God or dethrone the one true God.

Scientists Work between Heaven and Earth

Disdain for the Earthly Can Lead to Hubris

It is the mixture of the earthly and the heavenly in human beings that sets them up for great successes and failures. Adam was created as a heavenly creature, in the image and likeness of God, but he was also an earthly creature, distinct from God. Adam's first great temptation was to deny his earthly limitations and grasp at becoming like God with respect to being the ultimate authority to determine what is good and evil. Man is created to occupy a position between heaven and earth, and the mixture between the earthly and the heavenly in man is the battlefield on which God and Satan fight. Satan constantly urges people to cast off the shackles of their earthly limitations and enjoy the unfettered prerogatives of their heavenly status, while God commands people to obey Him and to do all they do as His representatives, His images.

Another way to characterize Adam's first great temptation is as an attack of Satan on Adam's vocation: "Vocation is a focal point of decision in the combat between God and the devil."[15] It is fascinating that the greatest temptation related to vocation is the same as the greatest temptation related to being created in the image of God—the temptation to set oneself up as God. "Evil officeholders want to make themselves God, rather than servants of God; they want to rule and not to serve, ascribing to themselves the power and the righteousness which belong to the office, to God, not man."[16]

When officeholders are allied with Satan rather than with God, their office

> is and continues good and divine just as the sun is still God's pure creation, even if some use the light of day to commit murder and other crimes . . . . The combat between God and the devil for all vocations and orders takes place within every single human being. If God is victor, then that part of external existence which lies within man's reach is made to serve God. If Satan wins, God's creation is used in the opposite way. But an office is good, even when it is misused, even as the spear that pierced Christ's side did not for that reason cease to be God's good creation.[17]

The office of scientist is a powerful office, full of potential for good or evil. It is so powerful that the specter of a scientist gone bad haunts the theologian. The scientist who makes himself God, caring nothing about the one true God or His laws of right and wrong, is like an incarnate devil. He has great power but refuse to acknowledge God's laws governing its use. At best, he is restrained from grievous evil by his own sense of right and wrong or that of society, but such restraints are not always as trustworthy or as powerful as they need to be. The scientist misuses his vocation when he makes himself God, refusing to acknowledge God's primacy, His created orders, or His revealed will.

One recent example shows the inadequacy of ethical standards that are based on individuals or societies rather than on God's moral laws. Many scientists have argued that they should be allowed to harvest stem cells from excess embryos at fertility clinics because those embryos would either be discarded or sub-jected to slow deterioration in perpetual storage. Because the embryos are originally created for other purposes and have such a dismal future in store, it seems to many as though it would be prac-ticing good stewardship to use the embryos to provide the stem cells that carry so much hope for medical breakthroughs. What is suppressed in this discussion is the fact that human beings do not have the right to take human life, even in its earliest stages. Once that moral absolute has been forgotten, it is not such a far step to the mindset of the scientists at the Jones Institute for Reproductive Medicine in Norfolk, Virginia, who have now *created* embryos *for the purpose of* harvesting their stem cells. They collected and inseminated 162 eggs, created fifty embryos, destroyed forty of them to harvest stem cells, and isolated three colonies of stem cells. It is not as if they completely disregarded ethical considerations. They "had carefully assessed the ethical implications in advance and concluded that the approach was at least as ethical as using spare frozen embryos. There are ethical advantages to having par-ents know and agree from the start that their embryos would be used only for research."[18] Their problem was that they depended on their own fallible reason and social norms rather than on the absolute moral standards revealed by God.

The faithful scientist operates under the authority of God and His absolute command to love one's neighbor (including embryos) as oneself. This immediately places the scientist under the cross, bringing special difficulties and inconveniences. The cross that Christians bear is here understood in a broad sense: "Under this cross are included even the most trivial of difficulties, such as: in marriage, the care of babes, which interferes with sleep and enjoyment; in government, unruly subjects and promoters of revolt; in the ministry, the whole resistance to reformation; in heavy labor, shabbiness, uncleanness, and the contempt of the proud."[19]

SCIENTISTS CALLED TO BE LIKE GOD

One of the ways the faithful scientist operates under the authority of God is by submitting to the authority of the government that God has ordained. Even when competing feverishly with other scientists to be the first to publish a scientific breakthrough or to gain a patent, the faithful scientist will not break duly established laws that regulate and sometimes hinder his research. If he loses to a competitor who engages in unscrupulous or illegal activities, that loss is a cross he bears for his faithfulness in vocation. Whenever he stifles the temptation to use illegal or unethical experiments or treatments to achieve some great result, the scientific sacrifice he makes is a cross he bears. It is unfortunate that the willingness to make this sacrifice is waning, even among Christians. As the *Washington Post* observes:

> Some antiabortion groups argue an absolute moral status for embryos and suggest that research be confined to "adult stem cells" taken from other body tissues. *But many other prominent antiabortion activists—and, a new poll shows, majorities of both American Catholics and evangelicals—reject the need for such a scientific sacrifice.* No one knows yet if adult stem cells have comparable potential and scientific progress can lose years when shunted into artificial pathways.[20]

When scientists disdain their earthly status and operate as if they are not bound by God's laws of right and wrong, they have the potential of doing great evil to one element of the world or another, including taking the lives of innocent embryos.

Fear of the Heavenly Can Lead to Failure to Thrive

On the other hand, there is a corresponding danger that comes from scientists disdaining their heavenly status. Setting one's sights too low can be as much of a problem as setting one's sights too high. Sins of omission can hurt one's neighbor as much as sins of commission. Just as failure to thrive can be deadly in an infant, so, too, it can be deadly in the vocation of scientist.

Man was not created in the image of dogs or trees but in the image of God. Man participates with God in ruling over the world, creating new life, preserving life, and so on. God is the one who "heals all my diseases" (Psalm 103:3), yet He often does so through human physicians and through drugs that scientists have discovered or invented.

There is simply no theological warrant for the comment attributed to skeptics of a previous era: "If God had wanted people to fly, He would have created them with wings." One might as well say: "If God had wanted people to eat, He would have created them with attached food dispensers" or "If God had wanted people to speak English, He would have created them with an innate knowledge of English." Such silliness assumes that whatever is God's will is accomplished without any effort on the part of man. On the contrary, it is God's will that man rules over the world, and the hard work that goes into inventing efficient transportation is one aspect of accomplishing that will of God.

The scientist misuses his vocation if he does not participate with God in the work he has been called to do. Since the fall into sin, this work includes efforts to ameliorate the effects of sin, such as healing diseases, increasing fertility (both of the ground and people), and reducing pain. Scientific discoveries and inventions that aid in such work are blessings that God gives man through scientists.

The Search for a Path Between Heaven and Earth

The scientist, then, struggles to follow the path to which he has been called, a path between heaven and earth. It is a struggle with twin dangers: that of flying too high or of not flying at all. Ovid immortalized this struggle in his retelling of the ancient Greek myth of Daedalus and Icarus:

Meanwhile Daedalus, tired of Crete and of his long absence from home, was filled with longing for his own country, but he was shut in by the sea. Then he said: "The king may block my way by land or across the ocean, but the sky, surely, is open, and that is how we shall go. Minos may possess all the rest, but he does not possess the air." With these words, he set his mind to sciences never explored before, and altered the laws of nature. . . . [He built wings of feathers and string and wax and was able to raise himself into the air.] Then he prepared his son to fly too. "I warn you, Icarus," he said, "you must follow a course midway between earth and heaven, in case the sun should scorch your feathers, if you go too high, or the water make them heavy if you are too low. . . . Take me as your guide, and follow me!" . . . [As they began their flight together,] some fisher . . . caught sight of them as they flew past and stood stock still in astonishment, believing that these creatures who could fly through the air must be gods . . . . [Part way through the journey,] Icarus began to enjoy the thrill of swooping boldly through the air. Drawn on by his eagerness for the open sky, he left his guide and soared upwards, till he came too close to the blazing sun, and it softened the sweet-smelling wax that bound his wings together. The wax melted. Icarus moved his bare arms up and down, but without their feathers they had no purchase on the air . . . . [When he fell into the ocean,] the unhappy father, a father no longer, cried out: "Icarus!" . . . As he was still calling "Icarus" he saw the feathers on the water, and cursed his inventive skill.[21]

One might say that the gods themselves had given Daedalus the idea to fly like a bird. Before he attempted to fly, Daedalus had seen his nephew fly with the help of the gods. The nephew had been sent to him to learn all he could from Daedalus. The nephew proceeded to invent the saw and the compass for describing circles. The great Daedalus became jealous of his nephew and threw him down from a citadel. "But Pallas [Athena], who looks favourably upon clever men, caught the lad as he fell and changed him into a bird, clothing him with feathers in mid-air."[22] Here the gods rescue the nephew from death by helping him to fly.

Why were these myths composed, and why have they proved so popular? A natural suggestion is that they capture the universal struggle of man to follow the path between heaven and earth. Generally the myth of Daedalus and Icarus is used as a cautionary tale against setting one's eyes too high, against altering the laws of nature, and against becoming too much like the gods. After all, the high-flying Icarus dies, and Daedalus "cursed his inventive skill." But the myths lose their potency if they do not also encourage lifting one's eyes up from the ground. There are times when man must fly to escape death or a fate similar to death. Daedalus escaped his prison, and his nephew escaped his fatal fall from the citadel because they flew between heaven and earth with the permission and aid of the gods. Even Icarus would have been saved if he had followed Daedalus's advice: "You must follow a course midway between earth and heaven, in case the sun should scorch your feathers, if you go too high, or the water make them heavy if you are too low."

What the Greek myths teach about human beings striving to follow the path between heaven and earth is similar to what the Bible teaches. This is the honor and challenge of being a human being. Man is created in the image and likeness of God and are called to various offices through which God performs His work. People who understand who they are and what they are to do realize that they are sojourners on the earth with an inheritance in heaven and that they are called to follow a path between heaven and earth.

Conclusion

Two biblical doctrines intersect to teach that scientists are called to be like God. They are made like Him when they are made in His image. They are called to act like God when they are called into the office of scientist, through which God carries out much important work in the world. To say that scientists are called to be like God means that they are called to travel a middle road between heaven and earth.

Pursuing the middle road in scientific matters applies both to the aims of science and to its epistemology. The greatest advances in scientific knowledge have been made not by empirical observation alone (keeping one's eyes on the ground) but by a combination of empirical observation and rational deduction (lifting one's eyes to the heavens). "This middle road to which Newton was driven back again and again by his scientific creativity was of a piece with his explicit conviction about the validity of going mentally from the realm of phenomena to the existence of God."[23] Going mentally from what is earthly to what is heavenly is a natural exercise for those who are in a Godly vocation, for those who have been called by God to perform His work.

Being called to travel the middle road also applies to the aims of science. It encourages scientists to look up from the ground, yet cautions them against flying too closely to heaven. Scientists look up from the ground when they follow their calling not only with the aim of discovering the wonders of creation but also with the aim of participating with God in His creative and preserving activity, especially as it relates to exercising God-pleasing rule over the world and relieving the suffering brought into the world through sin. Because nature is not God but has been corrupted by the fall into sin, scientists do not misuse their office when they search for positive ways to change nature.

Scientists are cautioned against flying too closely to heaven when they follow their calling to represent God faithfully, to act like God in working for the good of His creation, to do what pleases God, and to function as God's hands or His mask. Scientists who understand who they are and what they are to do realize that God is at the center of the universe, not themselves. They join in the praise of God raised by His people: "You alone are the LORD. You made the heavens, even the highest heavens, and all their starry host, the earth and all that is on it, the seas and all that is in them. You give life to everything, and the multitudes of heaven worship You" (Nehemiah 9:6).

Notes

1. Thomas Aquinas, *Summa Theologica* 1. 3. q. 47, art. 1.

2. Aquinas, *Summa Theologica* 1. 6. q. 93, art. 2.

3. Christ is unique as an image of God because Christ is both God and man. As man, He was created in the image of God, but as God, He always existed as the image of God, begotten of the Father.

4. C. F. W. Walther, *The Proper Distinction between Law and Gospel: Thirty-Nine Evening Lectures,* trans. W. H. T. Dau (St. Louis: Concordia, 1929), 6.

5. LW 34:152–53.

6. Natural processes can be improved by strengthening the body's immune system, developing irrigation systems, fertilizing crops, etc.

7. LW 14:114–15.

8. Gustaf Wingren, *Luther on Vocation,* trans. Carl C. Rasmussen (Philadelphia: Muhlenberg, 1957), 144.

9. Wingren, *Luther on Vocation,* 5.

10. Wingren, *Luther on Vocation,* 8.

11. LW 5:124.

12. Wingren, *Luther on Vocation,* 3.

13. Cf. Wingren, *Luther on Vocation,* 7.

14. LW 21:237.

15. Wingren, *Luther on Vocation,* 92.

16. Wingren, *Luther on Vocation,* 86.

17. Wingren, *Luther on Vocation*, 86.

18. *Milwaukee Journal Sentinel,* 11 July 2001.

19. Wingren, *Luther on Vocation*, 29.

20. *Washington Post,* 1 July 2001 (*emphasis added*).

21. Ovid, *Metamorphoses* 8.183–235.

22. Ovid, *Metamorphoses* 8.251–53.

23. Stanley L. Jaki, *The Road of Science and the Ways to God* (Chicago: University of Chicago Press, 1978), 87.

9

Science

Sacred Cow or Sacred Calling?

KURT MARQUART

Abstract

From within the left-hand kingdom of reason, it is shown that though Sir Karl Popper was not a Christian, a broadly Popperian understanding of science is congenial to Christian thought. In particular, Marquart examines Popper's defense of realism against instrumentalism and fallibilism against dogmatism, and argues that the combination of a robust sense of reality with modesty about human cognitive ability is both supremely rational and highly appropriate for the scientific calling. In the process, Marquart criticizes the dogmatic pseudo-religion of scientism, both for its unwarranted pretensions (e.g., making Darwinism a theory of almost everything) and for its dehumanizing consequences. Again, Popper aids a Christian perspective on the value of human life by denying its reduction to the categories of materialistic science. In all of this, Popper is exemplary in his humble acceptance of the intellectual and moral limitations of science.

~

The proximity of October 31, Reformation Day—and now also of the infamous September 11—suggests a certain perspective as the logical starting point for our considerations.[1] Unlike the other two so-called "religions of the Book"—that is, Judaism and Islam—Christianity differentiates sharply between God and Caesar, between spiritual and temporal power. Among the major Christian confessions, it is the Church of the Augsburg Confession that presses this distinction most consistently, as part and parcel of her sharp division between Law and Gospel. This implies the total rejection of the mingling of theology, Middle Eastern politics, and certain chiliastic fantasies into the mischievously intoxicating brew so beloved in certain circles.

But what does this have to do with science? Much indeed. The Reformation freed the ordinary, temporal callings of people from the stigma of being "unspiritual" and restored them to their noble status of their valuable and beneficent ways of serving God and humanity. Just as temporal government now had its own dignity (Romans 13) as God's "left-hand rule" and was not accountable, as such, to ecclesiastical potentates, so by analogy also the various callings within that temporal rule. This is the realm of reason, of natural law, of common sense—quite distinct and independent of the realm of faith and of theology, resting on divine revelation. It is to this realm of reason or common sense that science belongs. Science can be "Christian" no more than farming can be "Lutheran" or chemistry "Evangelical." Such expressions are simply "category mistakes." For the Christian practitioner of science that calling is fully justified—indeed, sanctified—by the Creator's command to subdue the earth and to "have dominion over the fish of the sea, and over the fowl of the air, and over every living thing that moveth upon the earth" (Genesis 1:28).

Oddly enough, the demand that science be "reasonable" is by no means as straightforward and unambiguous as it might seem. What it means for something to be "reasonable" turns out to be problematic after the fall!

It was shocking to see in a recent issue of the *British Journal for the Philosophy of Science* a reference to the distinguished philosopher of science, the late Sir Karl Popper, as one of several "modern irrationalists"![2]

Of course, there is no perfect philosophy on earth. However, to quote a famous saying: A great philosophy is not one against which nothing could be said but rather one which has something to say. And Popper's philosophy, it seems to me, has much of significance to say about science, its aims, its methods, and its limitations. Whilst not agreeing with Popper on some quite fundamental issues, I nevertheless consider his philosophy to have been, in the main, an eminently reasonable one. And I should like to refer to several features of Popper's thought and work as concrete examples of how one might think rationally about the nature and limitations of science.

Realism vs. Instrumentalism

As a realist, Popper contended for the commonsense view that there is a real world or universe out there, independent of our thoughts and wishes, and that it is the business of science to discover and describe this real world. Scientific theories deal not with mental constructs or mere sense data but with objective realities and approximate them ever more closely. The theories can be tested against the realities. Indeed, that is what makes a theory scientific. Mere ideology or metaphysics can coexist with virtually any factual state of affairs. But a scientific theory is one that can be checked against objective reality and, if necessary, corrected by it.

Popper's chief opposition on this score was directed against "instrumentalism," the notion that scientific theories do not describe objective realities but are mere instruments or devices for technical calculation, prediction, and control. Science, on the latter view, pursues not the whole truth about the universe but only certain answers to practical problems. It is pragmatic, not truth-oriented. Any theoretical entities science finds necessary to postulate are taken to have purely heuristic or auxiliary value: They help to arrive at the practical result, but they are not meant to describe what the world is "really" like or, better, what the realities and interconnections are *behind* the facade of appearances or phenomena.

But this would mean, Popper argues, that the discoveries of science

> are mere mechanical inventions, its theories are instruments—gadgets again, or perhaps super-gadgets. It cannot and does not reveal to us new worlds behind our everyday world of appearance; for the physical world is just surface: it has no depth. *The world is just what it appears to be. Only the scientific theories are not what they appear to be.* A scientific theory neither explains nor describes the world; it is nothing but an instrument.[3]

A passion for truth, for discovery of what the world is really like, argues Popper, is the driving force of science at its best:

> But with all respect for the lesser scientists, I wish to convey here a heroic and romantic idea of science and its workers: men who humbly devoted themselves to the search for truth, to the growth of our knowledge; men whose life consisted in an adventure of bold ideas. I am prepared to consider with them many of their less brilliant helpers who were equally devoted to the search for truth—for great truth. But I do not count among them

those for whom science is no more than a profession, a technique: those who are not deeply moved by great problems and by the oversimplifications of bold solutions.[4]

Popper scorned, by means of a verse from the German humorist Wilhelm Busch, the reduction of science to safe and obvious formalisms, or what he called the "epistemological nursery":

> Twice two equals four: 'tis true,
> But too empty and too trite.
> What I look for is a clue
> To some matters not so light.[5]

The most important task of science, according to Popper, is that of explaining the far from obvious connections that lie beneath the surface of things:

> Yet we also stress that *truth is not the only aim of science.* We want more than mere truth: what we look for is *interesting truth*—truth which is hard to come by. And in the natural sciences (as distinct from mathematics) what we look for is truth which has a high degree of explanatory power, in a sense which implies that it is logically improbable truth.[6]
>
> I shall distinguish the point of view of the theoretician—the seeker for truth, and especially for true explanatory theories—from that of the practical man of action; that is, I will distinguish between *theoretical preference* and *pragmatic preference.*[7]

The task of science, which, I have suggested, is to find satisfactory explanations, can hardly be understood if we are not realists. For a satisfactory explanation is one which is not *ad hoc*; and this idea—the *idea of independent evidence*—can hardly be understood without the idea of discovery, of progressing to deeper layers of explanation: without the idea that there is something for us to discover, and something to discuss critically.[8]

The opposite ("instrumentalist") view—that science seeks not the truth about the universe but only various practical ways of manipulating its surface features—Popper rejects as undercutting the real inner dynamic of science. And with the killer instinct of a practiced polemicist, he attributes the invention of instrumentalism to three theologians: a Roman Catholic cardinal (Robert Bellarmine), an Anglican bishop (George Berkeley), and a Lutheran theologian (Andreas Osiander)![9] Elsewhere Popper adds the non-theologian Francis Bacon to the mix.[10]

In the argument about the relative importance of empirical observations versus reason, Popper is solidly on the side of reason. As a classic instance of the defeat of mere sense-observation by reason ("bold conjecture") Popper cites Copernicus's discovery that the earth goes round the sun: "It was bold because it clashed with all then accepted views, *and* with the prima facie evidence of the senses. It was bold because it postulated a hitherto unknown hidden reality behind the appearances."[11]

Christian thinkers should find Popper's defense of realism against instrumentalism thoroughly congenial. Who would quarrel with Popper that "a realist who believes in an 'external world,' necessarily believes in the existence of a cosmos rather than a chaos; that is, in regularities"?[12]

Indeed, it can be argued that it was the centuries of Christian conviction that prepared the way for the origin of modern science. Stanley L. Jaki, for instance, showed "the crucial role played in the origin of science by a widely shared belief in the first article of Christian creed, an article placing the origin of all in the creative act of God, the Father Almighty, Maker of heaven and earth."[13] A number of factors are involved here. For one thing, scientific thinking was unlikely to arise in an animist environment in which every babbling brook had its elf and every tree its own sprite! It was Christianity that taught people to distinguish rigidly between the Creator and His creation—something Nikita Khrushchev should have remembered when he announced triumphantly that his cosmonauts had traversed the solar system and found no heaven nor God nor angels! As one wit responded: Would one expect to find a watchmaker inside a watch?

Belief in an arbitrary, capricious deity would also not encourage scientific thinking. But Christianity holds that behind the created order stands not chaos nor caprice but Logos, the Divine Word, from which we take our word *logic* (John 1:1–3). The universe is a reasonable, orderly entity, therefore open to reasonable inquiry. Moreover, if the physical universe was created "good," it is worthy of our study and exploration. F. M. Cornford makes the interesting observation that, given the mechanical materialism of ancient (pagan) Greek "science," Socrates "gave up all hope of an intelligible system of Nature, and turned away from the study of external things. . . . It was not only the man Socrates, but philosophy itself that turned, in his person, from the outer to the inner world."[14] Contempt for material creation is not the way of Christianity. Indeed, Popper, who was hardly known as a theist let alone a Christian, made the brilliant observation that Bishop Berkeley's "idealism clashes with his Christianity. The reason is . . . the doctrine of incarnation is essential to Christianity."[15]

Fallibilism Vs. Dogmatism

Does it follow from a realistic understanding of science that scientific knowledge is solid and certain, an impregnable bastion of absolute truth? Of course not. Sometimes science has been regarded in just this way. In the nineteenth century it was often seen as the educated person's substitute for the lost certainties of Christian dogma. To the optimistic progressivism of the Victorian age, it seemed self-evident that science was marching relentlessly forward, pushing back the frontiers of ignorance and superstition, forcing nature to yield up her secrets one by one, and ushering in a bright future of reason and commonsense. Then something quite unexpected happened: classical ("Newtonian") physics was challenged by the rise of relativity theory and quantum theory early in the last century.

Sir Isaac Newton had been the scientific genius of his age. Alexander Pope wrote of him: "Nature and Nature's laws lay hid in night: God said, *Let Newton be!* and all was light."[16] When the great certainties of the tidy Newtonian world collapsed into the weirdness of quanta and relativity, one could either give up confidence in science as purveyor of reliable knowledge about the universe or find a way of immunizing future science against similar surprises. One influential result was what came to be known as the Received View of scientific theories. This was a bare-bones approach that sought to rely only on (presumably objective) observational data and mathematical logic, eschewing all unobservables as "metaphysics." The rise and especially the decline of this Received View is well described in Frederick Suppe's 1977 book *The Structure of Scientific Theories*. In fact, this volume arose out of and reports the proceedings of the 1969 Illinois Symposium on the Structure of Scientific Theories, called specifically to deal with the "acute intellectual disarray" into which the philosophy of science had fallen, so as to "sort out prevailing chaos and to search for new, productive intellectual directions to follow."[17] Another classic treatment is *Revolutions and Reconstructions in the Philosophy of Science* by Mary Hesse.[18]

A central feature of the "logical positivism" that lay behind the Received View was the dogma that not only truth but also meaning itself lay in the empirical verification of a statement, indeed that "(t)he meaning of a term is its method of verification."[19] This stringent combination of mathematical logic and strict empiricism seemed to guarantee the infallibility of any scientific outcome. The cost, however, was too high. It reduced reality to a thin layer of the empirically observable. And physics itself had long since gone beyond the bounds of the directly observable.

A classic formulation of verificationism was Alfred J. Ayer's *Language, Truth and Logic*, which first appeared in 1936. With a glib combination of venom and glee, the book disposes of God and ethics as "meaningless." Statements about God and ethics, we are told, are neither true nor false; they simply have no meaning at all because, of course, they cannot be verified empirically. I quote from the 1946 edition:

> If now I . . . say, "Stealing money is wrong," I produce a sentence which has no factual meaning—that is, expresses no proposition which can be either true or false. . . . For in saying that a certain type of action is right or wrong, I am not making any factual statement, not even a statement about my own state of mind. I am merely expressing certain moral sentiments. And the man who is ostensibly contradicting me is merely expressing his moral sentiments. . .
>
> But in every case in which one would commonly be said to be making an ethical judgment, the function of the relevant ethical word is purely "emotive." It is used to express feeling about certain objects, but not to make any assertion about them.[20]

It was this astringent minimalism that guaranteed, for the Received View, science as the privileged realm of the infallibly verifiable. And it was Popper who modestly claimed to have "killed" this whole enterprise, virtually single-handedly, one gathers ("I fear that I must admit responsibility"[21]). His classic work, *The Logic of Scientific Discovery*[22] had first appeared in 1934 in German (two years before Ayer's book).

Popper's central argument was the logical nonsymmetry between verification and falsification. One single genuine counterexample would falsify a typical scientific generalization, but no limited number of positive examples could definitely verify it. One simply has no guarantee that the next observation would not contradict the previous ones. Now, the basic structure of scientific theories is this: If theory T is true, observation O will follow. But a whole series of observations O has followed; therefore, theory T is true.

But, says Popper, this is the fallacy of inductivism—or, more formally, the fallacy of the affirmation of the consequent, in statements of the form, *If A then B*. Take this example: If it is raining, the street is wet. But the street is wet; therefore, it is raining. That is an obvious fallacy. The street could be wet for other reasons, for example, a broken hydrant, a passing water truck, children playing with water, and the like. Thus the mere confirmation of the consequent "the street is wet" does not prove that it is raining. In other words, B could be the case for any number of reasons other than A. On the other hand, if A is true, B necessarily follows. It is sound, therefore, to argue: If A then B; but A, therefore B. It is not sound to reverse this: but B, therefore A.

This is why Popper argued that the important thing to look for is not verification—which, for infinite series, can never be completed—but falsification, which clearly and decisively disqualifies the relevant claims or statements. Therefore, Popper offered falsification as the real test or criterion of scientific discourse. A statement is scientific if and only if it can in principle be falsified, that is, if it entails claims or predictions that could be contradicted by future observations. This means that astrology is not a science—nor is Freudian psychoanalysis. Marxist economics, on the other hand, used to be scientific but degenerated into a dreary dogmatism by being protected against falsification. Similarly Darwinism is really "a metaphysical research programme."[23] Such were the views of the "early" Popper. By 1978 he had been persuaded to make a public volte-face on Darwinism in the most abject terms. *Nature* quoted him as follows:

The fact that the theory of natural selection is difficult to test has led some people, anti-Darwinists, to claim that it is a tautology. . . . I mention this problem because I too belong among the culprits. . . . I have changed my mind about the testability and the logical status of the theory of natural selection; and I am glad to have an opportunity to make a recantation.[24]

To return to the main argument, it is important to note that Popper offered falsification *not* as a criterion of *meaning*, as in the logical positivist verificationism, but as a criterion of *demarcation*, distinguishing scientific from nonscientific discourse. Yet Popper did not press this "demarcation criterion" in a rigid, doctrinaire way, so as to exclude everything except natural science. On the contrary:

Science, after all, is a branch of literature; and working on science is a human activity like building a cathedral. No doubt there is too much specialization and too much professionalism in contemporary science, which makes it inhuman; but this unfortunately is true of contemporary history or psychology also, almost as much as of the natural sciences. . .

Labouring the difference between science and the humanities has long been a fashion, and has become a bore. The method of problem solving, the method of conjecture and refutation, is practised by both.[25]

Before leaving the subject of verificationism, we should note what has always struck me as a self-contradiction: How can we know whether something can be verified or not unless we *first* know what it means? But if we know what the statement means before it is verified, how can its meaning depend on its verification?

What was it that drove Popper to his—pardon the alliterative pedantry—*falsificationist fallibilism*? In brief, it was the revolution in physics, which had driven others, including the young

Einstein, from realism into instrumentalism. The two chief factors, according to Popper, were "(a) difficulties in the interpretation of the formalism of the Quantum Theory, and (b) the spectacular success of its applications."[26] Einstein, wrote Popper, later "repented" of his instrumentalism[27] and told Popper "that he regretted no mistake he ever made as much as this mistake."[28] But "Einstein's withdrawal came too late. Physics had become a stronghold of subjectivist philosophy, and it has remained so ever since."[29] For instance, note the extraordinary statements by J. A. Wheeler, quoted in a different context by Popper's friend, Sir John Eccles, in his 1977–1978 Gifford Lectures in Edinburgh:

> No search has ever disclosed any ultimate underpinning, either of physics or mathematics, that shows the slightest prospect of providing the rationale for the many-storied tower of physical law. One therefore suspects it is wrong to think that as one penetrates deeper and deeper into the structure of physics he will find it terminating at some nth level. One fears it is also wrong to think of the structure going on and on, layer after layer, *ad infinitum*. One finds himself in desperation asking if the structure, rather than terminating in some smallest object or in some most basic field, or going on and on, does not lead back in the end to the observer himself, in some kind of closed circle of interdependences. . . .
>
> Could the universe only then come into being, when it could guarantee to produce "observership" in some locality and for some period of time in its history-to-be? Is "observership" the link that closes the circle of interdependences?[30]

Rather than abandon realism and join the flight to subjectivism and instrumentalism, Popper chose to stay with the commonsense view of science but to stress its unfinished, growing, nondogmatic nature. It seems to me that this attitude is supremely rational. Of course, those who yearn for infallible scientific oracles, in other words, for science as a sacred cow, will find Popper's demand for scientific modesty annoying. Thus Stove (1982) dismisses Popper as an irrationalist simply because Popper refuses to grant to *induction* the same conclusive logical force as that belonging to *deduction*. But Stove is wrong in caricaturing Popper as an armchair philosopher, far removed from actual scientific discovery. On the contrary, Popper paid close and rational attention to actual scientific developments and, therefore, to Einstein, "whose theories convinced Popper about the tentative character of all human knowledge, about the fallibility of the most entrenched theories, about the fact that no knowledge is absolute."[31]

The Problem of "World Views"— "Scientific" or "Christian"

On the one hand Popper wrote: "All science is cosmology, I believe, and for me the interest in philosophy, no less than of science, lies solely in its bold attempt to add to our knowledge of the world, and to the theory of our knowledge of the world."[32] But on the other hand he held: "Science does not rest upon rock-bottom. The bold structure of its theories rises, as it were, above a swamp. It is like a building erected on piles. The piles are driven down from above into the swamp, but not down to any natural or 'given' base."[33] Or again: "There is a reality behind the world as it appears to us, possibly a many-layered reality, of which the appearances are the outermost layers. What the great scientist does is boldly to guess, daringly to conjecture, what these inner realities are like. This is akin to mythmaking."[34]

I find this combination of realism and modesty refreshing. It does justice both to the value of science and to its limitations. There are no arrogant pretensions here to final truth and reality, embodied in the brittle dogmatism of "the Scientific World

View." Such grandiose, all-encompassing world views were nineteenth-century illusions, reflective, perhaps, of the rebellious adolescence of a science consciously at odds with its Christian origins. The new modesty, emanating particularly from physics, may be a sign of science having reached a certain stage of calm maturity.

The German mathematician Hans Rohrbach, in his thought-provoking *Naturwissenschaft, Weltbild, Glaube*, puts paid to the traditional "conflict between science and religion" that still spooks about in the minds of would-be modern (or post-modern?) theologians. He defends two theses: "(1) The so-called scientific world view [*Weltbild*] is not the world-view of natural science. (2) The so-called biblical world-view is not the world-view of the Bible."[35]

Rohrbach traces the collapse of nineteenth-century dogmatic materialism in the face of the sort of advances in physics mentioned earlier in this essay. Then he challenges the standard caricature of the "biblical world view" as consisting of three stories or layers: heaven on top, earth in the middle, hell below. Rather, Rohrbach argues, the biblical world view is that of a mutual interpenetration of visible and invisible worlds (just what we confess in the Nicene Creed)! Rohrbach cites several telling biblical examples, such as that of the invisible-made-visible heavenly armies in 2 Kings 6 and the opening of heaven at the stoning of St. Stephen in Acts 7. Then Rohrbach distinguishes between (1) a naïve, pre-scientific world-view that "had room in it for God"; (2) a modern-scientific world-view (spanning roughly the years 1600 to 1926) that did not have room for God; and (3) the contemporary scientific picture of nature "for which there is room in God."[36]

Similarly, the German physicist Werner Schaaffs cites a report by a theologian (Otto Weber) about a conference "under the chairmanship of the well-known demythologizer Bultmann, with renowned physicists in attendance." Weber said: "I must say how humiliating it was. Physicists sat there declaring their faith, and theologians sat there denying theirs." Then:

> In the course of the discussion, Weber reported, one of the physicists said to Professor Bultmann that it was not right that he and other professors tell their students nothing more about physics than what they had learned sixty years earlier from their school teachers. Physics has changed considerably since then, and the physicists in attendance wished to observe in all humility that they had had more than a little to do with bringing the changes about.[37]

We Christians also need to remember that divine revelation in the Sacred Scriptures does not supply us with a grand overall dogma about the nature of the universe. "We know in part and we prophesy in part" (1 Corinthians 13:9), writes St. Paul, that great theologian of the cross (1 Corinthians 1:18–25). Like the "strip-maps" provided by automobile clubs, which chart only the main road from origin to destination with no details beyond 5 or 10 miles to either side, so Holy Scripture clearly shows Him who is the Way, the Truth, and the Life (John 14:6) but does not distract us with all sorts of curiosities irrelevant to our pilgrimage.

Martin Luther's theology of the cross[38] refuses to ground theology in reason or philosophy, as scholasticism did. This means that genuine theology, founded entirely on divine revelation (Ephesians 2:20), and single-mindedly pursuing the transmission of divine life and salvation through the holy means of grace, God's Word and Sacraments, must avoid unnatural entanglements with the domain of reason, namely, science and philosophy. It will not do to mix up biblical texts and current science into a stew that is neither theology nor science. In a few years or decades, any such melange will be hopelessly out of date!

With theology and science both minding their respective business, and because the truth of divine revelation cannot contradict the truth of the divinely created nature, conflict between them will be minimal, the result in principle of misreadings of either Scripture or nature or both. A textbook example of this mutual respect and independence is the treatment of Copernicanism in sixteenth-century Lutheran universities. John Warwick Montgomery has traced the matter in fascinating detail. He writes: "The simultaneity of the Copernican and Lutheran revolutions suggests a more than accidental relationship between them."[39] The long and the short of it is that while Rome's Aristotelianism and Calvinist biblicism regarded Copernicanism as heretical, the new science was propagated freely at Lutheran universities, mainly by students of Melanchthon. Indeed, the Lutheran theologian Andreas Osiander wrote the introduction to Copernicus's classic. True, Osiander offered the instrumentalist escape route, just to be on the safe side. Yet, in principle, Lutheran theology was open to this sort of secular, independent use of scientific reason and observation. The Bible simply uses the normal language of appearance in describing nature—even as the best informed physicist today will quite naturally talk about the beautiful sunset to his wife and will not lecture her pedantically about how it is really the earth, not the sun, that is moving!

In concluding this section on worldviews, I cannot help but refer to Popper's ingenious suggestion of three worlds—not as an ironclad "worldview" but as a systematic paradigm for filing and relating all sorts of disparate phenomena. World One is the ordinary material world that we observe. World Two is the subjective realm of individual human consciousness. World Three is the intersubjective world of ideas, including culture, science, philosophy, and so on. A useful feature of this view is that it avoids the psychologism and subjectivism now so rampant—especially in "postmodernism." Ideas are seen to have an objective life of their own once they enter the public realm of World Three. Thus all sorts of things follow from Euclid's axioms or from Einstein's proposals that never occurred to these historical authors but which thinkers today can discover and make explicit. A particularly attractive deployment of the three-worlds scheme is found in the Popper-Eccles 1977 symposium on the mind-brain problem.[40] Here Popper and Eccles both profess themselves to be "radical dualist interactionists," which being interpreted means that they hold the mind and the brain to be two different entities that interact, to be sure, but that are not reducible to each other. The neuro-physiologist Eccles, it must be admitted, freed by his Christian convictions, presses his dualism rather vigorously, while the agnostic philosopher Popper seems more reticent and reserved about it.

That suggests one feature of Popper's thought that strikes me as falling short of rationality. He seems never to have outgrown his "lifetime's dislike of theorizing about God," quipping, typically: "Theology, I still think, is due to lack of faith."[41]

I conclude by citing one or two examples of a really scientistic worldview dogmatism, in keeping with the leading cultural myth of our time, namely, that everything came from nothing by itself. P. W. Atkins has written:

> Science will be forced to admit defeat if it has to stop at a seed of any size. That is the severity of the criterion that science sets for itself. If we are to be honest, then we have to accept that science will be able to claim complete success only if it achieves what many might think impossible: accounting for the emergence of everything from absolutely nothing. Not almost nothing, not a sub-atomic dust-like speck, but absolutely nothing. Nothing at all. Not even empty space.[42]

By way of another example, here is Jerry Fodor's debunking of Darwinist dogmatism in a volume on the mind-brain problem:

> It may be, of course, that natural selection explains some of our cognitive architecture; it may even be that natural selection explains our cognitive architecture in considerable detail. But, as a vocal minority keeps pointing out, it also may *not* be, consonant with a rigorously materialistic approach to mind and its etiology. The fact is *we don't know* whether natural selection explains our cognitive architecture. And, I think, we're not really in a position to speculate fruitfully: too many of the big pieces are missing. Most glaringly, there is no general *synchronic* account of human cognition that is remotely close to being well-evidenced; or even well articulated. *We don't know how the mind works,* so we don't know *what* got selected when selection selected us. (If it did.) Second, we know nothing about how psychological structure supervenes on brain structure. (If it does.) ... Indeed, it seems to me (though not to the present authors) that, in respect of the workings of cognition, there's a lot that we still don't know about almost anything. Does anybody really doubt that?[43]

Science and Morality

In his well-articulated protest against the dehumanizing tyranny of scientism, Bryan Appleyard writes:

> Science begins by saying it can answer only *this* kind of question and ends by claiming that *these* are the only questions that can be asked. Once the implications and shallowness of this trick are realized, fully realized, science will be humbled and we shall be free to celebrate our selves again.

And that should mean that science can become itself again rather than the quasi-religious repository of all our faith defined by the popularizers.[44]

When ethical issues become simply functions of medical technology, society becomes dehumanized and totalitarian. The dignity of human beings has been sacrificed to an allegedly "self-correcting" technical-scientific enterprise. That will never do. Morality is not reducible to technology. All sorts of horrors are medically feasible; that does not mean they should be allowed. Science itself cannot decide such matters because it has no adequate values. Science can tell us how to deprive human beings of their lives most efficiently or painlessly, but it cannot possibly tell us whether or when such measures ought to be taken. Society must decide such issues on independent, moral grounds—there is nothing in science or the scientific method that could possibly provide moral grounds or standards for respecting human dignity.

In a remarkable address about the scientist's moral responsibility, Popper referred to the oath he took when he graduated from the University of Vienna, an oath "which no doubt historically derives from the Hippocratic Oath."[45] Elsewhere he appealed to Kant's autonomy-principle.[46] In her interesting new interpretation of Kant's work, Susan Neiman has written: "Theoretical inquiry is a conditional good while moral action is not. The claim that morality is more important than science is simply rock-bottom. . . . Kant's claim that morality is more important than science is a moral one."[47]

Popper's defense of freedom against totalitarianism earned him the hatred of the Marxists, who blamed him for having "created 'ideological reserves' for the politics of contemporary imperialistic bourgeoisie."[48] Popper's best-known works on that theme are *The Poverty of Historicism*[49] and *The Open Society and Its Ene-*

mies.[50] Popper rejects so-called "laws of history" because they fail to do justice to the freedom and complexity of the human reality.

Although I do not have the documentation at hand, I clearly recall having read that Popper refused an invitation to serve as one of the editors of the humanist-oriented journal *Free Inquiry* on the grounds that he could not collaborate with B. F. Skinner, whose *Beyond Freedom and Dignity* assaulted the foundations of human dignity. Here, too, belongs that famous Cambridge confrontation between Popper and Wittgenstein, in which Popper insisted that the true object of philosophy is not an arcane realm of linguistic puzzles but the real, objective universe—and human morality to boot![51]

The overriding mandate requiring the ethical treatment of human beings as such is not derivable from any fact or proposition of science. It is, however, given in the human conscience (Romans 2:14–15). Science and the practice of it stand squarely under, not over, this moral reality. To the extent that society casts aside the moral constraints that even the anti-Christian philosopher Immanuel Kant regarded as the foremost object of reason, it sinks into a lingering self-destruction. Human society can, if need be, function without science but not without morality.

Concluding Observations

For the "young scientist" Popper had this advice: "Try to learn what people are discussing nowadays in science. Find out where difficulties arise, and take an interest in disagreements. These are the questions which you should take up."[52] One might add: "See what issues people are avoiding, and pursue those."

It is my own conviction that the most interesting scientific/philosophical problem today is that of the source of the prodigious amount of *information* (in the technical sense) represented by biological organisms. Consider the radical implications of Norbert Wiener's dictum: "Information is information, not matter or energy. No materialism which does not admit this can survive at the present day."[53]

If life is basically a vastly sophisticated information system—which cannot be doubted since the discovery of DNA—then it is not derivable simply from matter or energy! To quote the former atheist and present non-Christian Sir Fred Hoyle:

> The essence of his argument last week was that the information content of the higher forms of life is represented by the number $10^{40,000}$—representing the specificity with which some 2,000 genes, each of which might be chosen from 10^{20} nucleotide sequences of the appropriate length, might be defined. . . . The chance that higher life forms might have emerged in this way is comparable with the chance that "a tornado sweeping through a junk-yard might assemble a Boeing 747 from the materials therein." . . . Of adherents of biological evolution, Hoyle said that he was at a loss to understand "biologists' widespread compulsion to deny what seems to me to be obvious."[54]

Given the enormously far-reaching implications of the notion of "information," it is strange that there is not a great deal more scientific-philosophical exploration of it. Yet it is often ignored—for instance, in *The Oxford Companion to Philosophy* for 1995, which does not even have an entry under "information," though "chaos theory," for instance, is dutifully noted! With splendid publications such as William Dembski's *The Design Inference*[55] and Werner Gitt's *In the Beginning Was Information*,[56] there is some hope that the ramifications of the bio-information problem will begin to sink into our public consciousness.

To conclude, science is a gift of God—scientism is its malign distortion.

Notes

1. This chapter was delivered as a talk for the Cranach Institute Series on Science and Vocation on 7 November 2001.

2. Noretta Koertge, " 'New Age' Philosophies of Science: Constructivism, Feminism and Postmodernism," *British Journal for the Philosophy of Science* 51:4 (2000): 667–83. Koertege was citing David Stove, *Popper and After: Four Modern Irrationalists* (Oxford: Pergamon, 1982).

3. Karl Popper, *Conjectures and Refutations: The Growth of Scientific Knowledge* (New York: Harper Torch Books, 1968), 102.

4. Paul Arthur Schilpp, ed., *The Philosophy of Karl Popper* (La Salle, Ill.: Open Court, 1974), 2:977.

5. Popper, *Conjectures and Refutations*, 230.

6. Popper, *Conjectures and Refutations*, 229.

7. Karl Popper, *Objective Knowledge: An Evolutionary Approach* (Oxford: Clarendon, 1979), 13.

8. Popper, *Objective Knowledge*, 203.

9. Popper, *Conjectures and Refutations*, 99.

10. Popper, *Realism and the Aim of Science*, ed. W. W. Bartley III (Totowa, N.J.: Rowman & Littlefield, 1983), 116.

11. Schilpp, *Philosophy of Karl Popper*, 2:978.

12. Schilpp, *Philosophy of Karl Popper*, 1:14.

13. Stanley L. Jaki, *The Origin of Science and the Science of its Origin* (South Bend, Ind.: Regnery/Gateway, 1979), vii. See also Jaki, *The Road of Science and the Ways to God* (Chicago: University of Chicago Press, 1978).

14. F. M. Cornford, *Before and After Socrates* (Cambridge: Cambridge University Press, 1974), 3–4.

15. Popper, *Realism and the Aim of Science*, 110.

16. *The Oxford Dictionary of Quotations*, 3rd ed. (Oxford University Press, 1979), 378.

17. Frederick Suppe, ed. *The Structure of Scientific Theories* (Urbana: University of Illinois Press, 1977), 4.

18. Mary Hesse, *Revolutions and Reconstructions in the Philosophy of Science* (Bloomington: Indiana University Press), 1980.

19. Suppe, *Structure of Scientific Theories*, 13.

20. Alfred J. Ayer, *Language, Truth and Logic* (New York: Dover Publications, 1946), 107–8.

21. Popper, *Unended Quest: An Intellectual Autobiography* (La Salle, Ill.: Open Court, 1982), 88.

22. Popper, *The Logic of Scientific Discovery* (New York: Basic Books, 1959).

23. See Schilpp, *Philosophy of Karl Popper*, 1:134; 2:985.

24. *Nature*, 30 July 1981, 404.

25. Popper, *Objective Knowledge*, 185.

26. Popper, *Conjectures and Refutations*, 100.

27. Popper, *Conjectures and Refutations*, 114.

28. Schilpp, *Philosophy of Karl Popper*, 1:76.

29. Schilpp, *Philosophy of Karl Popper*, 1:122.

30. Sir John C. Eccles, *The Human Mystery* (Berlin: Springer-Verlag, 1979), 29–30.

31. Schilpp, *Philosophy of Karl Popper*, 1:484.

32. Popper, *Conjectures and Refutations*, 136.

33. Schilpp, *Philosophy of Karl Popper*, 1:488.

34. Schilpp, *Philosophy of Karl Popper*, 2:980.

35. Hans Rohrbach, *Naturwissenschaft, Weltbild, Glaube* (Wuppertal: R. Brockhaus, 1974), 76.

36. Rohrbach, *Naturwissenschaft, Weltbild, Glaube*, 43–53.

37. Werner Schaaffs, *Theology, Physics, Miracles*, trans. Richard L. Renfield (Washington: Canon, 1974), 25.

38. See "The Theology of the Cross," in Hermann Sasse, *We Confess Jesus Christ*, trans. Norman Nagel (St. Louis: Concordia, 1984), 36–54.

39. John Warwick Montgomery, *Cross, Constellation and Crucible: Lutheran Astrology and Alchemy in the Age of the Reformation* (Ottawa: Royal Society of Canada, 1963), 251.

40. Karl Popper and John Eccles, *The Self and Its Brain* (New York: Springer International: 1977).

41. Popper, *Unended Quest*, 18.

42. P. W. Atkins, "The Limitless Power of Science," in *Nature's Imagination*, ed. John Cornwell (Oxford: Oxford University Press, 1995), 131.

43. Jerry A. Fodor, Review of Peter Carruthers, and Andrew Chamberlain, eds., "Evolution and the Human Mind: Modularity, Language and Meta-Cognition," in *British Journal for the Philosophy of Science* 52 (2001): 623–28.

44. Bryan Appleyard, *Understanding the Present* (London: Picador, Pan Books, 1993), 249.

45. Paul Weingartner and Gerhard Zecha, eds., *Induction, Physics, and Ethics* (Dordrecht: D. Reidel, 1970), 325.

46. Popper, *Conjectures and Refutations*, 181ff.

47. Susan Neiman, *The Unity of Reason: Rereading Kant* (New York: Oxford University Press, 1994), 127.

48. Cited in Gerard Radnitzky, *Contemporary Schools of Metascience* (Chicago: Henry Regnery, 1973), 335 n. 212.

49. Karl Popper, *The Poverty of Historicism* (London: Routledge & Paul, 1961).

50. Popper, *The Open Society and Its Enemies*, vol. 2: The High Tide of Prophecy: Hegel, Marx and the Aftermath (Princeton, N.J.: Princeton University Press, 1971).

51. David Edmonds and John Edinow, *Wittgenstein's Poker* (New York: HarperCollins, 2001).

52. Popper, *Conjectures and Refutations*, 129.

53. Norbert Wiener, *Cybernetics, or Control and Communication in the Animal and the Machine* (Cambridge: MIT Press, 1948), 132.

54. Sir Fred Hoyle, *Nature*, 294 (12 November 1981): 105.

54. William A. Dembski, *The Design Inference* (Cambridge: Cambridge University Press, 1998).

56. Werner Gitt, *In the Beginning Was Information* (Bielefeld, Germany: Christliche Literatur-Verbreitung e. V.).

10

Science and
the Natural Law

WILLIAM POWERS

He set the earth on its foundations; it can never be
moved. You covered it with the deep as with a garment;
the waters stood above the mountains. But at your
rebuke the waters fled, at the sound of your thunder
they took to flight; they flowed over the mountains, they
went down into the valleys, to the place you assigned for
them. You set a boundary they cannot cross; never again
will they cover the earth. (Psalm 104:5–9)

Abstract

Inasmuch as science serves humanity, the scientist has an office.
This office has a function guided by a natural law. The office of
science, as any office, is established by God both to crucify the old
man and serve neighbor, either unwillingly under the Law, or

willingly under the Gospel. It is through the law of retribution, where disobedience to the natural law is temporally punished and obedience is temporally rewarded, that the scientist is taught the natural law and where service to one's neighbor is fulfilled. We examine the history of science through the eyes of three eminent historians of science: Thomas Kuhn, Larry Laudan, and Stanley Jaki. Through this examination, we will perceive the working of a natural law for science. Kuhn and Laudan are primarily concerned with describing the history of scientific theories and their method of evaluation. Because their chief focus is how science works, the picture provided of natural law is particularly associated with overall strategies for making progress, such as the need for a diverse pool of theories. Natural law is shown to affect this internal practice of human theory-making. Jaki, on the other hand, is principally concerned with the reality that underlies science, is necessary for its success, and is presumed by the scientist in the act of discovery. As such, what is revealed by the natural law is the imposition of a mind-independent, contingent, and intelligible reality on the scientist and scientific theories. With Jaki's emphasis on an external reality and its impact on the discovery of scientific theories, we especially find that aspect of the natural law that points humans to something beyond themselves, even to God.

Introduction

The office of science, as any office, is established by God for a dual purpose, functioning under both Law and Gospel. Under the law, "God compels man without the assent of his heart to serve others." This legalistic compulsion crucifies the old man, and by the conviction and despair of the Law, shows our need for a savior, yet cannot save us. However, under the Gospel, salvation is freely granted by grace through faith, and without compulsion, the new man in Christ "gives himself to the care of his neighbor, concerned about his well-being."[1] From the world's perspective, the establishment of the office of science presupposes that the aims of the office be perceived as potentially fulfilling certain higher communal values, namely, the preservation and prosperity of the community. Not just any human activity will be established as an office. The practice of science is a legitimate office today in the West. It is, however, not necessary that all societies at all times contain such an office. For science, or any office, to arise as an office it is necessary that a community's understanding of humankind and the world be such that the office is seen as a means for the preservation of and the welfare of the community, that is, the community must envision the office as meaningful labor.[2]

In this process of establishing an office, one begins with a general, perhaps ill-defined, need, the satisfaction of which entails a value or aim. In seeking to achieve that aim, one searches for a means to that end, a means that is fitted both to one's nature and the nature of the world.[3] Clearly one can at best find no other than such means, but it is possible to imagine and try those that will fail. This process, however, cannot go forward unless there is in place some measure of success or failure. We must have a means of knowing whether and to what degree we have obtained what we desire. Implicit in this search is the conviction or presumption that the world is orderly. If it is not orderly, we would not speak of means but of chance or luck. The search, then, is historical because we believe that today's events and our memories of them have something to do with yesterday's events. This means that our experience counts for something. Inasmuch as this process of discovery is accessible to our experience and faculties, it is natural.

In this natural process we encounter two kinds of laws: those we can choose to break and those we cannot break. Attempting to violate the law of gravity with unaided flight can result in more than a bruised ego. The inviolable laws, which we might call the laws of nature, are what we need to discover and employ to seek our ends. Equally important is another law, one that we are capable of violating. While we cannot choose to make bread with sand, we can choose to steal from our customers. It is this second law, this natural law, with which we are here concerned.

The natural law is moral because it is volitional. It is always associated with office because it is office that it seeks to preserve.[4] As Wingren reminds us, the office is the ethical agent.[5] It is God who works through office for the love of neighbor. We know this because it is office that binds and compels us. Breaking this law violates those purposes for which God established the office, and in breaking this law, there are consequences. These consequences may not be as immediate or universal as those attributed to breaking the laws of nature, but consequences occur in accordance with the law of retribution, which provides temporal rewards and punishments for obedience and disobedience respectively.[6] But it is not immediately clear to us what that natural law is because we resist it and because of our own inadequate knowledge of the world. Consequently, in seeking the means to our ends, we must not only obey this moral law but also discover it by the law of retribution. This process of discovery is itself, of course, bound by its own natural law, which will, should we violate it, result in a vain and fruitless search.

Office, were it not deliberately preserved, would decay through sin and lawlessness. This is the purpose of natural law and our institution of that law. That such decay can be seen as reform emphasizes that reform need not be progressive. However, at any given time it is not evident which reforms are good and which reforms are bad. As Wingren reminds us: "When we confront a concrete change on the earth, something new and revolutionary could well be the work of the devil, rather than God's work."[7] As a result, in its intention to preserve, office tends to resist change.

There is a dynamic, then, between what is presently the case and its reform, the reform being motivated positively by the law of retribution and negatively by the law of sin. There is, in addition, another law at work through the law of retribution: the law of stability, whereby no office is autonomous and isolated from all others.[8] All office is under compulsion not only to the demands of its own office but also to those of others. In this dynamic, stability demands that the office thrives without crippling the function of other offices, violation of which will be punished through the law of retribution, a violation of natural law. This implies that it is not only important to understand the natural law governing individual offices but also the natural law that is over all offices and engenders stability.

It is our intention to examine the history of science through the eyes of three eminent historians of science: Thomas Kuhn, Larry Laudan, and Stanley Jaki. Through this examination, we will perceive the working of a natural law for science. These three men see the history of science as supporting different philosophies of science. Crudely, Kuhn exhibits a relativist view of science, Jaki a realist perspective, and Laudan, lying somewhere between Kuhn and Jaki, a more rational, pragmatic view. This distinction between relativism and realism is important and worth understanding because it will likely influence the character of the office and its interaction with the natural law. A realist claims that there is an objective, mind-independent world and that our theories of the world, or aspects of them, can be true or nearly true.[9] Relativists deny this in varying degrees. They claim that in some sense science is relative to something: a community, a language, a model, and the like. Therefore, science cannot be said to be objective. Relativism is a type of skepticism. It starts with our perspective and cannot see how to get beyond that perspective. Realism, on the other hand, claims there is something transcendent about us and our knowledge. This debate is principally about the nature of humanity's knowledge. Pragmatism is more concerned with the utility of our ideas and practices in making measurable progress toward our goals. It is important for the pragmatist to determine whether an idea or practice makes a concrete difference in our lives than whether it is objectively true.[10]

In any case, no one denies that there is such an office as science and that it does something. And whatever that "something" is, science does it fairly well. It is this doing of something and doing it well that is under the natural law. It does not necessarily matter to the natural law what we think about what we are doing. What matters is the sense of doing this something well, some sense of doing it poorly, and that in the trying we know frustration, failure, and conviction. Although natural law works in relativist, pragmatist, and realist worlds, the manner it which it works is different in each, as we shall see.

Kuhn's Relativism

In the 1960s Thomas Kuhn's seminal work *The Structure of Scientific Revolutions* changed the thinking of many about science. In this book Kuhn describes science by means of a paradigm. A paradigm is a snapshot of science at a given time or at least within a certain community of scientists. Broadly, a paradigm consists in what is necessary for a community to go about its business. According to Kuhn, this would include a shared language, behavior, and commitments. The commitments include certain shared values, goals, methods, presumptions, and exemplars.[11] The fact that those who share a common paradigm have much in common does not imply that they are all in agreement. Shared values do not imply that everyone applies them identically.[12] It only implies that they can converse, argue, and persuade. They know how to go forward, despite their disagreement, and what it would take to settle the disagreement.

Kuhn sees the history of science as oscillating between periods of normal science and those of revolutionary science. During periods of normal science, the paradigm remains more or less static, and scientists work out the implications of the particular paradigm. It is a period of puzzle solving. Like puzzles, science actively pursues problems for which it expects to find solutions.[13] The paradigm serves to establish a context of shared commitments within which a class of paradigm-relative problems are studied with the expectation of finding solutions.[14] During periods of normal science, a sense of confidence and progress in attacking and solving problems reigns. However, during periods of revolutionary science, competing paradigms exist simultaneously. Problem solving comes to a halt, doubt reigns, and consensus breaks down.[15] Rarely can more than one paradigm endure for any length of time in a given field of study.[16] Eventually a new paradigm is established, and normal science begins again. The transition from normal science to revolutionary science occurs through the recognition of anomalies, "the recognition that nature has somehow violated the paradigm-induced expectations that govern normal science."[17] That is, when results are obtained that are unexpected by the theories and methods of the paradigm, some modification is called for. Often such adjustments can be accomplished within a particular paradigm. However, as the seriousness of unexplained anomalies increases, crisis grows, inducing a search for a paradigm better equipped to deal with those anomalies. When that new paradigm begins to show signs of solving the problems of the old paradigm, the scene is set for a paradigm shift.

Although Kuhn believes that paradigm shifts often result in a science that is in some sense improved, he does not think that a shift occurs because the new paradigm is clearly and convincingly superior. This is because he thinks comparisons between the two paradigms are not sufficient. They are what Kuhn refers to as "incommensurable."[18] Briefly, this is because different paradigms have generally different aims and standards for science.[19] The standards science uses to test and evaluate theories are, according to Kuhn, ambiguous and often inconsistent. As a result, a different application or prioritization of the standards will result in different conclusions. Moreover, there is often a problem of meaning variance, whereby similar terms can mean different things in the context of different theories[20] and more than one theory can fit the data.[21] Hence, according to Kuhn, "the competition between paradigms is not the sort of battle that can be resolved by proofs."[22] It is, rather, as if "the proponents of competing paradigms practice their trades in different worlds."[23] Kuhn, then, sees these scientific revolutions as involving large and discrete shifts in paradigms, which is why he speaks of "conversion" or a "gestalt switch."[24] It is not that there are not good reasons to support the new paradigm; instead, those reasons are insufficient to warrant the shift.[25] Kuhn concludes:

> [P]aradigm debates are not really about relative problem solving ability, though for good reasons they are usually couched in those terms. Instead, the issue is which paradigm should in the future guide research on problems many of which neither competitor can yet claim to resolve completely. A decision between alternate ways of practicing science is called for, and in the circumstances that decision must be based less on past achievement than on future promise . . . A decision of that kind can only be made by faith.[26]

Nevertheless, Kuhn thinks that the history of science evidences progress in greater accuracy of prediction and increasing numbers of problems solved.[27] However, he recognizes that what is determined to be the solution to a problem is paradigm-dependent; thus in some sense the perception of such progress is "self-fulfilling."[28] What Kuhn rejects is any absolutist notion of scientific progress: "That there is some one full, objective, true account of nature and that the proper measure of scientific achievement is the extent to which it brings us closer to that ultimate goal."[29] What Kuhn favors instead is more akin to a nonteleological Darwinian evolution of scientific theories.[30]

In looking to Kuhn for a manifestation of a natural law for science, one cannot overlook the priority of the paradigm. We cannot do science without one, yet Kuhn asserts that all paradigms are historically bound. We would like to think that somehow movement from one paradigm to another means something is learned and that in some sense paradigms have some cumulative history. But Kuhn does not intend to assure us of this. He views the history of science more as a blind, purposeless, evolutionary process. There is change, but to compare one period with another is difficult and inadvisable.

Because all judgments are formulated relative to the paradigm and the transition from one paradigm to the next is disconnected, this is no objectivist view of science's progress. It is, perhaps, more our view, not unlike what we might expect of sinful man guided by a natural law: a drunkard staggering between two walls, bouncing back and forth between the two. Although Kuhn is willing to speak of a type of progress toward increasing complexity, it is not a progress toward anything.[31] A paradigm is, nevertheless, indispensable because it guides and orders our comings and our goings.

According to this notion of progress, the scientist has some notion of what to do and what not to do, but only during times of normal science. During times of revolutionary science, on the other hand, everything appears broken and no way appears clear. If a natural law is in effect, it is more to tell us that we have gone wrong than to tell us how to find our way again. There apparently is no decisive way to adequately adjudicate between competing paradigms.

Despite the darkness of revolutionary periods, during periods of normal science scientists learn that progress is made if they remain faithful to the paradigm. Thus the scientist gains confidence in the paradigm by success and the continued expectation of success. The individual scientist and the community of scientists know how to proceed in the context of their paradigm. But the scientist's commitment is not merely to the various beliefs associated with the paradigm; but also to the progress of that paradigm and to working out in greater detail its scope and precision.[32] Thus during periods of normal science, the scientist trusts in the fruitfulness of the office. It is, indeed, through the shared commitment to the paradigm that consensus is achieved and progress made. In this way, the community recognizes and acknowledges that it is a community and dependent on that community for the success of the office.

Moreover, as scientists look back over the history of science, they recognize that this activity, requiring perseverance and patience, while not drawn in glory, was necessary and invaluable for the progress not only of the historically bound paradigm in which they work but also in laying the foundations for future paradigms and the greater progress of science. According to Kuhn, though it is not the intention of normal science to uncover novelty and anomaly, history has shown that it does. This revelation is only possible because of diligent and careful work.[33]

Today, looking back, the resistance to these revolutions of science seems foolish. These revolutions mark the advent of the Copernican revolution in astronomy, the Newtonian revolution in mechanics, the rise of modern electromagnetic theory, and the Einsteinian revolution. Everything that we today regard as the great advances in science originally were resisted with vigor. Kuhn would have us, however, be judicious with our criticism of such scientists because not only did they not see the great advances these "paradigm shifts" would accomplish, but, moreover, it is not easy to find a paradigm that will fit nature.[34] Hence, having found one, they are difficult to give up.

Instead, Kuhn argues that, at their inception, the advances of these new paradigms were not nearly so clear. He argues that resistance to them was always defensible,[35] and that paradigm-dependent standards of theory evaluation undermined any clear resolution.[36] When to resist the new and remain faithful to the old, and when to abandon the old and embrace the new is never certain. Too great a tendency to abandon the old paradigm and pursue every new possibility will cut short the necessary progress of normal science. Yet too great a commitment to the old paradigm makes it a sacrosanct dogma and a dead science. According to Kuhn, the darkness and uncertainty of our decision is made more manifest by our inability to know when we are closer to the truth or even if there is such a thing.[37] All we have to guide us is a sense that the problems we see in our understanding of the world are being addressed. When, as a result, the world seems more intelligible to us, we think we are making progress. But what relationship that bears to how the world "really is" is unknowable. Yet some scientists did pursue the new paradigms because if they did not, their success would never have been realized. For this reason Kuhn concludes that a diversity of responses to the crisis is essential for the success of science.[38] In either case, whether scientists chose to remain faithful to the old paradigm or to pursue the new one, they remained faithful to office, and that faithfulness has, over time, preserved and prospered the office of science.

Kuhn's views regarding the occupation of science bear some resemblance to Luther's view of office. Luther believes that office must be both free and bound: "In earthly orders God and the devil are both actively at work. Therefore these orders never stand still. They are always corrupted because men depart from God's will. But they are improved and reformed anew by God."[39] The orders or offices must be free to change. They cannot be fixed by rigid rules that govern their execution because office must be free to seek the greatest benefit for our neighbor.[40] Despite the need for freedom in office, however, Luther is wary of reform because "he is convinced that the devil is still present as change for the better is made."[41] Sinful man will use reform as an excuse to abandon office, to be free of the demands for love of neighbor, and to "make himself comfortable for his own sake."[42] For example, modern cosmology, confronted with understanding the beginning of the universe, has seriously considered literal creation out of nothing, an explicit denial of causality; and this because it refuses to acknowledge the limits of its office.[43]

For Luther, as well as for Kuhn, there is essential tension in office. For Luther that tension is between the law of love and that of sin, while for Kuhn there is an essential tension between divergent and convergent thinking, between a freedom to doubt, reject, and "go off in different directions" and one that accepts and is bound by tradition.[44] The law of love requires freedom to act, while the law of sin requires constraint. For Luther this tension serves both for the love of neighbor and the conviction and despair of humanity.[45] For Kuhn, however, it serves merely for "scientific advance."[46] In either case, the working out of the office is in doubt, especially during times of crisis when the tension is at its greatest. For Luther this uncertainty is inherent in the hiddenness of God and "the inevitability of [one's] desperation,"[47] wherein one must take a "decisive position, despite the fact that he is bound to the limits of the hour and unable to survey anything completely."[48] While for Kuhn, uncertainty is inherent in the nature of science, of mankind, and of the world, which is only to say that office and the natural law are masks of God.

For Kuhn science is blind, trapped in an historically bound context, yet it appears to progress in some sense. Why it does so and what it says of humankind and the world, Kuhn wonders but does not answer.[49] Perhaps he thinks those questions can go unanswered and science will still progress. That is, he may believe they are outside the scope of natural law. When we look at the work of Stanley Jaki, we will take up these questions in earnest.

Laudan's Rational Pragmatism

Larry Laudan, an historian, philosopher of science, and a student of Kuhn's, has considerably refined and criticized Kuhn's understanding of the progress of science. It is Laudan's intention to save science from the more radical aspects of Kuhn's relativism. Although he agrees with Kuhn that we cannot speak of science as a true or nearly true knowledge of the world, he rejects the view that science is thereby irrational or nonprogressive. Instead, Laudan believes that science can, on the basis of its own internal standards, objectively and rationally choose between competing theories.

Laudan offers a richer, more comprehensible, and less monolithic view of science. According to Laudan, the rigidity of Kuhn's conception of a paradigm is the cause for his mistaken incommensurability hypothesis. Kuhn believes that normal science is marked by the dominance of a single paradigm, which changes holistically in all its aspects simultaneously (i.e., in aims, methods, and accepted facts).[50] In place of paradigms, Laudan speaks of research traditions. Research traditions are more flexible and continuous than paradigms, though they share many of the same characteristics: a common belief regarding the nature of the world and methodology for constructing and testing theories.[51] However, despite some common commitments, "there are scarcely any interesting set of doctrines which characterizes any one of these research traditions [e.g., Aristotelianism, Cartesianism, Darwinism, or Newtonianism] throughout the whole of its history."[52] Research traditions respond to anomalies and crises for the most part by simply modifying some core assumptions of the tradition. Yet they remain sensibly part of the same tradition.[53] Laudan says: "There is much continuity in an evolving research tradition. From one stage to the next, there is a preservation of most of the crucial assumptions of the research traditions."[54]

Laudan replaces Kuhn's holistic view of paradigm shift with a more gradual and sequential model. The model of paradigm change that Laudan suggests—the reticulated model of scientific rationality—represents a "unitraditional" change.[55] He believes this model explains most paradigm shifts and both consensus and dissensus in the history of science. In this model, aims serve to justify methods, while aims must be realizable by methods; methods are used to justify accepted theories and facts, while theories constrain methods; and theories and aims must be consistent. All three—aims, methods, and theories—might change independently, thereby affecting the remaining two. In this sense, the model is "unitraditional." According to Laudan, Kuhn has presumed a more hierarchical model, whereby theories are resolved by methods and methods by aims. As a result, there is no means by which values and aims can be resolved, producing the Kuhnian incommensurablilty. Thus it is the rational revisablility of aims and the possibility of incremental change that makes Laudan's model of scientific change more commensurable than Kuhn's.

The rigidity of Kuhn's paradigmatic view of science is not, according to Laudan, the only cause for his thesis of incommensurability. It is Kuhn's notion of progress itself that is problematic. Laudan fundamentally agrees with Kuhn that the progress of science is in some sense related to the problem-solving ability of science. However, Laudan believes that Kuhn's notion of what is a problem for science is too restrictive. For Kuhn the progress of science is exclusively empirical, where "the only progressive modifications in a theory are those which increase the scope of its empirical claims."[56] With this narrow view of scientific advance, Kuhn views many changes in science to be caused by "a mixture of objective and subjective factors"[57] and, therefore, seemingly illegitimate.

Laudan, however, broadens the problems relevant to science to include conceptual problems, perhaps in part because he can see no reason to exclude them on the basis of utility. Among these conceptual problems are consistency with other scientific theories and disciplines, inconsistencies between the aims and methods of science, and conflicts with extra-scientific views, such as those in philosophy and theology. Unlike Kuhn's more monolithic conception of a paradigm, Laudan's understanding of the interactions between research traditions is more fluid and dynamic.[58] What appears to Kuhn as nonrational paradigm shifts is to Laudan the rational aim of resolving relevant empirical and conceptual problems.

Laudan, moreover, argues that Kuhn and others misconstrue the legitimate types of scientific activity, further confounding the intelligibility of science. In accordance with Kuhn's more rigid and monolithic conception, normal science is conceived as dedicated exclusively to the solution of the empirical problems of a particular paradigm. In this context, a theory or paradigm is accepted or rejected. Laudan agrees that this is one of the modalities of scientific activity. He would, of course, extend it to include not only empirical problems but also conceptual problems. But Laudan additionally argues that

> scientists often claim that a theory, even if unacceptable, deserves investigation, or warrants further elaboration. The logic of acceptance and rejection is simply too restrictive to represent this range of cognitive attitudes. Unless we are prepared to say that such attitudes are beyond rational analysis [as Kuhn might argue]—in

which case most of science is non-rational—we need an account of evidential support which will permit us to say when theories are worthy of further investigation and elaboration.[59]

Laudan's account of scientific progress distinguishes the activities of acceptance and pursuit. The acceptance or rejection of a theory or research tradition is evaluated on the basis of its effectiveness to solve problems. A theory or tradition that is more effective, in some weighted sense, at solving the most empirical and conceptual problems is accepted relative to another and judged to be of greater adequacy.

Distinct from the notion of adequacy is that of progress. A theory or tradition that is most progressive exhibits the greatest rate of problem-solving. "It is always rational," says Laudan, "to pursue any research tradition [or theory] which has a higher rate of progress than its rivals (even if the former has a lower problem-solving effectiveness)."[60] Hence, it is not surprising that scientists might be simultaneously pursuing incompatible traditions, accepting some, while pursuing others, and that the coexistence of conflicting traditions is common, with the character and fortunes of these traditions constantly evolving.[61] With this dynamic perspective on the historical flow of science, Laudan sees so-called scientific revolutions as less revolutionary than Kuhn. Laudan argues that what we see manifested instead is that revolutions grow out of theories and traditions that were previously pursued for their potential until their development could no longer be ignored relative to the adequacy of the prevailing tradition.[62] In this way, Laudan observes, "scientific revolutions are not so revolutionary and normal science not so normal as Kuhn's analysis would suggest."[63]

Laudan's position, as he describes it, is between positivism and relativism.[64] By this he means that science is not derived, as the positivists thought, by some strict logical analysis of the empirical data. The making and accepting of theories is more complex and inferential. But this does not imply, as Kuhn and the relativists believe, that science is irrational and incomprehensible. Both the positivists' and the relativists' response that followed are wrong about how science works. One of the mistakes that both make is in constraining theory evaluation exclusively to empirical problems. Instead, scientists use a broad array of conceptual and empirical criteria in theory evaluation.[65]

Laudan's description of how science works and of its natural law is different from Kuhn's. Scientists employ a wide range of rational criteria in guiding their problem-solving activities. Kuhn had been misled in his conclusions by constraining the set of rational criteria too narrowly. According to Laudan's view of the natural law, problems and their resistance to solution punish science, while the solution of problems reward it. Scientists respond to these problems in a more complex manner than they do in Kuhn's description. They more freely modify key elements of the tradition they are working in or rationally explore other available traditions. According to this view of the natural law, scientists dwell in a highly critical, freely changing, and adaptive environment, committed ultimately to and guided by the goal of solving a complex array of problems. One imagines, then, in accordance with that law, that science would stall were scientists not to act in this way but instead to act in a more rigid and less pragmatic fashion.

Laudan's pragmatic attitude toward the working of science is seen in his view of truth. He argues that if science is to prosper, it must have a workable problem-solving model. In particular, this means that we must be able to tell when the standards we employ to evaluate a theory are being satisfied. Because Laudan believes that we have no means of measuring the truth or relative truth of a theory, we ought to abandon it as an unworkable standard.[66] His conclusion would be that were we not to do that, we would be in violation of the natural law, a natural law that bars us from recognizing the truthfulness of our theories. This is so because Laudan believes science works according to a natural law that rewards problem-solving, not truth-finding. Progress is measured in problem-solving, not in increasing truthfulness. Laudan's message, and the one that the success of science affirms, is that our knowledge of the world is fallible. We have no absolute measures of that knowledge, but we do have internal measures, such as empirical accuracy, coherence, and simplicity. These are standards that work because we can apply them to solve our problems and generate human knowledge. In this way, the office of science serves its neighbors.

Where there is labor, there is frustration and a recognition of inadequacy. What science labors to produce, according to Laudan and Kuhn, is the solution of problems. Inasmuch as we are frustrated and struggle in this endeavor, we know our weakness. This is the conviction, the cross, the office engenders according to God's purposes. For Kuhn's scientist, this cross is seemingly more difficult to bear than for Laudan's scientist. In the former case, scientists ought never forget that their knowledge of the world is fragile. The progression of their office is doubtful and the utility of their knowledge dependent on the prevailing paradigm, which is a tentative and fragile cradle. Although scientists may naively rejoice during times of normal science, they are brought low during times of crisis and revolution.

By contrast, for Laudan's scientists the load appears light. Of course, they must still labor and struggle, but they have a higher view of their success and their struggle appears less tragic. Because they are more pragmatic and less dogmatic, they are less bound and less committed to a particular way of going forward. Instead, the way forward is guided by relatively simple utilitarian aims. In Kuhn's description, commitment to a paradigm is more strong, more dogmatic, almost, despite Kuhn's claims, as if the scientist were seeking some best or true paradigm. After all, if one believes in an absolute knowledge, one does not give up one's notion of it as easily as if one thought there were no such thing. If it is not the truth of the paradigm, then at least some form of love is reflected in this attachment. Kuhn identifies this resistance to paradigm shift with the difficulties associated with paradigm evaluation, but perhaps it is the quest for truth or some form of love of the ideas themselves that underscores the uncertainty of paradigm evaluation, making it all the more tragic because it belies the pragmatism Laudan finds in science.

If this is true, it may well be that what Kuhn has unearthed for the natural law of science is that the scientist must be something of a realist, in agreement with Jaki and despite Kuhn's relativist leanings. Moreover, the decision to go forward or resist is for a Kuhnian scientist a mixture of sin and pride with a natural law that works painful progress by dedicated commitment. Indeed, it is possible that it is just through this prideful resistance that the scientist is brought low through the collapse of all that is so dearly held.

Laudan, on the other hand, believes that scientists who are obedient to the natural law know when to bend and do so willingly and rationally because they are not so committed to a way of doing things as to the solution of problems, no matter from where they may arise. One wonders, however, whether it is that scientists in Laudan's world are willing to risk less than those in Kuhn's, and whether by risking less they are more willing to abandon a theory or tradition than those in Kuhn's. As a result, through this less dogmatic, more intelligible, and more pragmatic commitment, less progress might be made, in violation of the natural law. If this is the case, it is indeed odd that the relativist, if that is what the Kuhnian scientist is, may be closer to God than the more assured pragmatist. The relativist may cling desperately to his or her fragile paradigm as the sole beacon of light in an otherwise dark world, as one might cling to a friend, while the pragmatist, finding no further utility, will more readily abandon the paradigm for another.

Jaki and the Middle Road of Science

Stanley Jaki—a Benedictine priest, historian of science, and contemporary of Kuhn—might be called a "plain realist." He is not so much concerned with whether the entities of theories bear a one-to-one correspondence with reality[67] or whether its theories are "ontologically exact" as that there is a firm commitment to a plain reality: the existence of certain fundamental entities, including that of mind-independent objects, a coherent universe, free wills, and minds. What this evidences is a concern for the importance of philosophy, metaphysics, and ontology as the starting point in the making of science. But it is not a philosophy or metaphysics that constrains reality to the mind's own fancy but one in which the objectivity of reality can live out its own autonomy:[68] "Not to start with things is to make things subservient to one's learned whim and fancy."[69] Fundamental to Jaki's approach to reality is the "unconditional registering of particular things,"[70] of objects that *object*, a registering to which one must continually return for fear of losing sight of what is most alive in our theories: objective reality.[71]

Science is the "quantitative study of the quantitative aspects of things."[72] But clearly knowledge and science cannot be derived from quantities and numbers alone. Although "empirical reality first reveals itself by its quantitative properties,"[73] unless there is a fundamental coherence of that reality beneath the numbers and the mind is able to discover it, it will never be found. What is more, even if it is true, unless it is believed, no one will seek it. Science, then, "presupposes philosophy instead of providing it."[74] Science is a child of philosophy, but not just any philosophy, because science, knowing only quantities, cares not to ponder the nature of that reality that lies behind those quantities but only to presume it.[75] Science's business is only the quantitative aspects of matter. Of the nonquantitative, such as freedom and purpose, it can say nothing but only presume it.[76] This means science is blind without metaphysics to illumine the reality it seeks to sensibly quantify. Lacking that illumination, it cannot find its way through quantities back to reality,[77] resulting ultimately in "blind alleys" or stillbirths.

It is Jaki's aim to reveal the true nature of science and the many "blind alleys" into which science has gone because it started with false metaphysics. He argues that Kuhn, for one, has completely missed the fact that the great scientific revolutions "were sustained by this belief in an objective world and in an objective account of nature."[78] It is this, the common belief in an "objective, orderly, and contingent world,"[79] that has served as "a major propellant of intellectual and scientific history,"[80] making of science something objective and unified, not the "parceling of it into as many sciences as there are 'scientific revolutions.'"[81]

What Jaki finds is that "the most successful cultivators of science were driven toward that epistemological middle road,"[82] or a "moderate realism,"[83] which lies between idealism and empiricism, between an unwarranted exaltation of the mind over that of empirical observation, and an unwarranted exaltation of the evidence over that of the mind. Jaki writes: "[S]cientists always wanted to know something that had a strict connection with things."[84] Idealists, however, dissolve the object into ideas; empiricists prohibit the object from revealing what is intelligible in it. The idealist, starting with ideas, chokes off reality, never giving it sufficient autonomy to speak for itself; the empiricist, only knowing sensations, never unleashes the mind's inferential capability to know what is beyond mere observation.[85] Thus idealism is hindered by too much *a priorism* and empiricism by too little metaphysics. In both cases, it is too little reality that produces a stillbirth.

According to Jaki, science requires the conjunction of two hostile ideas: the radical contingency of the world and the rationality of the world. Scientists, especially the great ones, have always relied on two central metaphysical presumptions: "One is the existence of a world intrinsically ordered in all its parts and consistent in all its interactions. The other is the existence of a human mind capable of understanding such a world in an ever more comprehensive manner."[86] That the world is lawful implies that its behavior is ordered, predictive, and, in some sense, rational. More than this, science presumes that the world is more than a collection of objects, even objects with natures but otherwise uncorrelated. Science presumes that there is a universe, "the strict totality of consistently interacting things."[87] It presumes that matter behaves everywhere in the same way over space and time. Otherwise, there could be no laws. The autonomy of the world, however, implies that to know the world one must start with the world. The world, then, is both like us because its behavior is rational, and unlike us because it is autonomous; and it being like us is important. For how else might we expect to be able to know it at all? Knowing the world entails that we can act purposefully and freely to understand it with our minds.

This conjunction of metaphysical commitments denies any form of *a priorism* in which we, believing the world is like us, think we can know it better without looking. Where *a priorism* is adopted, it is founded on prior metaphysical commitments. Pantheism, for example, cannot imagine a creation that is both lawful and autonomous, one that is like us and not like us. For, since in pantheism everything is alike, if the world were lawful, we would have some expectation of being able to figure it out on an *a priori* basis.[88] Moreover, in pantheism or any divinized nature, "either all is free or there is no freedom at all."[89] Where there is no freedom, everything is determined and there is no place for the scientist and science. Where everything is free, the world is unpredictable.[90]

Science presumes a type of dualism that is consistent with Christianity: a free creation out of nothing by the Logos, God Incarnate, making the creation both contingent because it is freely done and lawful because He created it, cared for it, dwelled in it, and like us is fully man.[91] That dualism includes both a creation and a Creator, the universe and something outside it, and a history with a beginning and an end. It is consistent with the presumption of both a physical, lawful universe and a human nature that transcends that universe. Dualism, in this sense, denies also materialism and physicalism. If there is only matter, then what of purpose, free will, and minds? If we do not freely pursue understanding, can we rightly believe to have any understanding at all? Not only physicalism, but any conception of a universe that denies a Creator outside of it, one who creates it freely from nothing, engenders a diminished sense of contingency, surprise, and wonder, and an increased sense that we can know that universe fully. For in that case, there is nothing more to know and we are part of all that is. In such a universe there can be no conception of free will. Either all is free or nothing is. Either all is mind or there is no mind, meaning there is no coherent universe at all. Either we can know all or nothing at all. Dualism, however, affirms otherwise: There are individual minds and things that are not minds, and those minds can know the other.

What the mind-independence of the world entails is that "what physics looks for is the interconnectedness and coordination of nature and not merely some purely mental constructs having no relation to nature."[92] There is a real world with a real physics, and that world and its physics is independent of our minds and constructs. This is true even if our theoretical constructs should appear contradictory and inadequate for the task, as they seem to be regarding the supposed wave-particle dualism of matter. The fundamental recognition that "objects object" and keep objecting whether the mind pays attention to them or not[93] is elemental to our understanding and experience of the world, though we have no direct experience of that underlying reality. The quantities and measurements of science merely point to that reality. Jaki says:

> To know the real is already a recognition of causality, insofar as objects activate the mind, instead of minds activating objects. . . . The recognition that, apart from shaping this or that bit of reality, man cannot create it, because man can know that it exists in utter independence of him, is the ultimate basis for asserting the truth of causality . . . . Science . . . is never about causality, not even about reality as such. Science merely presupposes reality in order to make meaningful its special work about the quantitative aspects of reality.[94]

> The science of physics knows both enormously much and enormously little about the material world, because it can only know its quantitative properties. Science becomes involved in an identity crisis only when it ignores its own methods or when it lets philosophers, eager to promote their agnosticism and subjectivism, take over as the spokesman of science.[95]

Science knows enormously much because there is no end to its measuring, but it knows enormously little because quantities and measurements say nothing of what stands below—of substance, natures, and universals. Yet where these are denied, science can say nothing of any thing. Those philosophers and spokesmen of science that Jaki decries are men such as Kuhn and Laudan. This is not because either denies the existence of an objective world. They do not.[96] Rather, at best they underestimate that objectivity and our ability to know it and focus more on the internal and subjective problems of theory acceptance, which for them is not related to an objective and true metaphysics and ontology. This is because they are more interested in the manner in which science works than in the nature of science and what it says about the mind's ability to know something.[97]

"In order to do justice to science," Jaki asserts, "one has to render to the mind what is of the mind."[98] The mind is that entity that grasps the universal in the particular—strictly speaking, an inference—not a necessity, neither physically nor logically.[99] "Science is not the source of the notion of the universe and of man's intellectual trust in its reality."[100] It is the mind that integrates our disjointed sensory experience, even to inferring the existence of a universe.[101] The mind is what is responsible for the recognition of causality in a mere succession of events.[102] It is neither trapped inside the head, unable to know anything outside it, as in some Cartesian doubt, nor is it wholly limited to what is given to it by way of sensory impressions. Instead, the mind is capable of knowing what is intelligible in the particular. In this sense, the mind, more than merely thinking, knows. Thinking merely manipulates ideas; knowing speaks of that mysterious relationship without which all our talk is nonsense, a relationship between our ideas and a mind-independent reality.

Of itself, science, because it is a mere measurement of quantities, knows nothing of the mind, though it must presume its existence. Jaki argues that historicist accounts, such as those of Kuhn, that urge scientists to envision their enterprise as "a chain of disconnected visions or Gestalts,"[103] undermine the progress of science that they seek to explore. By making the notion of scientific progress meaningless, "it can hardly have a genuine appeal to great scientific discoverers."[104] What Kuhn's description of the history of science reveals is a "distrust in the ability of the mind,"[105] a distrust that is not warranted given the record in science of the mind's triumph. Although, as Jaki indicates, Kuhn makes reference to the genius of Galileo in making his discoveries, "about that genius, which through its intellectual exploits makes discoveries and through discoveries, science, not a word more was said in *The Structure of Scientific Revolutions*."[106]

Although philosophical discussions regarding the nature of science and its methods and the rationale for the acceptance and pursuit of theories have their place, Jaki emphasizes that what ought not be forgotten is that "discovery is the soul of science."[107] Without discovery there is no science. Discovery is dependent on the existence of minds, free wills, and purpose—none of which are known by science but are nonetheless evident metaphysical reality.[108]

Of particular importance for the role of mind in science is the relationship between the external world and the realm of ideas. According to Jaki:

> Science is inseparable from that process of comprehending which is conscious experience tying the real world and the knower into a unity. Once this tie is slighted, one is left either with solipsism or with physicalism. On the basis of the former one can build up oneself but not a world, on the basis of physicalism one will not have a physics which is a *comprehension* of the world.[109]

That creative process in which the facts are converted into a coherent, rational unity is, according to Jaki, a wonder that is in some sense transcendent. It cannot be understood in terms of, nor reduced to, physicalist or materialist descriptions. Indeed, "wonderment" is at the heart of scientific understanding.[110] Deeply seated in that understanding is an appreciation for the "miracle" that the profound ordered contingency of the world can be grasped by the human mind.[111] To undermine this surprising ability of the human mind, as physicalism does, is also to undermine the conviction humans have in their ability to know the world and thereby to undermine the pursuit of science.

According to Kuhn and Laudan, the natural law manifests itself through the solution of problems and anomalies. Because, for Kuhn, commitments to a way of proceeding are more rigid and complete, change is more painful than for Laudan, who sees change as occurring more gradually and with less trauma because commitments are more varied and diverse. Within these structures, science will progress in some sense by solving more problems.

This is what is fixed through time: man's pursuit of the solutions to problems. The emphasis is on justifying or explaining changes in science. Clearly, there must be something objective, or mind-independent, about that pursuit, for we do not desire this resistance to our understanding. But of this next to nothing is said. Both Kuhn and Laudan are interested in this pursuit, and they wish to explain its coherence or rationality. For them it seems more like a Cartesian enterprise, where none of us can get outside our own head to speak of something real outside of it. Because we cannot do so, only what goes on inside our head is spoken of.

Instead of traditions and the like, Jaki speaks of "blind allies." Science goes down a blind alley when it deviates from Jaki's middle road, that is, when it fails to abide by its metaphysical commitments and the methodology consistent with that fundamental metaphysics. This perspective is quite different from that of Kuhn and Laudan. A paradigm or research tradition is what one sees from the outside, but a blind alley is the experience of the discoverer. Kuhn and Laudan have both missed the discoverer and that reality that upholds his act of discovery.

This distinction is important, Jaki insists, because without a discoverer there is no science. Yet the discoverer, not being quantifiable, is outside of science. The natural law, then, is manifest at the level of the paradigm and the research tradition, but it is experienced at the level of the discoverer. One ought not expect to have a complete picture of science without an understanding of the discoverer. If the natural law's intention is not only to guide one's behavior but also to convict and save, can one expect to have an understanding of the natural law without an understanding of man? Jaki sees this understanding contained within an understanding of free will, purposeful activity, and the mind, none of which can be grasped by science. Were man a mere machine, even a supercomputer, could we speak of science at all?

There is hardly a word in Kuhn and Laudan about such concerns. Indeed, Laudan argues that if we are interested in the "evolution of research traditions," we ought not be so concerned with the processes by which ideas are generated but with the way in which those ideas themselves were received.[112] It is from the perspective of theory evaluation that both Kuhn[113] and Laudan object to realist concerns for truth. "We apparently do not have any way of knowing for sure (or even with some confidence)," argues Laudan, "that science is true, or probable, or that it is getting closer to the truth. Such aims are utopian, in the literal sense that we can never know whether they are being achieved. . . . They are not very helpful if our object is to explain how scientific theories are (or should be) evaluated."[114] Jaki's response probably would not, perhaps surprisingly, be one of total disagreement. He would agree that, with ever more complex mathematical theories of the physical world, the relationship between the terms of those theories and physical reality has become increasingly tenuous.[115] But that does not imply that truth is a useless measure. There are still some things of which one is certain. For example, Jaki declares the principle of complementarity—in which the wavelike properties of subatomic material and their particlelike properties were to be considered as complementary—to be an evasion of fundamental metaphysical reality. Although no one could grasp how anything could be both a wave and a particle, the principle counseled disregard for the apparent contradiction.

Thereby, counseling that we disregard that our theories are about something; and to deny this is to deny that our science must conform, if it is to be about reality, with what we believe to be fundamentally true about that reality.[116]

Theory evaluation is, according to Jaki, distinct from the creation of those theories. For it is only in the creation of the theory that the metaphysical reality that stands behind the measurements is preeminent. Once the theory is created, the connection with that reality is severed,[117] and the theory becomes no more than mathematics: a correlation of quantities.[118] It is just for this reason that theories can be accepted as well by realists and anti-realists.[119] Indeed, it might very well be that because Kuhn and Laudan are concerned principally with theory evaluation that they find metaphysics, reality, and truth so seemingly unimportant. What concerns Jaki is that such ideas derived from historical or sociological analysis may descend to the discoverer, thereby producing yet another blind alley. For it is at the level of the discoverer that such metaphysical commitments are alive.

In moving from Kuhn through Laudan to Jaki science finds itself ever more drawn into the larger community. In Kuhn science is somewhat isolated except in times of crisis, when it is near crumbling. In Laudan conceptual problems include those from the larger community, but this is little more than an acknowledgment that such influence occurs.[120] For Jaki, however, science is profoundly influenced by philosophy and religion inasmuch as they support or undermine the commitments of a middle way. In this association, man must acknowledge his dependence on a community that is outside science. Yet one cannot segregate science from these influences because science depends on their guidance and support. Indeed, to attempt to do so would be to turn science into a monastery, which would constitute an abandonment of office.[121] For to insulate man from his neighbor is to reject the love of neighbor and his preservation.

In contrast to Kuhn and Laudan, Jaki speaks of what stands below science yet not within its purview. Although this fundamental reality serves as a foundation for science, it might be better described as being above science because science cannot rise above it but must submit to it. Yet the commitment and obedience to this middle way, which is consistent with this reality, is fragile. If not in practice, at least in talk about science, the middle way is all too easily lost, as is evident in physicalism, talk of indeterminacy in quantum physics,[122] or purposeless Darwinism.[123] Not just any image of man and his origin will do. He must, in accordance with this reality, be in some sense exalted. This is the danger of collectively forgetting or never consciously acknowledging, as Kuhn and Laudan do not, these fundamental metaphysical realities: that we will think there is no such hard reality and might easily be led astray by talk that undermines that reality. In just this way, those who are taken in by the ability of science to cohere the quantitative aspects of the world will suggest that the mind and consciousness are no more than physical and quantitative realities, forgetting that their measurements presume that mind and consciousness are more than physical and that what they say of the reality below their measurements is not quantitative but metaphysical and, therefore, outside the purview of science.

In this is seen man's desire to be free of the demands of office, which is here manifest as the desire to be free of that objective reality that is the hand of God. This it cannot do entirely for man in any office must always know labor and frustration. This demonstrates, however, the burden of metaphysical truth and objectivity and its importance for a natural law and the working of office. It places us before God, where we are discoverers, not creators. Here we receive and bow in humble reverence to what might be graciously revealed to us. It is a groping in the dark, often a dark night of despair, a despair not seen were one to examine only the final work, as historians of science such as Kuhn and Laudan do, but a groping nonetheless until the day dawns.[124] It is in this wrestling for what is true and objective out of the labor of office that man is crucified, that office serves as the *larvae Dei*, the mask of God, to bring men to the cross of Christ.

Jaki, then, illumines the vocation of science from something beyond it, something mere "problem solving" cannot do. That something beyond science cannot, or at least ought not, go unnoticed because the fact that there is undeniably purpose and free will in the world is a mystery, no less so than that there is understanding and that something exists this way and not another. Jaki is careful never to imply that science, or its possibility, demonstrates the existence of God,[125] but it certainly ought to cause us to wonder. Jaki writes: "As long as the mind searches for an explanation that relates to the existence of things and not merely to their quantitative properties," one ought to be open to the possibility of God.[126]

Thus the natural law is manifest by Jaki in two ways. First, it demonstrates by blind alleys the essential nature of science: that it must presume a certain metaphysics, the existence of a mind-independent reality, and the ability of the mind to understand it. Second, it also relies on a reality that is beyond it, pointing to a reality that is best described as unphysical. In these two is manifest the two uses of vocation and the law. In the first, the scientist is shown how he might prosper and serve his neighbor while curbing unlawful behavior; in the second, something beyond the law and vocation is pointed to.

Notes

1. Gustaf Wingren, *Luther on Vocation*, trans. Carl C. Rasmussen (Philadelphia: Muhlenberg, 1957), 66.
2. However, matters are different for the ministerial "offices" or callings of the church, such as pastor and deacon. Here, there are biblical criteria for what counts as a calling that transcend the requirements of any

human community. It is God and His representatives that reveal the Gospel to a fallen world.

3. Beyond this, the Bible sees worldly offices as achieving maximal blessing when their duty serves God's covenant people and "thy neighbor" as both an ethical imperative in the present and as an eschatological sign of the eternal paradise.

4. Werner Elert, *The Christian Ethos*, trans. Carl J. Schindler (Philadelphia: Muhlenberg, 1957), 73.

5. Wingren, *Luther on Vocation*, 6.

6. Publisher's note: The law of retribution states: "An eye for an eye . . ." In this chapter, the use of the term "the law of retribution" is identical to that of Elert (*Christian Ethos*, 104), wherein he identifies it with the "second use of the law," evil being punished and good rewarded. Breaking the law certainly merits punishment, yet keeping it does not merit reward apart from salvation in Christ.

7. Wingren, *Luther on Vocation*, 145.

8. Elert, *Christian Ethos*, 126.

9. J. P. Moreland, *Christianity and the Nature of Science* (Grand Rapids: Baker, 1989), 142–43.

10. Samuel Enoch Stumpf, *Socrates to Sartre, A History of Philosophy*, 6th ed. (Boston: McGraw-Hill College, 1999), 361.

11. Thomas S. Kuhn, *The Structure of Scientific Revolutions*, 2nd enlg. ed., Foundations of the Unity of Science (Chicago: University of Chicago Press, 1970), 176–90.

12. Kuhn, *Structure of Scientific Revolutions*, 186.

13. Kuhn, *Structure of Scientific Revolutions*, 37.

14. Kuhn, *Structure of Scientific Revolutions*, section IV.

15. Kuhn, *Structure of Scientific Revolutions*, 69, 71.

16. Kuhn, *Structure of Scientific Revolutions*, 162.

17. Kuhn, *Structure of Scientific Revolutions*, 52.

18. Kuhn, *Structure of Scientific Revolutions*, 148.

19. Kuhn, *Structure of Scientific Revolutions*, 148–49, esp. section XII. Cf. Larry Laudan, *Beyond Positivism and Relativism, Theory, Method, and Evidence* (Boulder: Westview, 1996), 89–99.

20. Kuhn, *Structure of Scientific Revolutions*, 149.

21. Kuhn, *Structure of Scientific Revolutions*, 76.

22. Kuhn, *Structure of Scientific Revolutions*, 148; cf. 199.

23. Kuhn, *Structure of Scientific Revolutions*, 150.

24. Kuhn, *Structure of Scientific Revolutions*, 150–51.

25. Kuhn, *Structure of Scientific Revolutions*, 152, 169, 199.

26. Kuhn, *Structure of Scientific Revolutions*, 157–58.

27. Kuhn, *Structure of Scientific Revolutions*, 206.

28. Kuhn, *Structure of Scientific Revolutions*, 169.

29. Kuhn, *Structure of Scientific Revolutions*, 171.

30. Kuhn, *Structure of Scientific Revolutions*, 172.

31. Kuhn, *Structure of Scientific Revolutions*, 170.

32. Kuhn, *Structure of Scientific Revolutions*, 42.

33. Kuhn, *Structure of Scientific Revolutions*, 64.

34. Kuhn, *Structure of Scientific Revolutions*, 135.

35. Kuhn, *Structure of Scientific Revolutions*, 159.

36. Kuhn, *Structure of Scientific Revolutions*, 148.

37. Kuhn, *Structure of Scientific Revolutions*, 206.

38. Kuhn, *Structure of Scientific Revolutions*, 186.

39. Wingren, *Luther on Vocation*, 37.

40. Wingren, *Luther on Vocation*, 49, 147.

41. Wingren, *Luther on Vocation*, 118.

42. Wingren, *Luther on Vocation*, 35.

43. One might additionally argue that the suggestion some have made of pursuing a Christian science, wherein scriptural evidence is permitted in theory evaluation, represents an abandonment of office.

44. Thomas S. Kuhn, *The Essential Tension: Selected Studies in Scientific Tradition and Change* (Chicago: University of Chicago Press, 1977), chapter 9.

45. Wingren, *Luther on Vocation*, 118.

46. Kuhn, *Essential Tension*, 227.

47. Wingren, *Luther on Vocation*, 145.

48. Wingren, *Luther on Vocation*, 146.

49. Kuhn, *Structure of Scientific Revolutions*, 173.

50. Kuhn, *Structure of Scientific Revolutions*, 162. Cf. Larry Laudan, *Science and Values, The Aims of Science and Their Role in Scientific Debate*, Pittsburgh Series in Philosophy and History of Science (Berkeley: University of California Press, 1984), 69.

51. Larry Laudan, *Progress and Its Problems, Towards a Theory of Scientific Growth* (Berkeley: University of California Press, 1977), 97.

52. Laudan, *Progress and Its Problems*, 97.

53. Laudan, *Progress and Its Problems*, 98.

54. Laudan, *Progress and Its Problems*, 98.

55. Laudan, *Science and Values*, 80.

56. Laudan, *Progress and Its Problems*, 77.

57. Kuhn, *Essential Tension*, 325.

58. Laudan, *Progress and Its Problems*, 105.

59. Laudan, *Beyond Positivism*, 82.

60. Laudan, *Progress and Its Problems*, 111.

61. Laudan, *Progress and Its Problems*, 136.

62. Laudan, *Progress and Its Problems*, 138.

63. Laudan, *Progress and Its Problems*, 134.

64. Laudan, *Progress and Its Problems*, 4.

65. Laudan, *Beyond Positivism*, 18.

66. Laudan, *Progress and Its Problems*, 127.

67. Stanley L. Jaki, *Means to Message: A Treatise on Truth* (Grand Rapids: Eerdmans, 1999), 55.

68. Jaki, *Means to Message*, 206.

69. Jaki, *Means to Message*, 21.

70. Jaki, *Means to Message*, 15.

71. Stanley L. Jaki, *A Mind's Matter, An Intellectual Autobiography* (Grand Rapids: Eerdmans, 2002), 247.

72. Jaki, *Means to Message*, 168.

73. Jaki, *Means to Message*, 168.

74. Jaki, *Means to Message*, 58.

75. Jaki, *Means to Message*, 168, 169.

76. Stanley L. Jaki, "The Biblical Basis of Western Science," in *The Limits of a Limitless Science*, by Stanley L. Jaki (Wilmington, Del.: ISI Books, 2000), 54.

77. Jaki, *Means to Message*, 169.

78. Stanley L. Jaki, *The Road of Science and the Ways to God*, The Gifford Lectures 1974–75 and 1975–76 (Chicago: University of Chicago Press, 1978), 241.

79. Jaki, *Road of Science*, 242.

80. Jaki, *Road of Science*, 242.

81. Jaki, *Road of Science*, 242.

82. Jaki, *Road of Science*, 242.

83. Jaki, *Road of Science*, 276. Following Etienne Gilson, Jaki later prefers to call it "methodological realism." Cf. Jaki, *Mind's Matter*, 88.

84. Jaki, *Mind's Matter*, 92.

85. Jaki, *Means to Message*, 14.

86. Jaki, *Road of Science*, 247.

87. Jaki, *Means to Message*, 144.

88. Jaki, *Means to Message*, 207.

89. Jaki, *Means to Message*, 73.

90. Stanley L. Jaki, "The Physics of Impetus and the Impetus of the Koran," *Modern Age* 29 (1985): 159.

91. Jaki, *Means to Message*, 207; Stanley L. Jaki, "Science: Western or What?" in *Patterns or Principles and Other Essays* by Stanley L. Jaki (Bryn Mawr, Penn.: Intercollegiate Studies Institute, 1995),173; and Stanley L. Jaki, *The Savior of Science* (Grand Rapids: Eerdmans, 2000), 79–84.

92. Stanley L. Jaki, *The Relevance of Physics* (Chicago: University of Chicago Press, 1966), 365.

93. Jaki, *Mind's Matter*, 246.

94. Jaki, *Means to Message*, 108.

95. Jaki, "Science and Religion in Identity Crisis," in *Limits*, 175.

96. Laudan, *Beyond Positivism*, 110. Kuhn comes close to denying any objective ontology by saying, "There is, I think, no theory independent way to reconstruct phrases like 'really there' " (Kuhn, *Structure of Science Revolutions*, 206).

97. Jaki, *Mind's Matter*, 92.

98. Jaki, *Road of Science*, 246.

99. Jaki, *Means to Message*, 137.

100. Jaki, "Beyond Science," in *Limits*, 103.

101. Jaki, *Means to Message*, 137, 144.

102. Jaki, "Beyond Science," in *Limits*, 95.

103. Jaki, *Road of Science*, 246.

104. Jaki, *Road of Science*, 246.

105. Jaki, *Road of Science*, 244.

106. Jaki, *Road of Science*, 247.

107. Jaki, *Road of Science*, 247.

108. Jaki, *Means to Message*, 65, 87, 137.

109. Jaki, *Road of Science*, 261. Solipsism is the skeptical view that nothing exists except oneself. Physicalism is the "view that everything is constituted of the entities taken to be basic by the physical sciences" (*Dictionary of Philosophy*, ed. Thomas Mautner [New York: Penguin, 1997], 424).

110. Jaki, *Road of Science*, 258.

111. Jaki, *Road of Science*, 258.

112. Laudan, *Progress and Its Problems*, 183.

113. Kuhn, *Structure of Science Revolutions*, 206.

114. Laudan, *Progress and Its Problems*, 127.

115. Jaki, *Means to Message*, 55; Jaki, "Science and Religion in Identit.y Crisis," in *Limits*, 171.

116. Jaki, *Means to Message*, 53.

117. Jaki, *Means to Message*, 50, 51.

118. Jaki, *Means to Message*, 58.

119. Jaki, *Means to Message*, 58.

120. Laudan, *Progress and Its Problems*, 32, 64.

121. Wingren, *Luther on Vocation*, 31.

122. Jaki, "Determinism and Reality," in *Patterns*, 114–44.

123. Jaki, *Savior of Science*, 165–73.

124. Jaki, *Road of Science*, 250.

125. Jaki, *Mind's Matter*, 93.

126. Jaki, *Means to Message*, 172.

Contributors

PETER BARKER became Professor of the History of Science at the University of Oklahoma in 1995. He previously served as the first director of Virginia Tech's interdisciplinary graduate program in Science and Technology Studies, and taught in the program from 1986 to 1995. Originally trained in philosophy, Barker is the author of more than forty papers on the history and philosophy of science. In the course of a collaborative study of Johann Kepler, with historian of astronomy Bernard R. Goldstein (University of Pittsburgh), Barker became convinced that the religious ideas of sixteenth century Lutherans actively supported their work in science. His most recent book project, co-authored with Hanne Andersen (Copenhagen) and Xiang Chen (California Lutheran) is *The Cognitive Structure of Scientific Revolutions*.

PAUL R. BOEHLKE is Professor of Biology and has served as Chair of the Life Sciences Department at Wisconsin Lutheran College in Milwaukee. Before coming to Wisconsin Lutheran he taught biology at Martin Luther College in New Ulm, Minnesota, for 24 years. He holds a B.S. from Martin Luther College, an M.S. from Winona State University, Minnesota, and an M.S.T. in chemistry from Union College in New York. Boehlke's Ph.D. from the University of Iowa is in science education and biology. He has done research in cognitive preferences and in plant-animal interactions: studying the wild parsnips webworm and also the monarch butterfly. Always interested in larger issues, he did postgraduate work in ethics at Marquette University. Boehlke has received awards from the Association for the Advancement of Science (AAAS) and also from the Governor of the State of Minnesota for his educational work. He is a frequent presenter at conferences. Recently, he published an article on terpenes and the sense of smell in *American Biology Teacher*. He and his wife, Jeanette, live on the south side of Milwaukee.

EDWARD B. DAVIS, professor of the History of Science at Messiah College (Grantham, PA), is editor (with Michael Hunter) of *The Works of Robert Boyle* (London, 1999–2000). Dr. Davis has a B.S. in Physics (Drexel University, 1975) and a Ph.D. in History and Philosophy of Science (Indiana, 1984). Although best known for his work on Robert Boyle, his main area of interest is Christianity and science since 1650, on which he has written widely in professional literature. Dr. Davis' research on Boyle and theology and science in the seventeenth century has been aided by grants from the Charlotte W. Newcombe Foundation, the National Science Foundation, and the Mellon Foundation. His teaching and writing on religion and science has been recognized several times with grants and awards from the Lilly Foundation and the John M. Templeton Foundation. His current project examines the religious beliefs of American scientists in the early 20th century.

PETER HARRISON is professor of History and Philosophy at Bond University, Australia, and is a Fellow of the Australian Academy of the Humanities. He has written extensively on early modern thought, with a particular emphasis on the interactions of science, philosophy, and religion. His publications include *'Religion'* *and the religions in the English Enlightenment* (Cambridge, 1990) and *The Bible, Protestantism, and the Rise of Natural Science* (Cambridge, 1998).

NATHAN JASTRAM was born and raised in Japan, the son of missionary parents. He received a bachelor's degree in the classical languages at the University of South Dakota in Vermillion, South Dakota, and a master's degree in theology at Concordia Theological Seminary in Fort Wayne, Indiana. His doctor's degree in Ancient Near Eastern Languages and Civilizations, with a dissertation on the Dead Sea Scrolls, was from Harvard University in Cambridge, Massachusetts. He has published several articles and made many presentations on the Dead Sea Scrolls, Bible translations, and the image of God. He taught at Concordia University, River Forest, Illinois, from 1990–1999, and has been teaching at Concordia University Wisconsin, Mequon, Wisconsin, from 1999 to the present. He is currently the chairman of the theology division.

KURT MARQUART was born in Estonia. The family fled from the Soviets before World War II and came to the U.S. in 1949 as refugees. Rev. Marquart attended Concordia, Bronxville, NY (AA, 1954), then Concordia Seminary, St. Louis (BA, 1956; BD, 1959). His first parish was Trinity Church, Weatherford, Texas, then Redeemer Lutheran Parish, Toowoomba, Queensland, Australia, 1961–1975. Rev. Marquart has been associate professor of systematic theology at Concordia Theological Seminary, Springfield/Ft. Wayne since the end of 1975. The Marquarts spent the academic year 1981–82 in London, Ontario, where Kurt earned his MA at the University of Western Ontario, concentrating on the philosophy of science. Books include *Anatomy of an Explosion* (1978), an account of The Lutheran Church—Missouri Synod controversy on biblical authority, and *The Church and Her Fel-*

lowship, Ministry, and Governance (1990, vol. IX in the *Confessional Lutheran Dogmatics* series). At the 2001 Spring Graduation, Kurt Marquart was awarded an honorary doctorate of divinity by Concordia University, Wisconsin in gratitude for his contributions to the church.

ANGUS J. L. MENUGE is professor of Philosophy and associate director of the Cranach Institute at Concordia University Wisconsin (www.cranach.org). He received his BA in philosophy from the University of Warwick and his Ph.D. on action explanation from the University of Wisconsin-Madison. In addition to this collection, Dr. Menuge is editor of *C. S. Lewis: Lightbearer in the Shadowlands* (Crossway, 1997) and *Christ and Culture in Dialogue* (Concordia Academic Press, 1999). With the help of William Dembski, Menuge hosted the Design and its Critics conference in June 2000, which inspired the present volume. Dr. Menuge has written a number of recent articles on intelligent design, including a book defending a robust notion of agency against reductionist theories, entitled *Agents Under Fire: Materialism and the Rationality of Science* (Rowman & Littlefield, 2004).

NANCY RANDOLPH PEARCEY is the Francis A. Schaeffer Scholar at the World Journalism Institute, where she teaches a worldview curriculum based on her book *Total Truth: Liberating Christianity from its Cultural Captivity.* She has authored or contributed to several works, including *The Soul of Science* and the bestselling, award-winning *How Now Shall We Live?* In addition, she has contributed chapters to several books, including *Mere Creation, Of Pandas and People, Genetic Ethics, Signs of Intelligence, Uncommon Dissent,* and a Phillip Johnson *festschrift* titled *A Man for This Season.* For nearly nine years she was policy director of the Wilberforce Forum and executive editor of "BreakPoint," a daily radio commentary program analyzing current issues from a Christian worldview perspective. Her articles have appeared in publications such as *Washington Times, Human Events, First Things, Books & Culture, World, The American Enterprise, The World & I, Christianity Today,* and *Regent University Law Review.*

WILLIAM POWERS earned his Ph.D. in physics from University of California, San Diego in 1985 on the scattering of HF pulses from ionospheric plasma turbulence. Dr. Powers came to Los Alamos National Laboratory, after a short stay with the Naval Ocean Systems Center in San Diego, in 1985 as a Postdoc. For almost four years he worked on the remote sensing of vegetative canopies (e.g., trees and crops) through the atmosphere. In particular, Dr. Powers developed theoretical models of the reflection characteristics of vegetative canopies for the purpose of inversion. In 1989, Dr. Powers joined X Division, a computational physics group at Los Alamos National Laboratory, where he has remained to this day. Here he has worked on the development of hydrodyamics, remeshing, and remapping algorithms. For the last couple of years his efforts have been focused on the development and implementation of parallel techniques in various physics packages.

HENRY F. SCHAEFER III was born in Grand Rapids, Michigan in 1944. He received his B.S. degree in chemical physics from the Massachusetts Institute of Technology (1966) and Ph.D. in chemical physics from Stanford University (1969). For 18 years (1969–1987) he served as a professor of chemistry at the University of California, Berkeley. During the 1979–1980 academic year he was also Wilfred T. Doherty Professor of Chemistry and inaugural director of the Institute for Theoretical Chemistry at the University of Texas, Austin. Since 1987 Dr. Schaefer has been Graham Perdue Professor of Chemistry and Director of the Center for Computational Quantum Chemistry at the University of

Georgia. His other academic appointments include Professeur d'Echange at the University of Paris (1977), Gastprofessur at the Eidgenossische Technische Hochshule (ETH), Zurich (1994, 1995, 1997, 2000), and the David P. Craig Visiting Professor at the Australian National University (1999). He is the author of more than 900 scientific publications, the majority appearing in the *Journal of Chemical Physics* or the *Journal of the American Chemical Society*.